DREAMS, "EVOLUTION," AND VALUE FULFILLMENT

VOLUME II

BOOKS BY JANE ROBERTS

How to Develop Your ESP Power • 1966
The Seth Material • 1970
Seth Speaks: The Eternal Validity of the Soul • 1972
The Education of Oversoul Seven • 1973
The Nature of Personal Reality (A SETH BOOK) • 1974
Adventures in Consciousness: An Introduction to Aspect
    Psychology • 1975
Dialogues of the Soul and Mortal Self in Time • 1975
Psychic Politics: An Aspect Psychology Book • 1976
The "Unknown" Reality (A SETH BOOK), Two
    Volumes • 1977–1979
The World View of Paul Cézanne: A Psychic
    Interpretation • 1977
The Afterdeath Journal of an American Philosopher: The
    World View of William James • 1978
The Further Education of Oversoul Seven • 1979
Emir's Education in the Proper Use of Magical Powers • 1979
The Nature of the Psyche: Its Human Expression (A SETH
    BOOK) • 1979
The Individual and the Nature of Mass Events (A SETH
    BOOK) • 1981
The God of Jane: A Psychic Manifesto • 1981
If We Live Again: Or, Public Magic and Private Love • 1982
Oversoul Seven and the Museum of Time • 1984
Dreams, "Evolution," and Value Fulfillment: Volume I (A SETH
    BOOK) • 1986

A SETH BOOK
DREAMS, "EVOLUTION," AND VALUE FULFILLMENT

VOLUME II

Jane Roberts

Introduction by
Robert F. Butts

PRENTICE HALL PRESS
New York   London   Toronto   Sydney   Tokyo

Prentice Hall Press
Gulf+Western Building
One Gulf+Western Plaza
New York, New York 10023

PRENTICE HALL PRESS and colophon are registered
trademarks of Simon & Schuster, Inc.

Library of Congress Cataloging-in-Publication Data

Roberts, Jane, 1929–1984.
    Dreams, "evolution," and value fulfillment.

    Include index.
    1. Spirit writings.   2. Reincarnation.   I. Seth.
II. Title.
BF1301.R589   1988   133.9'3   88-17907
ISBN 0-13-219395-7 (v. 2)

Manufactured in the United States of America

10   9   8   7   6   5   4   3   2   1

First Edition

*This book is dedicated to
my husband, Robert F. Butts,
for his love and devotion.*

Contents

* Chapters 1–6 (pages 1–288) are in Volume 1 of *Dreams, "Evolution," and Value Fulfillment.*

Quotation from
Jane Roberts

"I kept looking for a logic that would explain life. It never occurred to me that instead love is the vital synthesis."
—December 1981

Quotations from Seth in ESP Class

(A note by R.F.B.: Jane had formally ended her ESP classes by March 1975, when we moved from our downtown apartments in Elmira, New York, to the hill house at the edge of the city. These quotations are from sessions she gave at the house through Seth, her trance personality, for visiting groups of former students.)

". . . you are a part of nature, and that is your saving grace—that no matter how you try to leave that framework you exist within it, so that you communicate with earth at other levels, even if you refuse to be aware of that communication. You help the earth survive, no matter how you might at times deny that heritage."

—FEBRUARY 11, 1977

"Each breath you take is a breath of quality. All you have to do is realize that each breath you take ultimately reaches to the ends of the universe and helps uphold your world."

—DECEMBER 12, 1978

"Now, the creative abilities do not just help you write books, paint pictures, play the piano, compose. The creative abilities are largely responsible for keeping you alive. Your cells are creative. You are alive because you wanted to create. Every act you perform is creative. Your creative self, your spontaneous, creative self—<u>that</u> self that speaks through your impulses—keeps you alive."

—SEPTEMBER 29, 1979

299

Poems by Jane Roberts
with Commentary by Robert F. Butts

(*Jane hadn't shown me any of these poems as she wrote them over a period of some four and a half years. She didn't keep them from me deliberately. In one way they're like casual jottings that she left half finished and unseen in her journals, until I found them when I began searching for fresh material for the frontmatter of this Volume 2 of* Dreams. *In another way they contain deep and private insights, ranging from her free, marveling childhood yearning and intuitive knowing up to her present physically impaired condition—her arthritic-like "symptoms," as we call them—and beyond to the final state of her work after her death. I found each poem to be a revelation, stirring sad and questioning wells of emotion. I can't help but mourn as I write this piece; I tell myself that had I seen the poems as Jane produced them I might have learned a little more about her each time; I might have been able to help her more than I had over the years. At the same time, it's as though she's just finished the poems, so fresh and consistent do they seem to me. And as I reread them I understand once again that my wife is still teaching me about her courage, and about the ineffable, unending mystery of the universe that each one of us is creating moment by moment, separately and all together.*

I offer each one of these poems with a brief commentary. The spelling and punctuation are always Jane's own. The third poem is the only one she formally titled.

In this deceptively simple but moving poem about her magical childhood responses to the world she lived in, Jane foreshadows from that viewpoint the innate knowledge she was to express a quarter of a century later in the Seth material. When she actually wrote the poem, she'd had her physical symptoms for some nine years; for her own creative and challenging reasons she had allowed them to gain a deep hold upon her, and I think that she drew her inspiration for this poem from that context.)

lord let me remember how it was
when i nudged my skin
against the touch of each new morning
and bounded through
the thick thought-forests
that stretched between dawn and noon,
when like magic my lunch was put before me.
lord let me remember how it was
when i was so new
that i thought i was part of the morning.

i didn't want to sleep
for fear the world would disappear
but new days kept coming and coming.
the old ones slipped away one by one,
but were always replenished.

lord let me remember how it was
when i nuzzled the air in the morning
and thought i could wiggle a distant leaf
just as i moved my own ears and toes.
i thought that i caused rain to fall
just as the tears from my own eyes
wet my cheeks,
and that my thoughts turned into clouds
that circled the top of my head.

—SEPTEMBER 1974

*(I hadn't realized four years ago that Jane was speculating about leaving
physical reality. Had I known, I would have been bewildered—at least at first.
She was 47; I was 10 years older. As Jane wrote then about drawing strength
from me by touching my arm, in April 1980 she touched my heart when I found
this poem:)*

(ideas while driving with Rob Sun.)

I was walking past the world
one day,
half deciding not to stay,
when I saw you standing there,
ten years ahead of me in time
but so close in space

that I reached out
and touched your arm.

—APRIL 26, '76

*("With all of her mental and physical challenges, my wife could still write a
poem of humble thanks to the earth. Amazing!" Such was my first thought when
I found this poem. Jane loved physical life with a deep, intuitive and psychic
innocence then—and she still does. I don't see how she can express that earthly
love more clearly, simply, and beautifully than she does here. Yet, to me this poem
also contains many other layers of meaning:)*

letter to earth

I've done the best I could
with thy sweet heritage of blood,
one creature like all the rest
born from your power and benevolence,
graced to share in what you are
for your love's multiplication
knows no prejudice,
so let me humbly state my thanks

—1976

*(In this poem, which she wrote just a year ago, Jane deals not only with her
transformation of her work into its inevitable literary, physical form, but restates
her belief that her individualized consciousness will live after her physical death.
Yet, just as it had been in the first poem in this series, her death was still on her
mind some four and a half years later. I see now that given the lifetime challenges she's chosen, such thoughts will continue to play a prominent role in the
reality Jane is creating for herself:)*

I've always transferred my life to letters,
and one day it will reside
exclusively in written nouns and vowels,
clean paragraphs
distilled from mysterious life's days.
Even before death's event
I plan my mind's resting place
as if there is a second life
in thought's products that defies
the brain's shorter span, and rises

sans blood, flesh, hand or eye,
self-contained, truly alive at last;
like some mental balloon
set on a safe course finally
through unexplored skies
when the hand that holds it
lets it go.

—APRIL 17, 1979

Introduction
by Robert F. Butts

As soon as I realized that *Dreams, "Evolution," and Value Fulfillment* was going to be so long that it would require publication in two volumes, I began to think about how I was going to summarize here all of the material that Jane, Seth, and I had contributed to Volume 1. I developed the hilarious notion that if I did the job the way I really wanted to, this introduction would be as long as that first volume is itself! Then I realized that a lengthy, elaborate introduction for Volume 2 is hardly necessary, and I began to relax about the challenge.

What *is* necessary is for the reader to closely review Volume 1 before digging into Volume 2. There isn't any better way to grasp the complex themes of that first book. However, I can help initiate that process by presenting here three short blocks of material—from Seth-Jane, myself, and from Jane's and my editor at Prentice-Hall, Inc., Tam Mossman. Then I'll add a few later comments of my own.

First, Seth's headings for the six chapters of Volume 1 give a broad outline of his material in that book:

Second, here's the closing paragraph of my last note for Volume 1:

"Seth used Session 909 as a bridge between chapters 6 and 7 in *Dreams*. This means that now the session also serves as a connective—a very effective lure, say—between volumes 1 and 2. Indeed, in retrospect it almost seems as though Seth, that 'energy personality essence,' planned it that way! And Jane and I look forward with intense interest to the final version of *Dreams*, for as always this work will be as revealing and educational for us as it will be for anybody else. I thank each reader for his or her patience in accepting the publication of *Dreams* in two volumes."

Third, I quote from a letter Tam wrote to officials of Prentice-Hall, Inc. after Jane and I had finished Volume 2 of *Dreams*. Tam and others at our publishing company had very patiently waited for several years while Jane and I struggled to produce the book; in all that time no one ever exerted pressure upon us to hurry up and finish the job. We have always been, and still are, most grateful for that freedom. In his letter Tam enthusiastically recommended the publication of the book. I think that he very deftly sums up my own goals in putting together *Dreams* the way I did (with the approval of Seth and Jane, of course).

"It's been worth the wait! This is really three books in one, two of which the Seth fans have been waiting for, and a third that they're getting as an unexpected bonus.

"The 'Seth Book' core of the manuscript, as dictated by Seth, is fine as is. But to that, Rob has added a detailed, often harrowing account of exactly *why* Jane, with all the psychic and creative resources at her disposal, allowed herself to get in such [deep physical distress]. (I am being asked this question repeatedly by correspondents.) Suffice it to say that Rob does a complete and careful job of it, and the results—while not always light reading by any means—answer the hard questions the Seth readers have been asking.

"The 'third' portion of the book entails Rob's effort—again in notes—to develop the ideas that Seth is coming up with and relate them to two events then unfolding in the 'real' world—namely, the Three Mile Island near-disaster and the hostage crisis in Iran. Though it *seems* that this is unnecessary digression, by the end of the book Rob has pulled it all together very well indeed. More importantly, these news bulletins furnish an important ballast, giving the book a larger perspective and 'opening it up'—which is almost needed, as Jane becomes increasingly immobile and discouraged.

"The Seth material, too, includes not just book dictation, but a good deal of relevant private material given to Jane about her condition, as well as other parallel sessions. So all in all, the Jane Roberts fans are going to be treated to one of the best books in the series, and one that both poses—and answers—crucial questions about the entire course of the meaning of Seth's work.

"My enthusiasm for this work is tempered only by its necessary chronicle of Jane's suffering and Rob's own baffled looking for a way out—thus, there's more than a note of tragedy here, but one that should not deter Jane's readers. They know the 'facts' and are eager now for the *story*. In fact, I would put this on a crash [rapid publishing] schedule if at all feasible."

Finally: Tam Mossman wrote that some of my descriptive passages in *Dreams* are "harrowing" as I deal with Jane's personal challenges. Tam is right, of course. They *are* harrowing; they strike at the very heart of our fears of illness and disability, and even death, leading us to consciously face those possibilities while at the same time they perfectly mirror our equally profound inner needs and drives. In *Dreams* I'm presenting the account of Jane's struggles with her "physical symptoms" in the clearest light I can manage. I'm also demanding the very best insight, an excellence of understanding, from each reader, even though it may not be easy to summon those qualities. But in my opinion they're vital for understanding what the Seth material is all about.

I learned long ago that Jane's great creative abilities are so intimately bound up with her personal challenges that they're inseparable. Neither of us were ever interested in turning out a series of just "psychic books" *per se*, devoid of all of those human and intimate details that are piling up during our lifetimes, enriching the moments and the days, the weeks and the years, creating the seamless wholes of our lives. I also believe that in ordinary terms each living entity on earth employs such a process of enrichment, tailoring it for its unique, individual purposes. Obviously, in larger terms Jane and I believe that the earth—indeed, the universe itself—is alive.

I do feel that part of that enrichment involves a worldwide

(and possibly universal) healing action, contributed to by each living form—that here on earth, at least, this vital force of our own creation sustains us in an unending grand synthesis of re-generation. Yet I haven't read anything about this, at least put in just this way. Our species should study the whole subject of global healing, so that it can use the knowledge gained to lead itself into new areas of thought and feeling.

In her own creative way, Jane is doing just this; her physical symptoms are the signposts of her personal struggle, and of mine, and of our joint incomplete knowledge. With her suc-cesses and failures Jane leads the way for many, even while she and I keep trying to learn more. Yet it's an exceedingly lonely journey that my wife is taking, even with my help. The varieties of consciousness springing out of this global healing process must literally be without end—always creative, always forward-looking.

7

Genetics and Reincarnation. Gifts and "Liabilities." The Vast Sweep of the Genetic and Reincarnational Scales. The Gifted and the Handicapped

(See the beginning of this Session 909 in Chapter 6 for Volume 1 of Dreams. *As Seth, Jane had started delivering the session at 9:05 P.M. on Monday, April 21, 1980.)*

(Pause at 9:34.) Give us a moment. . . . Next chapter *(7)*: "Genetics and Reincarnation. Gifts and 'Liabilities.' The Vast Sweep of the Genetic and Reincarnational Scales. The Gifted and the Handicapped."

(Long pause.) Your species as a species includes the idiot and the genius, the stupid and the wise, the athletic, the deformed, the beautiful and the ugly, and all variations in between. There are genetic cultures operating, then, of literally infinite variety *(intently)*, and they each have their place and their reason, and they each fit into the overall picture—not only of man's reality but of the planet's reality, including all of nature.

Your religious ideas have often told you that deformities at birth were the result of the parents' sins cast upon the children, or that another kind of punishment was involved in terms of "karma." In terms of biology, people talk about coming from good stock or bad stock, and even those designations imply moral judgments.

The entire idea of reincarnation has been highly distorted by other religious concepts. It is not a psychological arena composed of crime and punishment. Again, you have free will in the conditions of your life, given the characteristics that are your own. The great facility and adaptability of the human species are dependent upon an amazing interplay between genetic preciseness and genetic freedom. The very characteristic attributes of the species, its dependability and integrity, are dependent upon constant checks and balances, the existence of divergent characteristics against which the species can measure itself.

The species is also always in the process of keeping within its genetic bank millions of characteristics that might be needed in various contingencies, and in that regard there is a connection, of course, between, say, viruses of many strains and the health not only of man but of other species.

The possibility of creative change must always be present to insure the species' resiliency, and that resiliency can show in many ways—in conditions that you consider deformities, disabilities from birth, or in any physical variation from a hypothetical physical norm. You all look quite alike, with one head *(amused)*, two arms and legs, and so forth, as a rule. Such differences or variations are very noticeable at a certain level, if you have more fingers than you are supposed to, or less, or two thumbs to a hand, or any other condition that is considered an abnormality.

(9:52.) There are mental conditions also: the so-called retarded people who do not use their reasoning minds as others do. There are also, again, highly gifted people, physically or men-

tally, people who seem to be at times as far from the ordinary person on the gifted scale as an idiot might be [on] the other. So as we progress, I hope to show where all of these situations fit in with the development of the individual and the species.

At a smaller level of activity such variances of course escape your notice. You do not know if you have any errant genes unless their effects show themselves. At microscopic levels, in fact, no one fits any norm, and there is no way to predict with complete certainty the development of any genetic element. You can make group predictions, and overall make certain judgments, but other elements are involved, so that any particular genetic element cannot be pinned down in terms of its development. This is because its activity is also involved with relationships that do not show in any of your calculations.

Your thoughts, feelings, desires and intents, your reincarnational knowledge[1] as well, modify that structure, bring certain latent characteristics into actualization, minimize others, as through the experience of your life you use your free will and constantly make new decisions.

End of dictation (forcefully). Do you have a question?

(10:04. "Do you want to say something about the little out-of-body Jane had this noon?"

Jane's consciousness had left her sleeping body in the bedroom and traveled to her writing room at the back of the house. She'd encountered me there, in my own out-of-body state, and we engaged in a very animated conversation. Afterward she insisted that I'd been out-of-body too, although I have no conscious memory of such an event. We estimated that at the proper time I'd just quit painting for the morning and was washing my brushes at the bathroom sink—a routine task I perform each day, and one that could leave a portion of my psyche free to engage in other adventures. Yet, since I'd been awake while she slept, we speculated that those same habitual cleaning chores had also occupied me enough consciously to mask my awareness of what another part of me was up to.)

Give us a moment. . . . The out-of-body was the result of a change in attitude, and made possible also because of his *(Ruburt's)* body's relaxation. He was exercising his consciousness, allowing himself greater freedom. A certain portion of your mind was drifting at the time.

Now people may wiggle their feet, or doodle, or tap a desk while they are concentrating on other things. They also exercise their consciousnesses in the same fashion—doodle with their minds, relaxing themselves in such a fashion, wandering off to refresh themselves—and you were both doing that, but Ruburt caught himself in the act, so to speak.

You were mentally wandering through the house, the both of you, and Ruburt caught himself where his mind was—only his physical body was not in the same place. Because this was like a mental doodle, the colors were not complete, the picture was not filled in.

The entire conversation was an attempt to make the event seem reasonable, an attempt to color in the picture.

End of session.

("Thank you.")

You are both doing very well. A fond good evening.

("Good night, Seth."

10:10 P.M. "I'm surprised I even had the session," Jane said. "He did go into that chapter I picked up on earlier today, but I don't remember what he called it.")

NOTE. Session 909

1. In Volume 1 of *Dreams*, see Note 3 for the 885th session. I quoted a poem (on animal consciousness) from a book of sketches and untitled poetry that Jane had created for my birthday last June. These two poems from the same little book fit in well here:

> *I've always felt*
> *that I've always known you,*
> *yet you surprise me daily*
> *with new versions*
> *of your personhood*
> *that* then *I remember.*

> *I clap my mental hands*
> *and say, "Of course,"*
> *and you change again*
> *into a new version*
> *that I've always known before!*

And:

> *This private probability*
> *isn't half bad*
> *when you consider*
> *the public worlds*
> *we had to travel*
> *to get here:*
> *molecules waiting*
> *in the wings,*
> *looking for*
> *the precise*
> *time-space*
> *to leap into,*
> *tiny strands of*
> *consciousness*
> *reuniting*
> *after centuries,*
> *sorting out ourselves*
> *from a million*
> *other forms*
> *we've taken part in—*
> *reassembling*
> *just those we wanted*
> *to call Rob and Jane.*

SESSION 910——April 23, 1980
9:06 P.M. WEDNESDAY

(The Dominican Republic is an economically very poor country occupying the eastern portion of the island of Hispaniola in the West Indies. Yesterday Jane and I reread an article I'd filed last September, then forgotten about: In the area surrounding a certain village in the Dominican Republic, 38 girls have turned into boys at the onset of puberty. These remarkable physical changes stem from a genetic "defect" carried by a common ancestor who lived more than a century ago. The men have low sperm counts and may not be able to sire children in the normal manner, yet Jane and I think that this rare group event—the only one of its kind on record—fits in with Seth's material about the millions of

variations contained within our species' vast genetic pool. For whatever mysterious reasons, then, our overall consciousness wants and needs this particular "genetic culture." See the portion of the last session given as the opening of this chapter.

Then today we read how scientists at a company that markets animals for medical research have bred a strain of hairless laboratory mice without thymus glands. The thymus gland helps a body create immunity against outside infections. Scientists often use "athymic" mice in cancer research, for example, since the mice do not reject tumor transplants. [Indeed, these animals are so sensitive to disease of any kind that they must be raised under sterile conditions.] Jane was very upset by the article and mentioned it to me several times.[1]

Before the session she said that she felt material from Seth "around," concerning genetics.)

Now: Good evening.

("Good evening, Seth.")

Dictation. *(Pause.)* If there were no idiots among you, you would soon find that geniuses were absent also.

Those human abilities that you consider to be characteristic of your species are, again, dependent upon the existence of infinite numbers of variations that appear in the aggregate, to give you often obviously opposing states. What you think of then as the average intelligence is a condition that exists because of the activity of constant variables, minute variations that give you at one end of the scale the idiot, and at the other the genius.

Both are necessary to maintain that larger "norm" of mental activity. I am using the word "norm" here for your convenience, though I disagree with the ways in which the term has been used, when it has been set up as a rule (underlined) of measurement, psychologically speaking. The genetic system[2] is not closed, therefore. The genes do not simply hold information without any reference to the body's living system. It does not exist, then—the genetic structure—like some highly complicated mechanism already programmed, started and functioning "blindly," so that once it is set into operation there is no chance for modification.

Particularly in your own species there is a great give-and-take between human genetic systems, the environment, and cultural events—and by cultural events I mean events having to do with your peculiarly unique field of activity that includes the worlds of politics, economics, and so forth.

(Pause.) Genetic events are not irrefutable in a deterministic fashion. They represent strong inclinations toward certain bodily or mental activity, certain biological preferences. They lead toward the activation of certain events over others, so that the probabilities are "loaded" in certain directions. *(Pause.)* Genetic events are (underlined) then events, though at a different level of activity than you are used to thinking of.

We are speaking of chromosomal messages. These are not written within the chromosomes as words might be written upon paper, but the information and the chromosomes are a living unit. The information is alive *(intently)*. We are speaking about a kind of biological cuneiform, in which the structures, the very physical structures, of the cells contain all of the knowledge needed to form a physical body—to form themselves. This is indeed knowledge in biological form, and biologically (underlined) making its clearest living statement.

(9:27.) The cells [with their] genetic packages, like all cells, react to stimuli. They act. They are aware of all of the body's events biologically. In ways impossible to verbalize, they are also aware of the environment of the body as it is perceived at biological levels. I have said before that in one way or another each living cell is united with each other living cell through a system of inner communication. "Programmed" genetic activity can be altered by conditions in the environment.

(Long pause.) I am not simply saying that genetic activity can be changed, for example, through something like a nuclear accident, but that highly beneficial alterations can also take place in genetic behavior, as in your terms the genetic structure not only prepares the species for any contingency, but also prepares it by triggering those characteristics and abilities that are needed by the species at any given time, and also by making allowances for such future developments *(all quite forcefully)*.

Your genetic structure reacts to each thought that you have, to the state of your emotions, to your psychological climate. In your terms, it contains the physical history of the species in context with the probable future capabilities of the species. You choose your genetic structure so that it suits the challenges and capabilities of the species. You choose your genetic structure so that it suits the challenges and potentials that you have chosen. *(Long pause.)* It represents your physical reference point, your bodily framework. It is your personal physical property. It is a portion of physical matter that you have identified, filled out with your own identity. It is like a splendid ship, the body, that you have chosen ahead of time for a splendid challenging adventure—a ship that you have personally appointed that is equipped to serve as much as possible as a physical manifestation of your personhood.

Some people, in beginning such a venture, will indeed insist upon an excellent vessel, with the most sophisticated mechanisms, equipped with grand couches and a banquet room. Others would want much more excitement, much more zest, and order then instead a less grand vessel, but one that went faster. Some would set goals for themselves that demanded that their powers of seamanship be tested. The analogy may be a simple one, yet each person chooses the living vessel of the body, with his or her own intents and purposes in mind.

(Long pause.) In physical reality, if you will forgive me, life is the name of the game—and the game is based upon value fulfillment. That means simply that each form of life seeks toward the fulfillment and unfolding of all of the capacities that it senses within its living framework, knowing that in that individual fulfillment each other species of life is also benefited.

(9:45.) In no way do I mean to demean the indisputable value of geniuses, or their great contributions to the quality of life—but the quality of life is, again, also benefited by the existence of idiots. Not only because both ends of the scale are necessary for genetic reasons, but also because idiots themselves are in no way considered failures or defects by nature. Those terms are human judgments. Idiots also serve their role by moderating the sometimes fierce hold that the reasoning mind can (underlined) have upon human activity.

The idiot is often able to experience in his or her own reality a freer, more generous, more faithful flow of emotional states, unhampered by reason's sometimes stern dictates, and it is important that such a moderating tendency does operate genetically.

I will have more to say on that subject later in the book.

The reasoning mind, as you have used it thus far, roughly (underlined) since the birth of Christianity, has used—instead of used, confined—has confined its reasoning abilities to a very narrow spectrum of reality. It has seen the value of life largely only as that life conforms to its own standards. *(Pause.)* That is, the reasoning mind, as you have used it, considers that only reasoning creatures are capable of understanding life's values. Other forms of life have almost seemed beside the point, their value considered only insofar as they were of service to man. But man's life is obviously dependent upon the existence of life's other species, and with him those species share certain values. Life is sacred—all life—and again, all life seeks value fulfill-ment, not simply physical survival.

Ruburt read an article about the development of a strain of mice without thymus [glands]. Since the thymus is very impor-tant in the necessary process of maintaining bodily resistance to disease, these particular mice have little resistance. They are bred and sold for experimental purposes. The intent of such procedures is to promote the quality of human life, to study the nature of diseases, and hopefully apply what is learned to some of the lives of human beings. Mice are not considered human. They are not. So like any animal, they are thought of as dispen-sable, sacrificed to a fine humanitarian end.

(Long pause.) Perhaps at first that prejudice of the reasoning mind might escape you, since after all mice are far divorced from your own species. *(Louder:)* There were Jews sacrificed to the same end not too long ago, and the reasoning was largely the same, though in that case you were dealing with your own spe-cies.

(10:05.) Jews were considered almost not human, however, and whenever such atrocities against your own species are con-cerned, you indulge in the same kind of twisted reasoning (un-derlined). Because the Jews were considered less than human—or, at best, human defects—they were thought of as justifiable sacrifices on the altar of "the genetic betterment of mankind." You cannot improve the quality of your own lives by destroying the quality of any other kinds of life. There is no genetic master race. The very classification of the species into races to begin

with is based upon distinctions that are ridiculously minute in the overall picture of the similarities.

Ruburt was incensed by the article that he read, and he said indignantly that such procedures involve a biological immorality. I usually avoid terms like "morality" or "immorality," since their definitions vary according to the individual. The proceedings, however, do involve a biological violation, a going against nature's flow and intent, a process in which a form of life is made to go against its own value fulfillment, and it is because of such attitudes involving other kinds of life that the horrors of the Jewish war camps were made possible.

End of dictation *(louder)*. Do you have a question?

(I was shaking my head no, grinning, before Seth finished asking his question. My amusement wasn't directed at the seriousness of his material, but arose because of the intense scrutiny Seth directed at me. All during her trance tonight, Jane's blue-gray eyes had been especially dark and luminous.)

Then I bid you a fine good evening.

("Thank you. The material's very good.")

(With humor:) Naturally.

("Okay. Good night."

10:14 P.M. "I know he went into that article on the mice." Jane laughed, almost against her will. "I also know he's going to redeem it all, in spite of everything. Although I don't know how you can redeem it for the mice. . . . Once again, she was surprised that she'd delivered so much material in so short a time.

See Note 3 for a few comments relative to Seth's discussion of genetics in the session.)

NOTES. Session 910

1. Jane and I are both aware of and frustrated by the obvious ambiguities in our own feelings about the use of animals in medical research. We also think that most other people have such mixed feelings, whether they realize it or not. Were either of our own physical lives saved—perhaps even before birth—by those using knowledge gained from animal experimentation? We don't know. We do know that it's much easier to condone a philosophy espousing traumatic and repetitive animal research if one is relatively shielded from it.

However, if given a choice, Jane and I now *would* forgo the "benefits" stemming from animal experimentation, even if our own future welfares were to suffer because of a subsequent lack of knowledge—and providing that at a time of crisis we didn't weaken in our joint resolve! Following such a course would actually be most difficult, so pervasive in our society are the results flowing from animal research: I even think it might be necessary to live as a hermit in the wild to get away from them. Using animals in the laboratory *is* imposing human goals and values upon other life forms, even though the modern scientific method is supposed to be value-free. For such research is carried out in the name of progress and the practical common good, of course—and that progress applies also in the remedial treatment of other animals, let us remember. We think that every reader of this book has benefited, and still does, from animal experimentation, some of it most cruel, in ways that he or she can hardly suspect, let alone specify: even benefiting from the use of animals in the study of medical and chemical, beauty and recreational products that can be found in practically every home in the country. Jane and I live in one of those homes. I see the passive, thinking and unthinking tolerance of animal experimentation as a classical case of a society using ends to justify means—yet in the United States, at least, we carefully teach each generation of our species that such rationalizations aren't morally acceptable. . . .

2. In Chapter 6 for Volume 1 of *Dreams*, see Note 1 for the 905th session.

3. Originally I'd planned a series of notes for this session, in which to explore Seth's ideas on genetics versus those held by the scientific establishment. Those plans gradually evaporated as I realized that it would take many pages to compare the two viewpoints in any detail. We're in the early stages of an extensive scientific growth involving genetics, and certainly by the time this book is published much more information will have been acquired, even if it's of the same general kind. If they knew about it, I expect that most members of the scientific community would disagree with much of the excellent material Seth gave in this session. Not all would—or will—of course. But Jane and I don't try to bend others to our way of thinking; the reality that our species is creating is too big and varied for that; we believe

only that we'll have to explore questions like those involving genetics and consciousness in our own ways, and with Seth's help.

I *also* believe, however, that generally speaking science still views our genetic systems in mechanical, deterministic, and reductionistic terms, and will continue to do so for a long time: So that evidence is being accumulated to support that overall view that at this time science has no *need* to seek for other, larger, and more unsettling frames of reference encompassing consciousness, intent, and genetics. Indeed, I seldom see consciousness mentioned in connection with genetics, except as its quality may relate to genetic "defects" like mental retardation, say.

Nor do I think that establishment science will soon be interested in Seth's ideas that exchanges take place involving our genetic systems, the environment, and cultural events like politics and economics; or that our genetic systems react to our thoughts and emotions—let alone that there's any genetic planning for future probabilities! I do not know whether, or how, any of those factors could be measured and/or manipulated in the laboratory. Science could grant Seth's ideas their own realities *outside of* the scientific framework, of course, and thus be free of them.

But granted or not, the idea of any sort of genetic preparation for future contingencies collides with the very powerful theory of evolution, which holds that evolutionary, genetic changes take place only through natural selection and chance mutations (although random or chance mutations are generally regarded as mistakes on nature's part). There are many unsolved challenges here. I can even see Seth's material in this session being scientifically dismissed as another version of old, discredited Lamarckian theories. (Jean Baptiste de Monet de Lamarck [1744–1829] was a French naturalist who advocated that certain modifications of an organism's structure and function could develop in response to environmental factors, and that these "acquired characters" could be inherited. Lamarck's work has been widely misunderstood, however. It still has value, and recently has been employed in some remarkable scholarly studies that show how, in scientific teams, evolution can take place through means other than natural selection and chance mutations.)

I'm sure that Seth would be the first to agree that consciousness obviously contains an unlimited number of viewpoints, regardless of which ones we humans may choose to call "true" at any particular time. Consciousness is just as amenable to having some of its physical manifestations scientifically studied, its parts manipulated through "genetic engineering," as it is to encompassing Seth's material. All of our species' actions represent our keen and creative interests in studying ourselves in the finest details possible. That the scientific approach has limitations is obvious. So do all others in this physical realm. A discipline, of whatever nature and motivation, can erect barriers to "outside" influences—and those barriers are often artifacts growing almost automatically out of the very nature of the belief system in question.

SESSION 911——April 28, 1980
8:55 P.M. MONDAY

(Last Friday, April 25, was day 174 of the taking of the American hostages in Iran. Until that day the 53 prisoners had been held at two locations in Tehran, the capital city of that very turbulent land. As we ate breakfast early Friday, Jane and I were astounded by television news reports that in the predawn hours of the 25th, Iranian time, American commandos had failed in a very complicated attempt to rescue the hostages. Actually, our forces hadn't come close to reaching the prisoners: Responsible were mechanical failures and two dust storms that the American helicopters had to struggle through before joining a group of transport planes at a remote airfield, code-named Desert One, in central Iran. By then three of the eight "choppers" were out of action. Since six of them were considered vital for a successful rescue, the mission was canceled at that point—but eight crewmen were killed when one of the remaining helicopters collided with a transport plane during a refueling attempt. The resulting fires and explosions could be seen and heard for miles through the desert night.

Many in the United States now feel that our country looks the fool before the rest of the world. The mildest epithet being applied to us in the Middle East is "stupid." A few of our European allies, however, have expressed concern and sympathy. Our President's main challengers for his office haven't publicly criticized him, but neither have they defended him from foreign and domestic censure—and today our Secretary of

State resigned in protest of the rescue mission. Our government is sup-
posed to have begun preparing for the rescue shortly after the hostages
were seized more than five months ago. All details of the failed attempt
may not be released for months, or even years, but already critics are
questioning whether the excessive secrecy surrounding the operation led
to basic errors in planning and judgment, as well as poor anticipation of
the mechanical factors involved.

At this time Jane and I think the mission's failure is a blessing: Based
upon our limited knowledge of the factors involved, we do not see how it
could have succeeded. We mourn the dead servicemen and wonder how
many more Americans—military people and hostages—would have been
killed had our commandos penetrated to the American Embassy com-
pound, and the Iranian Foreign Ministry, in the heart of Tehran.

As soon as they learned of the rescue attempt, the furious and con-
temptuous leaders of Iran announced that they were dispersing the hos-
tages around their country in order to block another such endeavor. In
spite of their previous threats, however, the Iranians have not harmed the
hostages in reprisal for the operation, and our Administration has
strongly warned them not to do so. And there for the moment events seem
to swirl in place—storms of consciousness that, I think, are bound to
combine in new patterns to further explore certain large challenges.[1]

Just before dusk, a fine rain began to fall. Jane sat in the doorway
that opens from her writing room onto the screened-in back porch of the
hill house, and watched the birds searching out the wet remnants of the
feed I'd scattered in the driveway this morning. Because of her walking
difficulties she'd stayed in her office chair, which is on wheels, and
pushed the sliding glass door wide open from that position. The rain
didn't bother the birds at all: a pair of cardinals, several red-winged
blackbirds, some phoebes, various warblers, and a group of mourning
doves. Jane grew very relaxed as she sat there at that quiet hour—yet she
wanted to hold the session anyhow; she called me early; she felt Seth
around. . . .)

Good evening.

("Good evening, Seth.")

Dictation: The genetic system is an inner, biological, "universal" language.

In your terms that language speaks the flesh—and it speaks
the flesh equally in all races of mankind. There are no inferior
or superior races. Now dreams also provide you with another
universal kind of language, one that unites all peoples to one

extent or another, regardless of their physical circumstances or nationalities or alliances.

The cataloging of separate races simply involves you in organizations of variances played upon a common theme—variances that you have used for various purposes. Often those purposes led you to overexaggerate the differences between groups, and to minimize man's biological unity.

(Long pause.) The most important aspects of individuality are those subjective characteristics that on the one hand distinguish each person from the other, and that on the other hand are each like sparkling psychological mosaics, giving separate, exquisite individual versions of that larger pattern from which mankind emerges. The security, the integrity, and the brilliance of each individuality rises in these terms from that universal genetic language, and also from the inner subjective universal language of dreams. There are great connections between the two, and both are spoken together.

Let us become more practical, and see how these issues merge in your reality. Some of this requires a great honesty on your own parts, as you try to recall some feelings and daydreams that you have tried to put away or forget or disown. Why are some people, then, born with conditions that are certainly experienced as genetically defective, granting even the overall value of such variances on the part of the species? For, again, I must stress the fact that in its way nature makes no such judgments, regardless of the beliefs of your science or religions.

Science seems to be of the opinion that the individual is important only insofar as *(louder:)* he or she serves the purposes of the species' survival—and I am not saying that. I am saying that the existence of each individual is (underlined) important to the value fulfillment of the species. And moreover, I am stating that the value fulfillment of the individual and the species go hand in hand.

(Long pause at 9:13.) I am also stating that the species is itself aware of those conditions that lead to its own value fulfillment, and that of its members. No species basically (underlined) biologically considers its own existence with other species except in a cooperative manner—that is, there is no basic competition between species. When you think that there is, you are reading nature wrong. Whatever man's conscious beliefs, on a biological

level his genetic structure is intimately related to the genetic structure of all other species.

In man, the probabilities of development are literally numberless. No computer could count the combinations of characteristics possible. It is highly important, then, that the species retain flexibility, and not become locked into any one pattern, however advantageous *(intently)*—and I am referring to physical or mental patterns. Within the framework of established specieshood, there must be every kind of leeway—leeways that are biologically activated, so that variances are constantly active. Those genetic variances may appear as defective or eccentric. They may appear as the handicapped. They may appear as superior characteristics of one kind or another, but they must be biologically stated as the variations from the genetic norm.

By themselves, whether they appear as superior or defective conditions, they necessitate a different kind of adaptability, a change of subjective or physical focus, the intensification of other abilities that perhaps have been understressed. Yet granting all this, why, again, would some individuals choose situations that would be experienced as defective conditions? For this, we need to examine some human feelings that are often forgotten.

Now I have often said that suffering of itself is not "good for the soul." It is not a virtue, yet certainly many individuals seem to seek suffering. Suffering cannot be dismissed from human experience as a freak matter of distorted emotions or beliefs.

(Long pause.) Suffering is a human condition that is sought for various reasons. There are gradations of suffering, of course, and each person will have his or her definitions of what suffering is. Many people do indeed equate a certain kind of suffering with excitement. Sportsmen, race-car drivers, mountain climbers—all seek suffering to one extent or another, and find the very intensity of certain kinds (underlined) of pain pleasurable. You might say that they like to live dangerously.

(9:29.) Some s-e-c-t-s *(spelled)* have believed that spiritual understanding came as the result of bodily agony, and their self-inflicted pain became their versions of pleasure. It is usually said that animals, and also man, avoid pain and seek pleasure—and so any courting of pain, except under certain conditions, is seen as unnatural behavior.

(Pause.) It is not unnatural. It is an eccentric *(pause)* behavior

pattern. Many children daydream not only of being kings or queens, or given great honors, they also daydream about being tragic figures. They daydream of cruel deaths. They glory in stories of wicked stepmothers. They imagine, in fact, every situation that they can involving human experience. To an extent adults do the same thing. They are drawn to cinema or television dramas that involve tragedies, sorrows, great dramatic struggles. This is because you are alive as the result of your great curiosity for human experience. You are alive because you want to participate in human drama.

While I admit that many people will not agree with me *(smile)*, I know from experience that most individuals do not choose one "happy" life after another, always ensconced in a capable body, endowed by nature or heritage with all of the gifts most people seem to think they desire.

Each person seeks value fulfillment, and that means that they choose various lives in such a fashion that all of their abilities and capacities can be best developed, and in such a way that their world is also enriched. Some people will choose "defective" bodies purposely in order to focus more intensely in other areas. They want a different kind of focus. *(Long pause.)* They want to sift their characteristics through a certain cast. Such a choice demands an intensification. It is made on the part of the individual and on the parts of the parents as well, so that a certain group of people will relate to the world in a highly characteristic way. In almost all such cases *(pause)*, such people will be embarked upon subjective issues and questions also that might not be considered otherwise. They will ask questions on their own parts that need to be raised, not only for themselves but for the society at large.

(9:48. Pausing in trance, Jane poured herself some wine.)

Those questions help bring out psychological maturities and insights about the nature of the species in general. Many such conditions also serve to keep man's sympathies alive. I make a distinction between sympathy and pity, for a lively sympathy leads toward construction, toward the utilization of abilities, even to social discourse, while pity can be deadening.

Your overreliance upon physical norms, and your distorted concepts concerning survival of the fittest, help exaggerate the existence of any genetic defects, of course. Many religious dogmas consider such conditions, again, the result of a god's punishment. The survival of the species is far more dependent upon your subjective activities than your physical ones—for it is your subjective behavior that is responsible for your physical acts. Science of course looks at it the other way around, as if your physical acts are the result of a robot's mechanical, formalized behavior—a robot miraculously programmed by the blind elements of an accidental universe formed by chance. The robot is programmed only to survive at anyone's or anything's expense. It has no real consciousness of its own. Its thoughts are merely mental mirages, so if one of its parts is defective then obviously it is in deep trouble. But man is no robot, and each so-called genetic defect has an internal part to play in the entire picture of genetic reality. The principle of uncertainty must operate genetically, or you would have been locked into overspecializations as a species.[2]

(*Pause.*) There are states of consciousness, one within the other, and yet each connected, of course, so that genetic systems are really systems of consciousness. They are intertwined with reincarnational systems of consciousness. These are further entwined with the consciousness that you recognize. The present is the point of power. Given the genetic makeup that you now have, your conscious intents and purposes act as the triggers that activate whatever genetic or reincarnational aspects that you need.

The state of dreaming provides the connecting links between these systems of consciousness.

End of dictation. Do you have a question?

(*10:05. "Well, I thought some of your material tonight, about focusing and bodily states, sounded like Jane's own situation—her troubles with stiffness and walking." Seth stared at me for a long moment.*)

Do you want a comment, or was that a statement?

(*"Both."*)

In Ruburt's case, there is no particular genetic connection. The same kind of process could occur, of course.

In Ruburt's case, patterns of behavior were concerned—picked up for the purposes of intensification. Ruburt's mother, and to a large extent your father, had some similar behavior problems. In Ruburt's case, we are still dealing with functioning—impaired functioning—rather than genetic results. Tell Ruburt the end does not justify the means (*with humor*) in his particular situation, any more than in any other. The idea still is to love and protect and cherish, and express the body that you have.

The statement also applies to people who have genetic handicaps. End of session, and a fond good evening.

("Thank you."

10:12 P.M. "There was something there toward the last," Jane said. "I didn't quite get it through, about the end justifying the means. He doesn't want people to apply that to genetic handicaps. . . . Was that a good session?"

"Very good," I said. Indeed, her delivery had been stronger and longer—both by large margins—than I'd expected it would be before the session.)

NOTES. Session 911

1. I suggest that in connection with this note the reader review the 891st session for December 26, 1979, in Chapter 3 for Volume 1 of *Dreams*, where Seth referred to the American hostage affair as "a materialized mass dream."

Over the centuries, in our terms, there have been numerous religious and secular (or worldly or nonreligious) consciousnesses at work and play in the Middle East. In Note 2 for Session 899, in Chapter 5 for Volume 1, I wrote that I could "only hint at the enormously complicated situation involving the whole Middle East these days." I mentioned the Russian invasion of Afghanistan, on Iran's eastern border, and how the coldly secular Russian philosophy clashed with the Iranians' fanatical Moslemic orientation. I also referred to our own country's entanglements in that section of the world. One of the complications I didn't mention is Iran's deepening confrontation with Iraq, another Moslem nation on Iran's western border. Currently the two are arguing over territorial rights concerning a waterway between them that flows into the Persian Gulf; Iran and Iraq have exchanged border clashes for several months now, and each country has threatened heavier military action against the other.

Historically, the animosity between Iran (which until 1935 was called Persia) and Iraq goes back to at least the seventh century, when Arabic conquests brought Islam to the area. A major difference between the two countries is that Iran is Indo-European, and Iraq is Arab. Mohammed, the founder of the Moslem religion, died in 632; conflicts over his successor led to an overall division of the religion into the Shiite and Sunni branches (although this is a simplification). But this great split is also a factor in the current challenges being explored by the two nations: Iran is ruled by Shiite Moslems, Iraq by the Sunni.

In just that one area on our globe, then, a group of consciousnesses has chosen to "evolve" into a number of religious and secular forces that are both internal and external as far as national borders go. Surely one of the larger, long-term questions those consciousnesses must be exploring concerns the confining aspects that very restrictive fundamentalistic interpretations of a certain religion must impose upon large population groups (which accept such conditions for their own collective reasons, of course). In Iran, for instance, present-day Islamic law reaches into and defines acceptable and nonacceptable behavior in every facet of individual and mass life—from the most explicitly sexual to that with the broadest social and national implications. Imagine this zealous and comprehensive orientation encountering the Russian and American world views (which in themselves oppose each other) at this time!

From our viewpoint, it's almost as though our country has become transfixed by its involvements in the Middle East. I even think that the dust storms the American helicopters had to struggle through to reach Desert One were not only symbols but conscious manifestations of our challenges there. The failure of our rescue mission represents another learning step as we grapple with some of the "modern" convolutions of religious and secular forces. Actually, the proliferations of consciousness on our planet are seamless: In those terms, the overall challenges are ancient indeed.

2. Seth delivered the 823rd session for *Mass Events* on February 27, 1978—over two years ago. See Note 2 for that session, in Chapter 4, wherein I wrote that as a physical principle the uncertainty principle of quantum mechanics "sets definite limits to the accuracy possible in measuring both the motion and position of atoms and elementary particles simultaneously," and that

"there is an interaction between the observer (with his instruments) and the object or quality being measured."

Here in *Dreams* Seth uses the uncertainty principle as an analogy (and an excellent one), meaning that as the positions and motions of elementary particles, say, cannot be simultaneously measured precisely, so our genetic qualities and their motions can not always be specifically determined. In *Dreams* he's already said (in Session 909) that the human species has an "amazing interplay between genetic preciseness and genetic freedom," and (in Session 910) that "your genetic structure reacts to each thought that you have, to the state of your emotions, to your psychological climate." Choices and probabilities apply. Thus do we avoid genetic rigidity.

SESSION 912——April 30, 1980
9:04 P.M. WEDNESDAY

(Yesterday Jane finished typing Chapter 15 of God of *Jane. The chapter actually consists of her long poem, "A Psychic Manifesto," which she wrote in July 1979. I'm quoting the first verse of the poem in the front matter for* Mass Events. *"Among other things," I note there, "the poem is a passionate declaration of psychic independence, written in response to Seth's ideas in this book." Jane also described events relative to her creation of "A Psychic Manifesto" in Chapter 14 of* God of *Jane [I expect to finish the notes for* Mass Events *within a couple of weeks.]*

The last evening of the month was quite warm for our area at this time of year—66 degrees—and we had front and kitchen windows of the hill house open so the cats could go out on the porches as they pleased. Incredible, Jane and I thought, that 1980 was already four months old. Many of the birds have returned. I've started mowing a little grass each day.)

(With an elaborate smile:) Now, good evening.

("Good evening, Seth.")

Dictation.

("Right.")

Again, the genetic system is a far more open one than is usually supposed. It not only contains and conveys information, but it also reacts to information from the physical and <u>cultural</u> worlds.

In a way I hope to explain, then, the genetic system also reacts to those beliefs and events that are paramount in any given civilization. Events can <u>trigger</u> genetic activity—not simply through, say, chemical reactions, but through individual and mass beliefs about the safety or lack of it in the world at large.

There are also what I will call genetic dreams, which are inspired directly by genetic triggering. These help form and direct consciousness as it exists in any given individual from before birth.

The fetus dreams. As its physical growth takes place in the womb, so the shaping of its consciousness is also extended by genetic dreams. These particular fetus-oriented dreams are most difficult to describe, for they are actually involved with forming the <u>contours</u> of the individual consciousness. Such dreams provide *(pause)* the <u>subjective understanding</u> from which thoughts are developed, and in those terms complete thoughts are possible before the brain itself is fully formed. It is the process of thinking that helps bring the brain into activity, and not the other way around *(all quite intently)*.

Such thoughts are <u>like, now</u> (underline "like, now"), electrical patterns that <u>form their own</u> magnets. *(Long pause.)* The ability to <u>conceptualize is present in the fetus</u>, and the fetus does conceptualize. The precise orientation of that conceptualizing, and the precise orientation of the thinking patterns, wait for certain physical triggers received from the parents and the environment after birth, but the processes of conceptualization and of thought are already established. This establishment takes place in genetic dreams *(again, all intently)*.

Infants think long before they can speak. Thought must come before language. Language is thought's handmaiden.

(Long pause at 9:22.) Give us a moment. . . . The ability to use language is also genetically built-in, through the precise orientation, again, with the physical triggering of the parents' native language. Children learn such languages mentally long before they are physically capable of speaking them; but again, in genetically inspired dreams, children—or rather, infants—practice language. Before such infants hear their parents speak, however, they are in telepathic communication, and even in the

fetus genetic dreams involve the coding and interpretation of language. Those dreams themselves inspire the physical formations necessary to bring about their own actualizations.

Genetic dreams of one kind or another continue throughout your lives, whether or not you are consciously aware of them. They were of prime importance in "man's evolution," as you think of it. They were the source of dreams, mentioned earlier, that sent man on migrations after food, that led him toward fertile land. Those dreams are most closely related to survival in physical existence, and whenever that survival seems threatened such dreams arise to consciousness whenever possible.

They are the dreams that warn of famines or of wars. Such dreams, however, can also be triggered often, as in your own times, when the conscious mind is convinced that the survival of the species is threatened—and in such cases the dreams then actually represent man's fears. Overanxiety, then, can confuse the genetic system, and in a variety of ways. The existence of each of the species is dependent upon trust, indeed a biological optimism, in which each species feels the freedom to develop the potentials of its members in relative safety, within the natural frameworks of existence. Each species comes into being not merely feeling a natural built-in trust in its own validity, but is literally propelled by exuberance in its ability to cope with its environment. It knows that it is uniquely suited to its place within life's framework. The young of all species exhibit an unquenchable rambunctiousness. That rambunctiousness is built in.

(With emphasis, while Billy slept curled up against my left elbow as I sat on the couch writing down Seth's material:) Animals know that their own lives spell out life's meaning. They feel their relationship with all other forms of life. They know that their existences are vitally important in the framework of planetary existence. Beyond that, they identify themselves with the spirit of life within them so fully and so completely that to question its meaning would be inconceivable. Not inconceivable because such creatures cannot think, but because life's meaning is so self-evident to them.

(Long pause.) Whenever man believes that life is meaningless, whenever he feels that value fulfillment is impossible, or indeed nonexistent, then he undermines his genetic heritage. He sepa-

rates himself from life's meaning. He feels vacant inside. Man for centuries attached faith, hope, and charity to the beliefs of established religions. Instead, these are genetic attributes, inspired and promoted by the inseparable unity of spirit in flesh. *(Pause.)* The animals are quite as familiar with faith, hope, and charity as you are, and often exemplify it in their own frameworks of existence to a better extent. Any philosophy that promotes the idea that life is meaningless is biologically dangerous. It promotes feelings of despair that directly hamper genetic activity. Such philosophies are extremely disadvantageous creatively, since they dampen the emotional spirits and exuberance, and sense of play, from which creativity itself emerges.

Such philosophies are also deadening on an intellectual basis, for they must of necessity close out man's great curiosity about the subjective matters that are his main concern. If life has no meaning, then nothing else really makes any difference, and intellectual curiosity itself also ends up withering on the vine.

(9:49.) The intellectual ideas of societies, therefore, also have a great effect upon which genetic systems are triggered, and which ones are not.

Rest your hand.

(I was amused to see that Jane paused in trance just long enough to add a little wine to her glass. Resume at 9:51.)

You have genetic systems, then, carrying *(long pause)* information that is literally incalculable.[1] Now: Through your technologies, through your physical experience, you are also surrounded by an immense array of communication and information of an exterior nature. You have your telephones, radios, televisions, your earth satellites—all networks that process and convey data. Those inner biological systems and the exterior ones may seem quite separate. They are intimately connected, however. The information you receive from your culture, from your arts, sciences, fields of economics, is all translated, decoded, turned into cellular information. Certain genetic diseases, for example, may be activated or not activated according to the cultural climate at any given time, as the relative safety or lack of it in that climate is interpreted through private experience.

In one way or another, the living genetic system has an effect upon your cultural reality, and the reverse also applies. All of this is further complicated by the purposes and intents of the generations in any historical period, and the reincarnational influences.

Value fulfillment always implies the search for excellence—not perfection, but excellence. Excellence *(pause)* in any given area—emotional, physical, intellectual, intuitional, scientific—is reflected in other areas, and by its mere existence serves as a model for achievement. This kind of excellence need not be structured, then, into any one aspect of life, though it may appear in any aspect, and wherever it appears it is an echo of a spiritual and biological directive, so to speak. There are different historical periods, in your terms, where the species has showed what it can do—and what is possible in certain specific directions when the genetic and reincarnational triggers are touched and opened full blast, so that certain characteristics appear in their clearest, most spectacular light, to serve as individual models and as models for the species as a whole.

Again, such times are closely bound with reincarnational intents that direct the genetic triggering, and that meet in the culture the further stimulus that may be required. The time of the great masters in the fields of painting and sculpture is a case in point *(humorously and louder)*—so you see, I am getting to one of your favorite questions,[2] and we will continue the discussion at our next session.

Do you have any questions otherwise?

(10:09. I did have a question for Seth now—one made up of a number of questions, actually, and another one of my favorites. It's easily the longest I've asked in a session. It grows out of Seth's philosophy, obviously, yet it also reflects my own, and concerns man's attempts to both fight and grasp his heritage. Here's a condensation of what I said:

"The other day Jane and I were talking about people who maintain that the universe is an accident, or that it has no meaning, or that there's no such thing as life after death, or that psychic abilities don't exist—that sort of thing. People who call themselves skeptics, who seem to have a very rigid focus only within what they call physical reality. Those attitudes are very common. Some people have built careers around negative beliefs like that, and Jane and I were wondering how they react after physical death, when they discover that they still live—that they may have spent their professional lives maintaining belief systems which after death they begin to understand are quite wrong. How do they react? Are those individuals

even aware of their earlier beliefs? Do they care what they used to think? Are they shocked, do they have feelings of regret or embarrassment, or what? Or is there such a variety of responses possible that you can't answer the question simply? And how do such people react after death when they start to get glimmerings about the workings of reincarnation,[3] *for example?"*

Seth had listened politely while I expressed myself.)

Well, a tidbit: It is a highly individual matter, so that an overall answer is difficult.

Reincarnational patterns apply also. Some people, having lived lives believing in one religious system or another, being completely immersed in them, give themselves shock treatments of sorts, then, living lives in which they believe in nothing, or at least freeing themselves from any beliefs—only to discover, of course, that a belief in nothing is the most confining belief of all. That realization is the eye-opener, in such cases.

There are those who overrelied upon religious beliefs, using them as crutches, and in [later lives] then, they might—such people—throw those crutches away overreacting to their new-found "freedom"; and through living lives as meaningless they then realize, after death, that the meaningfulness of existence was after all not dependent upon any religious system. It was there all along, but they had not seen it.

The variations are endless. On the whole, in the vast scheme of reincarnational reality, a belief in life's meaning is by far the rule, and other excursions are indeed eccentric variations. Specifically, however, such life episodes will of course involve their "moments" of after-death realization—dismay, shock, or what have you.

If you will remind me, I will say more from time to time on that subject.

(Heartily:) End of session.

("Thank you, Seth.")

And a fond good evening to you both.

("The same to you."

10:20 P.M. I told Jane that the session is excellent. Her delivery had often been rather fast and intent—even impassioned. She laughed. "See, I wanted him to come through and say something about me, without my asking, but he didn't." She hadn't mentioned such a desire to me. "I got something about genetic dreams while I was doing the dishes tonight—

just the phrase," she said. "Anyhow, I feel better after the session than I did before it.

"But tonight I had the feeling after the session that it's a real full one—that I really got to the heart of something," Jane added. "I like that. The last session didn't give me that feeling, but when I read it, it was fine. . . .")

NOTES. Session 912

1. There isn't any such word as "incalculatable," of course, but that's what Jane came through with as she spoke for Seth. She obviously meant to say "incalculable." Seldom indeed does she make such slips while delivering the Seth material—much less often than any of us may do in daily life.

2. Seth referred to a question I periodically ask Jane, but seldom discuss with others simply because they don't seem to be interested: What's happened to all of the Rembrandts? Why isn't there at least one artist in all of the world painting today whose ability equals Rembrandt's, and who uses that great gift to evoke the depths of compassion for the human condition as Rembrandt did? For in my opinion there isn't such a one around. By extension, why isn't there a Rubens or a Velázquez or a Vermeer operating now? My choices are personally arbitrary, of course— yet *why don't we* have a Rembrandt contributing to our current reality? Just those four artists, whose lives spanned a period of only 98 years (from 1577 to 1675), explored human insight in powerful ways. To link the "great masters" with our species' reincarnational intents and drives, as Seth mentions in this session, opens up a new field for understanding my question, and a very large and intriguing one indeed.

Our many excellent "modern" painters inevitably work within a different world ambience. Our species' art is just no longer the same—a fact I both applaud and mourn. However, I do feel that in the course of ordinary time we have either lost certain qualities of art or no longer stress them.

3. I've been saving the following untitled poem of Jane's for a spot like this. She wrote it on November 7, 1979, almost a month before delivering Session 886 for Chapter 2 of *Dreams* (in Vol-

ume 1) on December 3. I suggest that in connection with the poem the reader review the opening paragraphs of that session.

If there is no life after life,
then what cosmic spendthrift formed
the universe,
for Chance alone can't be
that prolific, or fake an order in which
an accident of such proportions
as the creation of a world
seems so inevitable,
each random element
falling pat, into place,
and each consciousness promptly appearing
with body parts all neatly assembled—
only to be squandered,
falling apart, dissolving into nothingness
while Chance grinds out newer odds.

If there is no life after life,
then what a lack
of cosmic economy,
for nature strings one molecule
on to another so craftily
that each seed can grow a tree,
and contains the properties
of an entire forest,
while multiplications
are hidden everywhere.

SESSION 913——May 5, 1980
9:02 P.M. MONDAY

(After lunch today Jane and I were visited by our old friend David Yoder, who's been in Florida recuperating from the heart bypass surgery he underwent early this year.[1] David brought news that was at first startling, then quickly developed into several conflicting emotions and ideas for us: He'd just learned from a relative of hers that a few weeks ago Mrs. Steffans [not her real name], the wife of the couple we'd purchased the hill house from in March 1975, had committed suicide at

her home in a Western state while her husband was away on a business trip.

Now there are several "house connections" here, involving David, the Steffanses, and ourselves. We actually bought the hill house through the real-estate agent for the Steffanses, a few months after they'd moved out of Elmira. I never met the couple. Jane met Mrs. Steffans just once, in 1973, when she came through with a spontaneous "reading" for the lady at an informal party David Yoder gave in the apartment he was renting at the time. Jane and I think it most interesting that we were living in the same downtown apartment house as David was, and that Jane met— just that once—a person living in the house we were to buy two years later. Furthermore, Mrs. Steffans is the last individual for whom Jane has given a reading under such public circumstances.[2]

Her relative, David told us now, had informed him that Mrs. Steffans had suffered bouts of deep depression while living in the hill house. After David left we began to wonder if either one of us had ever picked up on such psychic lows, so to speak, either before or after we'd moved into the place. Jane certainly hadn't done so during her reading for Mrs. Steffans, and that made us speculate about when those depressive states had begun.

I was curious as to how often such a "negative psychology" oper-ated—when, simply because of his or her own hang-ups, an individual [or more than one person] is attracted to a site where strongly negative events had taken place. Surely this happens just as often as it does with positive situations. Later this afternoon Jane said she didn't think she'd ever tuned into Mrs. Steffans's depressions in that manner: "If I thought I had, or still was," she said, "I'd move out." We'd have to. I have no feeling that I'd been affected, either. Still, we found it strange indeed—unreal, even—to consider that a person so intimately connected with a place we love had killed herself.[3]

Jane was very relaxed by session time. The evening was still warm, following our hottest day of the year so far: 86 degrees.)

(*Whispering:*) Good evening.

("*Good evening, Seth.*")

(*With many pauses to start:*) Dictation. Your established fields of knowledge do not grant any subjective reality to c-e-l-l-s (*spelled*).

Cells, however, possess an inner knowledge of their own shapes, and of any other shapes in their immediate environ-ment—this apart from the communication system mentioned earlier that operates on biological levels between all cells.

To some important degree, cells possess curiosity, an impetus toward action, a sense of their own balance, and a sense of being individual while being, for example, a part of a tissue or an organ. The cell's identification biologically is highly connected with this [very] precise knowledge of its own shape, or sometimes shapes. Cells, then, know their own forms.

In highly complicated cellular structures like yourselves *(pause),* with your unique mental properties, you end up with a vital inborn sense of shape and form. The ability to draw is a natural outgrowth of this sensing of shape, this curiosity of form. On a quite unconscious level you possess a biological self-image that is quite different from the self that you see in a mirror. It is a knowledge of bodily form from the inside out, so to speak, composed of cellular shapes and organizations, operating at the maximum. The simple cell, again, has a curiosity about its environment, and on your much more advanced cellular level your own curiosity is unbounded. It is primarily felt as a curiosity about shapes: the urge to touch, to explore, to feel edges and smooth places.

There is particularly a fascination with space itself, in which, so to speak, there is nothing to touch, no shapes to perceive. You are born, then, with a leaning toward the exploration of form and shape in particular.

(9:19.) Remember that cells have consciousness, so while I say these leanings are biologically entwined, they are also mental properties. Drawing in its simplest form is, again, an extension of those inclinations, and in a fashion serves two purposes. Particularly on the part of children, it allows them to express forms and shapes that they see mentally first of all. When they draw circles or squares, they are trying to reproduce those inner shapes, transposing those images outward into the environment—a creative act, highly significant, for it gives children experience in translating inner perceived events of a personal nature into a shared physical reality apparent to all.

When children draw objects they are successfully, then, turning the shapes of the exterior world into their personal mental experiences—possessing them mentally, so to speak, through physically rendering the forms. *(Long pause.)* The art of drawing or painting to one extent or another always involves those two processes. An astute understanding of inner energy and outer energy is required, and for great art an intensification and magnification of both elements.

The species chooses the best conditions in which to display and develop such a capacity to the utmost, taking into consideration all its other needs and purposes. The particular, brilliant, intensified flowering of painting and sculpture that took place, say, in the time of Michelangelo *(1475–1564)* could not, in your probability, have occurred after the birth of technology, for example, and certainly not in your own era, where images are flashed constantly before your eyes on television and in the movies, where they are rambunctiously present in your magazines and advertisements. You are everywhere surrounded by photography of all kinds, but in those days images outside of those provided by nature's objects were highly rare.

People could physically only see what was presently before their eyes—no postcards with pictures of the Alps, or far places. Visual data consisted of what the eye could see—and that was indeed a different kind of a world, a world in which a sketched object was of considerable value. Portraits [were] possessed only by the priests and nobility. You must remember also that the art of the great masters was largely unknown to the poor peasants of Europe, much less to the world at large. Art was for those who could enjoy it—who could afford it. There were no prints to be passed around,[4] so art, politics, and religion were all connected. Poor people saw lesser versions of religious paintings in their own simple churches, done by local artists of far lesser merit than those [who] painted for the popes.

The main issue, however, in that particular era, was a shared belief system, a system that consisted of, among other things, implied images that were neither here nor there—neither entirely earthly nor entirely divine—a mythology of God, angels, demons, an entire host of Biblical characters that were images in man's imagination, images to be physically portrayed. Those images were like an entire artistic language. Using them, the artist automatically commented upon the world, the times, God, man, and officialdom.

(9:40.) Those mythological images and their belief system were shared by all—peasants and the wealthy—to a large degree. They were, then, highly charged emotionally. Whether an

artist painted saints or apostles as heroic figures, as ideas embodied in flesh, or as natural men, he commented on the relationship between the natural and the divine.

In a fashion, those stylized figures that stood for the images of God, apostles, saints, and so forth, were like a kind of formalized abstract form, into which the artist painted all of his emotions and all of his beliefs, all of his hopes and dissatisfactions. Let no one make God the Father look like a mere human, for example! He must be seen in heroic dimensions, while Christ could be shown in divine and human attributes also. The point is that the images the artists were trying to portray were initially mental and emotional ones, and the paintings were supposed to represent not only themselves but the great drama of divine and human interrelationship, and the tension between the two. The paintings themselves seemed to make the heavenly horde come alive. If no one had seen Christ, there were pictures of him.

This was an entirely different kind of art than you have now. It was an attempt to objectify inner reality as it was perceived through a certain belief system. Whether the artist disagreed with certain issues or not, the belief system was there as an invisible framework. That intense focus that united belief systems, that tension between a sensed subjective world and the physical one, and the rarity of images to be found elsewhere, brought art into that great flowering.

Later, as man insisted upon more objectivity of a certain kind, he determined that images of men should look like men—human beings, with weaknesses and strengths. The heroic mold began to vanish. Artists decided to stick to portraying the natural world as they saw it with their natural eyes, and to cast aside the vast field of inner imagery. Some of da Vinci's sketches already show that tendency, and he is fascinating because with his undeniable artistic tendencies he also began to show those tendencies that would lead toward the birth of modern science.

(9:57.) His notebooks, for example, dealt with minute observations made upon aspects of nature itself. He combined the forces of highly original, strong imagination with very calculated preciseness, a kind of preciseness that would lead to detailed sketches of flowers, trees, the action of water—all of nature's phenomena.

Now: Drawing of that nature flourishes in your times in an

entirely different fashion, divorced to some extent from its be-ginnings—in, for example, the highly complicated plans of engineers; the unity of, say, precise sketching and mathematics, necessary in certain sciences, [with] the sketching [being] required for all of the inventions that are now a part of your world. In your world, technology is your art. It is through the use of technology and science that you have sought to understand your relationship with the universe.

(Pause.) Science has until recently provided you with a unified belief system that is only now eroding—and if you will forgive me *(smile)*, your space voyages have simply been physical attempts to probe into that same unknown that other peoples in other times have tried to explore through other means. Technology has been responsible for the fact that so many people have been able to see the great paintings of the world, either directly or through reproductions—and more people are familiar with the works of the great masters than ever were in their lifetimes.

The species uses those conditions, however, so that the paintings of the great masters can serve as models and impetuses, not simply for the extraordinary artwork involved, but to rearouse within man those emotions that brought the paintings into being.

(10:05.) Give us a moment. . . . Man always does best, or his best, when he sees himself in heroic terms. While the Roman Catholic Church gave him a powerful, cohesive belief system *(pause)*, for many reasons those beliefs shifted so that the division between man and God became too great. *(Pause.)* Man the sinner took over from man the child of God. As a result, one you see in art particularly, man became a heroic figure, then a natural one. *(Pause.)* The curiosity that had been directed toward divinity became directed toward nature. Man's sense of inquiry led him, then, to begin to paint more natural portraits and images. He turned to landscapes also. This was an inevitable process. As it occurred, however, [man] began to make great distinctions between the world of the imagination and the world of nature, until finally he became convinced that the physical world was real and the imaginative world was not. So his paintings became more and more realistic.

Art became wedded, then, to phenomena directly before the

eyes. Therefore, in a way it could present man with no more data than he had before. Imaginative interpretations seemed like pretensions. Art largely ended up—in those terms, now—as the handmaiden of technology: engineering plans, mathematical diagrams, and so forth. What you call abstract art tried to reverse that process, but even the abstract painters did not believe in the world of the imagination, in which there were any heroic dimensions, and the phase is largely transitory.

I did mean to mention that man's use of perspective in painting was a turning point *(early in the 15th century)*, in that it foreshadowed the turning of art away from its imaginative colorations toward a more specific physical rendering—that is, to a large degree after that the play of the imagination would not be allowed to "distort" the physical frame of reference.

All of this involved the triggering of innate abilities at certain points in time by the species at large, and on the parts of certain individuals, as their purposes and those of the species merged.

(Long pause at 10:19.) End of dictation. Do you have a question?

("Earlier today we were talking about the suicide of Mrs. Steffans, who used to live in this house—")

I am familiar with the discussion. Ruburt has not been picking up on any of the woman's past depressions. In a fashion you were attracted to the house, as I mentioned *(in 1975),* because of its contemporary nature, and the neighborhood—but also because it put you in a different position, in a different social context. And that was the context that Mrs. Steffans operated in in a different way.

The house, as you recall, was highly formal, impeccably clean. [Mrs. Steffans] tried to live on the outside, while she was always concerned with inner issues, and it was on your parts indicative of a creative tension between the two. That is, you could certainly put that atmosphere to use, where she was unable to.

(Pause.) In a fashion the house itself yearned toward a flexibility, more openness with the elements, and the woman was attracted to it for that reason. You have not reacted to any negative influences in that regard, but in a fashion through your creativity helped reconcile what were conflicting elements.

End of session. Ruburt was correct about your dream *(of last night),* and if you remember, I have always encouraged the two of you in such *(dream recall)* activities.

("Yes, Seth. Thank you very much. Good night."

10:28 P.M. Once she'd moved past a slow beginning, Jane had accelerated her delivery considerably. "The session's really good," I told her. "I want to read over the material on art especially."

She laughed. "I hope it fits in with the book. I never heard of a book on evolution talk about dreams and art.")

NOTES. Session 913

1. In Chapter 4 of *Dreams,* for Volume 1, see the opening notes for Session 895, which Jane delivered on January 4, 1980.

2. For a brief description of Jane's encounter with Mrs. Steffans, see Note 13 for Session 744, in Volume 2 of *"Unknown" Reality.* Seth, and Jane and I, described a number of our house-hunting adventures in the two volumes of that work. Those complicated, interrelated happenings are just as fascinating to us now as they were when they were unfolding; we have yet to publish their full story. We think that the events surrounding our purchase of the hill house furnish many clues to the spontaneous and creative workings of individual consciousnesses in our chosen physical reality.

3. In none of our conversations involving Mrs. Steffans did Jane and I talk of blame or guilt in connection with suicide. As we searched for understanding, we reviewed the excellent material on death, as well as suicide, that Seth had given in the very first session for *Mass Events:* In Chapter 1, see the 801st session for April 18, 1977.

4. Right away I began to wonder when Seth stated that "There were no prints to be passed around. . . ." Presumably he referred to the time of Michelangelo. However, my reading indicates that Seth was probably right about prints being unavailable to the "poor peasants" of those times.

Woodcuts and wood blocks were used for a variety of purposes by the ancient Chinese and Egyptians, for example, and even by the Romans. Many of the early prints created in Europe illustrate religious subjects. One of the first dated European woodcuts, showing a religious figure, appeared in 1423; a book bearing woodcut illustrations was produced circa 1460; the first Roman book containing woodcuts was made in 1467. Bibles were illustrated with woodcuts in the late 15th century. The earliest known engravings, printed on paper, date from around 1450; pictorial engraving and etching were evidently developed in Germany in the early 1500s. Leonardo da Vinci (1452–1519) experimented with his own method of copper engraving. But all of these efforts were beginnings: There couldn't have been any mass circulation of printed material in those days.

SESSION 914——May 7, 1980
9:02 P.M. WEDNESDAY

(Jane will be 51 years old tomorrow.

"I've had a rough day," she said as we sat for the session. Actually, she was twice irritated. First had come her reactions to a group of upsetting letters she'd received this noon: One is a 20-page missive from a mental patient who wants returned to him all of the notes, objects, manuscripts, and books of poetry he's sent her over the years: another is from a woman who informed us that she's writing a book dictated by Seth: a third is a long letter from a man who's claiming us as his counterparts, for reasons we can't agree with. There are others. In these cases, it seems impossible that we'll ever be able to communicate effectively with the individuals involved, although we're sincerely trying to understand why each of them contacted us.

And: "I'm pissed off," Jane said now by way of further irritation. She referred to a "psychic fair" she'd accidentally tuned in to on television, while waiting for me to come into the living room for the session. I saw the last few minutes of the program: At a large open-air site, a medium, evidently speaking for "a great council" sitting on one of the outer planets like Saturn or Uranus, was delivering a ringing, generalized message to us earthlings. The several hundred people present applauded when the medium finished. "If we'd had any inkling of what we were getting into with the Seth material, I'd never have done it," Jane said. She meant that she wouldn't have become associated with "the cheap psychic field," not that she'd have given up working with the Seth mate-

rial. I had to laugh, as I remarked that we hadn't sought out such associations; others had made them for us. I asked her just how one could go about speaking for a personality like Seth, yet remain aloof from all of the psychic playing going on around us. I said I think we're doing reasonably well as it is.[1]

"Maybe I'd better concentrate on those great letters we got today," Jane said—for she had indeed received some of those, too. "Like from that actress, and the birthday cards, and the flowers. . . ."

Just before the session she showed me a page of notes she'd picked up from Seth today, about the subject matter for tonight's session—but we had no time in which to discuss them.)

Now: Dictation.

(I nodded.)

People have a biologically built-in knowledge that life has meaning. They share that biologically ingrained trust with all other living creatures. A belief in life's meaning is a necessity on the part of your species.

It is vital for the proper workings of genetic systems. It is a prerequisite for individual health and for the overall vitality of any given "stock." Your greatest achievements have been produced by civilizations during those times when man had the greatest faith in the meaningfulness of life in general, and in the meaningfulness of the individual within life's framework.

(Pause.) You are, I hope, coming toward a time of greater psychological synthesis, so that the intuitions and reasoning abilities work together in a much more smooth fashion, so that emotional and intuitive knowledge regarding the meaningfulness of life can find clearer precision and expression, as the intellect is taught—as the intellect is taught—to use its faculties in a far less restricted manner.

No matter what science says about certain values being outside of its frame of reference, science implies that those values are therefore without basis. The reasoning qualities of the mind are directed away from any exploration that might bring about any acceptable scientific evidence for such values, therefore. The fact is that man lives by those values that science ignores *(quietly emphatic, and repeated).*

For that reason, science—after its first great adventurous era—had its own flaws built in, and so it must expand its definitions of reality or become a tin-can caricature of itself, a prostituted handmaiden to an outworn technology, and quite give up its early claims of investigating the nature of truth or reality. It could become as secondary to life as, say, the Roman Catholic Church is now, losing its hold upon world dominance, losing its claim of being the one official arbiter of reality.

There are, overall, some processes important in man's development, and in the development of the species. Efforts, methods that work against value fulfillment phase themselves out, for in the long run they do not work.

(Slowly at 9:20:) There is nothing wrong with technology. Man has an innate inclination toward the use of tools, and technology is no more than an extension of that capacity. *(Pause.)* When men use tools in accord with *(pause)* the "dictates" of value fulfillment, those tools are effective. Your technology, however, as it stands, has to some important degree—but not entirely—been based upon a scientific philosophy that denies the very idea of value fulfillment. Therefore, you end up with a technology that threatens to work no longer. You end up with affairs of great national and world concern, such as the Three Mile Island episode, and other lesser-known near-nuclear accidents.

(Sometimes I become a bit puzzled as I prepare Seth's material for publication. My first thought was to recast his subjunctive mood in the next paragraph entirely in the present tense. My second thought was to leave the paragraph as it is—but to add the two bracketed inserts for greater clarity. I do not like to change Seth's information, and almost always avoid doing so.)

The control panels of the nuclear plants, many of them, were designed as if consciousness did not enter into the picture at all, as if the plants were [to be] run by other machines, not men—with controls that are not handily within reach, or physically inaccessible, as if the men who drew up the plans had completely forgotten what the species [is] like mentally or physically.

Now, the overall purpose supposedly is the utilization of energy—a humanitarian project meant to bring light and warmth to millions of homes. But that intent was sabotaged because the philosophy behind it denied the validity of the very subjective values that give man his reason for living. Because those values were forgotten, life was threatened.

There are grass-roots organizations—cults, groups of every

persuasion—growing up in your country as small groups of people together, once again, search for intellectual reasons to back up their innate emotional knowledge that life has meaning. These groups represent *(long pause)* the beginnings of new journeys quite as important to the species as any sea voyage ever was as man searched for new lands.

Seeds are blown by the wind, and so reproduce their kind. Many people speculate about the physical journeys of early man from one continent to another. It is said that in "the struggle to survive" man was literally driven to expand his physical boundaries.

(9:38.) Give us a moment. . . . The true motion of the species, however, has always been psychological, or psychic if you prefer, involving the exploration of ideas. And again, the survival of the species in those terms is basically dependent upon its belief in the meaningfulness of its existence. *(Emphatically:)* These new cults and groups, however—these new cults and groups, therefore—therefore—are following the paths of genetic wisdom, opening up new areas of speculation and belief. And if some of their present beliefs are ludicrous in the light of the intellect's reason, in the end—because [such groups] are following the dictates of value fulfillment, however feebly—they are significant. It is easy for the intellect, as you are used to using it, to see only the antics of such groups, and they can appear ridiculous in that light.

A scientist who would threaten the very survival of life on the planet in order to increase life's conveniences (underlined) is, however, truly displaying ludicrous behavior *(with irony)*.

The trouble with most ideas concerning evolution is that they are all one-sided—all loaded, of course, at man's end at the expense of the other species, and [with] all thinking in terms of progress along very narrow consecutive lines. Such ideas have much to do with the way you think of yourselves, and what you consider human characteristics, and the light in which you view those who vary in one way or another from those norms.

Take a brief break.

(9:48 to 10:04.)

Now: Man needs the feeling that he is progressing, but technological progress alone represents a comparatively shallow level

unless it is backed up by a growth of emotional understanding—
a progression of man's sense of being at one with himself and
with the rest of the natural world.

There are people who are highly intellectually proficient,
whose reasoning abilities are undisputed, and yet their considerable lack of, say, emotional or spiritual development remains
largely invisible as far as your assessments are concerned. Such
people are not considered retarded, of course. I will always be
speaking about a balance between intuitional and reasoning abilities and, I hope, [be] leading you toward a wedding of those
abilities, for together they can bring about what would certainly
appear in your world to be one completely new faculty, combining the very best elements of each, but in such a fashion that
both were immeasurably enhanced.

I also want to emphasize that your present beliefs limit the full
and free operation of your intellects, as far as your established
fields of knowledge are concerned, for science has placed so
many taboos, limiting the areas of free intellectual inquiry. I am
not, however, promoting dependence upon feelings above the
intellect, or vice versa.

The fact remains that when you assess your fellows, you put a
far greater stress upon intellectual achievement than emotional
achievement. Some of you may even question what emotional
achievement is, but it is highly important spiritually and biologically. Some people, who would rate quite high on any hypothetical emotional-achievement test, might very possibly under certain conditions be labeled as retarded, according to the dictates
of your society. The species is at least embarked upon its journey
toward emotional achievement, as it is upon the development of
its intellectual capacities, and ultimately the two must go hand in
hand.

A brilliant mathematician or scientist, or even an artist, or an
accepted genius in any field, can be an emotional incompetent,
but no one considers him as retarded. I am not speaking now of
eccentric behavior on the part of, say, creative people or anyone
else, but of a lack of understanding of emotional values.

Now as far as the species is concerned, all variations are necessary—and it is as if (underlined) in one instance a member of the
species—for its own reasons, but also on behalf of the whole—
decides to specialize in one particular area, to isolate certain

abilities, so to speak, and display them with the greatest tenacity and brilliance, while nearly completely ignoring certain other areas. In your society, however, the capacities of the reasoning mind have been considered in opposition to the intuitive abilities, so that your ideas of what a person is or should be largely ignore the idea of emotional achievement, emotional understanding.

Other people may be sophisticated, brilliantly aware of their own feelings and those of other people, intuitively knowledgeable in the handling of relationships, even, as adults, exquisite parents—yet they may be labeled as retarded if they do not live up to certain artificial intellectual standards. They are actually in the same position at the other end as the people mentioned earlier.

It is as if certain members of the species, for their own reasons, and again on the part of the whole, specialized this time in the use of <u>emotional</u> capacities. But those people are usually considered <u>retarded.</u>

I will have more to say about that particular issue, for I am speaking about certain cases only.

(*10:28.*) Now: (*Long pause.*) Mankind is a species (*long pause*) that specializes in the use of the imagination, and without the imagination language would be unnecessary. Man from his particular vantage point imagines images and events that are not before his eyes. The applied use of the imagination is one of the most distinguishing marks of your species, and the imagination is your connection between the inner worlds of reality and the exterior world of your experience. It connects your emotions and your reason. All species are interconnected, so, as I said earlier, when you think you think for yourselves, you also specialize in thinking <u>for the rest of nature</u>, which physically sustains you.

I want to discuss reason and imagination, then, and those subtle variations that unite the two. Through doing so, I hope to give a truer picture of your own dimension, and to continue our discussion about the gifts and seeming defects that are genetically inspired.

End of session, end of dictation, end of chapter, and a fond good evening.

(*"Thank you, Seth. Good night."*)

10:36 P.M. Although it had ranged from being slow to fast, Jane's delivery had often been quite forceful. She told me that Seth had changed the beginning of the session because of her reactions to the mail this noon, but that finally he'd gotten into some of the material she'd picked up from him today, and written down. Seth hadn't covered her notes about caveman art, however; she'd especially looked forward to his comments on that subject.

"But I don't want the Seth books to end up criticizing everything," Jane said.

"Well," I asked, "how are the three of us going to discuss what's going on in the world, and disagree with a lot of it, without appearing to criticize?"

"I know. But I want the books to be reassuring. . . .")

NOTE. Session 914

1. Jane's particular mood today, and my own remarks, shouldn't be taken to mean that we don't understand why people attend psychic fairs, for example. I think that each person at that gathering shown on television was looking for news about man's origin and nature—even if, in our opinions, it's too simplistic to postulate the existence of a great council on one of the far planets of our solar system. To us, that concept is an exteriorized distortion of the "great council" that each one of us carries within ourselves. But there are many ramifications here, and it's obvious that studying the Seth material is hardly the only way to explore reality. Human beings are far too diverse to be satisfied by any one system of thought, or even by any related group of them.

CHAPTER 8

When You Are Who You Are. The Worlds of Imagination and Reason, and the Implied Universe.

SESSION 915——May 12, 1980
9:10 P.M. MONDAY

(As she enthusiastically noted in her journal recently, Jane has had "loosenings all over" of her physical symptoms. What a pleasure it is to see her walk more easily, if only for a few steps at a time—and even if she leans upon a table for support, or whatever else may be handy.

She's just as enthusiastic over having organized the rest of her God of Jane. She finished Chapter 17 today, and wrote in her journal after supper: "Very very very good on Chapter 17—oodles of new insights! Pleased!" She envisions at least another half dozen chapters for the book, but at the same time she's leaving final decisions up to her creative self. And her book of poetry, If We Live Again, *hovers in the background of her consciousness. She's done little with it since late February. I last mentioned it a month ago; in Chapter 6 for Volume 1 of* Dreams, *see the opening notes for the 907th session.)*

Sue Watkins has informed us that she's approximately halfway through writing Volume 2 of her Conversations With Seth.

Jane was so much at ease tonight that she thought of skipping the session, but she decided to try for it because she'd picked up material on it from Seth today, and made a few notes. "I'm sort of confused," she said now, "because the stuff I got from him is kind of difficult, and I don't know whether I'm up to it or not. . . . But I feel him around. I guess I'll start in a minute, but it's amazing to me. . . ."

And Billy and Mitzi, who had been racing through the house, came as if on signal to play beneath Jane's rocker when she began speaking for Seth. Even as I took notes I couldn't help noticing how amazingly quick the cats' reflexes were—how joyously *they operated within their chosen physical realities.)*

Now: Dictation. New chapter *(8)*. Give us a moment for the heading.

(Pause.) "When (underlined) You Are Who You Are. The Worlds of Imagination and Reason, and the Implied Universe."

(Pause.) When you are determines where you are. *(Long pause.)* Space is in many ways more "timely" than you think. I am not speaking of the usual time concepts, of course, of consecutive moments, but of a certain dimension of activity in which your space happens.

(9:15.) As long as we are trying to explain the origin of your world in a new fashion, we will be bringing in many subjects that may not usually appear in such discussions. The world as you know it emerges from an inner, more extensive sphere of dimensions into actuality. It is supported then by a seemingly invisible framework.

Beyond certain levels it is almost meaningless to speak in terms of particles, but I will for now use the term "invisible particles" because you are familiar with it. Invisible particles, then, form the foundation of your world. The invisible particles that I am referring to, however, have the ability to transform themselves into mass,[1] or to divest themselves of it. And the invisible particles of which I speak not only possess consciousness—but each one is, if you will, a seed that contains within itself a potential for an infinite number of gestalts. Each such invisible particle contains within itself the potential *(pause)* to embark upon an infinite number of probable variations of consciousness. To that degree such psychological particles are at that stage unspecialized, while they contain within themselves the innate ability to specialize in whatever direction becomes suitable.

(9:26.) They can be, and they <u>are</u>, every<u>where</u> at once. Sometimes they operate with mass and <u>sometimes without</u> it. Now you are composed of such invisible particles, and so is everything else that you can physically perceive. To that degree—to that <u>degree</u> (underlined)—portions of your own consciousness <u>are</u> everywhere at once. They are not lost, or spread out in some generalized fashion, but acutely responsive, and as highly alert as your familiar consciousness is now.

The self that you are aware of represents only one "position" in which those invisible particles happen to intersect, gain mass, build up form. Scientists can only perceive an electron <u>as it is to</u> them. They cannot really track it. They cannot be cert<u>ain of</u> its position and its speed at the same time, and to some extent the same applies to your consciousness. The speed of your own thoughts takes those thoughts away from you even as you think them—and you can never really examine a thought, but only the thought of a thought *(with quiet amusement).*

Because you are, you are everywhere at once. I am quite aware of the fact that you can scarcely follow that psychological motion. As we will see later, your imaginations can lead you toward some recognition, even toward some emotional comprehension, of this concept. While your reasoning abilities at first may falter, that is only because you have trained your intellect to respond in a limited fashion.

There are what I will call "intervals of perception." *(Pause.)* You are usually conscious of events that are significant neurologically, and that neurological timing is the end result of an [almost]² infinite series of sequences. *(Pause.)* Those sequences are areas in which activities happen. Each consciousness within each area is tuned into its proper sequence. Each area builds on the others. The invisible particles are the framework upon which your body is formed, for example—<u>they</u> (underlined) move faster than the speed of light, yet you <u>are</u> not dizzy. You are aware of no such motion. You are tuned into a different sequence of action.

There are, then, different worlds operating with different frequencies at different intervals. They are conscious in other times, though you are neurologically equipped to perceive your own interval structures. When I speak of time, I do not merely refer to other centuries as you think of them. But between the moments that you know, and neurologically accept, there are other kinds of moments, if you prefer, other versions of time, and other kinds of accomplishments and fulfillments that are not dependent upon your usual ideas of, say, growth through time.[3]

Some of this may seem quite difficult at first reading, but I know that you are all far more intelligent than you realize you are—far more intuitive. I know also that you are tired of simple tales told to you as if you were children, and that your minds and hearts yearn for worthwhile challenges. You want to extend yourselves as far as possible, because each of you has been born with that urge toward value fulfillment.

It is only because, particularly in your times, you have trained yourselves to limit the nature of your own consciousnesses that such ideas seem strange. You have thus far believed that you must train your great imaginations and your intelligences to confine themselves and their activities to the physical world as you have been told it exists. In childhood, before you so leashed your imaginations, however, you each had your own dreams— dreams that awakened you to other portions of your own identities. There are many experiences open to you now—if you can be free enough to allow them—that will give you glimpses of those other intervals in which you have a reality.

I will deal with some such exercises later on in the book. All such methods, however, are useless if your beliefs hold you back, and so the main thrust of all of my books is to increase your own areas of thought and speculation.

Take your break.

(9:52. Jane's delivery for Seth had become quite fast by break time. "Wow," she exclaimed as she put on her glasses, "I was so far out of it, and the material got so complicated, that I didn't know what was going on. I remember the stuff on particles, but I don't even know if I got it all. I do know there's a certain amount I'm supposed to get through tonight. I got confused. . . ."

Apropos of that "certain amount," she read me her notes on the subjects she'd felt Seth would cover tonight. He'd touched upon a few of them. As we talked I heard Billy helping himself to some dry cat food in

the kitchen, on the other side of the room divider. Then he made himself
comfortable beside me on the couch, preparing for a nap.

"I think Seth's just going to come back briefly," Jane said as she
removed her glasses. Resume at 9:59.)

Now: End of dictation.

In material like tonight's, but in general during sessions, you
end up with information *(pause)* that does indeed come from
outside of time in certain important fashions.

It requires that Ruburt forge imagination and reason together
in a highly accelerated fashion, and at levels obviously not conscious in usual terms—levels that propel him into my domain. I
have my own consciousness at other intervals—intervals that in
your terms encompass your own.

Now Ruburt is undergoing some profound therapeutic
changes. Probabilities intersect at each point with your time, and
those probabilities are psychologically directed so that, in your
terms once again, he is at an excellent intersection point, where
the prognosis is excellent. Tell him I said this. And you are both
responsible, for both of your lives merge in their fashions.

(Heartily:) End of session, and a fond good evening.

("Thank you, Seth."

10:07 P.M. Once Jane was out of trance, I told her that most of Seth's
material since break can also be considered book work, including his hint
about his own reality. He'd alluded to her notes a little more, but I was
disappointed that he hadn't developed two particular thoughts Jane had
picked up from him today. I could almost hear his amused elaborations
upon: "Alone, reason finally becomes unreasonable. Alone, the imagina-
tion becomes less imaginative over time."

I had several other questions concerning Seth's use of the term "invisi-
ble particles," but decided to discuss them with Jane later.)

NOTES. Session 915

1. In Volume 2 of *"Unknown" Reality*, see Note 8 for Appendix
19. In it I wrote: "Ordinarily we think of mass as meaning the
bulk and/or weight of an object. In classical physics, the amount
of matter in a given object is measured according to its relation
to inertia, which in turn is the tendency of matter to keep moving in the same direction, if moving, or to stay at rest if at rest.

An object's mass is arrived at through dividing its weight by the acceleration caused by gravity."

That note makes a handy reference for related concepts, for in it I also briefly discussed subatomic "particles"; the components of atoms; molecules; supposed faster-than-light particles (tachyons); Seth's CU's, or units of consciousness; his assertion that consciousness can travel faster than light in out-of-body states; Jane's scientific vocabulary; and Einstein's special theory of relativity. In addition, I gave references to other material, including some by Seth, on several of those topics.

2. Just for my own study, I later inserted "[almost]" in Seth's sentence because I hadn't been quick enough to ask him to elaborate upon "the end result of an infinite series of sequences" when Jane delivered his material for him. After the session I began to wonder if Seth hadn't contradicted himself by saying there could be an end result of something infinite. Yet I also felt that he meant just what he'd said—and that even from our human positions alone the ramifications of our individual and joint realities are enormously greater than we ordinarily conceive them to be. Seth had indicated in the preceding paragraph of the session that such faltering of the reasoning abilities may occur. I also thought my intellectual hang-up over the concept of infinity was inevitably mixed up with the limitations of meaning that we usually assign to words.

3. Seth's material in this paragraph reminded me at once of Jane's own early, intuitive concept of the moment point. In Volume 1 of *"Unknown" Reality*, see Note 5 for the 681st session, which was held on February 11, 1974. I wrote that at the age of 25, nine years before initiating the sessions, Jane expressed the moment point in her poem, "More Than Men." I still think these lines are most evocative:

> Between each ticking of the clock
> Long centuries pass
> In universes hidden from our own.

In the very next session for Volume 1, which Jane gave two days later, Seth stated: "There are systems in which a moment, from your standpoint, is made to endure for the life of a universe. I do not mean that a moment is simply <u>stretched</u>, or that time is slowed down alone, but that all the experiences possible within a moment become realities within that framework."

SESSION 916——May 14, 1980
9:20 P.M. WEDNESDAY

(The first session in the Preface for Volume 1 of Dreams *is a private one that Jane delivered on September 13, 1979. In the Preliminary Notes for the session I wrote that Seth had finished dictating* Mass Events *a month ago [in the 873rd session for August 15, to be exact], and that a week later I began finishing my own notes for the book. I completed those notes yesterday afternoon—and on that score suddenly found myself free after nine months of concentrated labor. [And wouldn't you know it, I told Jane: My last paragraph for* Mass Events *is about the biannual migratory flights of the geese.]*

I estimate that it'll take me five or six weeks to type the final manuscript of the book for our publisher. Then I'll need another week to go over the manuscript, with colored pens marking instructions of each page as to what copy we want set in roman [upright] type, and in italics; while doing that I'll also check spelling, punctuation, references, dates, times— all of those mundane details so necessary in helping our publisher produce a finished, good-looking book for the marketplace.[1]

Last night, as I began typing Monday's 915th session, I asked Jane why Seth hadn't just called his "invisible particles" CU's, or units of consciousness, as he'd done earlier in Dreams,[2] *and as he'd always done in his other books. The question upset her, especially when I added that I was afraid Seth was repeating old material under a new term. In order to help Jane feel better, I speculated that he must have had his reasons for doing this, and that of course a certain amount of repetition is necessary in each book in a series: The restatements not only furnish a foundation for new material, but enable each book to be complete in itself. After all, I said, I try to achieve those same goals with the notes.[3]*

In spite of those thoughts, Jane was still rather upset and out of sorts a day later as session time approached. Even with her unease, however, she wanted to begin the session early, as she's been doing lately. She also thought of giving me the night off, by way of celebrating a bit because I've finished the notes for Mass Events, *but I told her I'd rather keep the sessions going as long as both of us feel like it. This afternoon I'd started my first tentative typing for* Mass Events, *and felt good about that.*

Then, as we waited for a delayed session, Jane received material from Seth in which he very nicely explained his use of "invisible particles" on Monday evening—and since tonight he goes into his reasons for doing so, there's no need to give them here. Of course we were both relieved. And of course, Seth hadn't been concerned at all.)

Now: Good evening.

("Good evening, Seth.")

Dictation. When Joseph *(as Seth calls me)* read the last session, he wondered whether or not the invisible particles I referred to were the same as the units of consciousness I have spoken of before.

He was supposed to ask the question, and so was each reader. For one thing, while I realize the importance of specific terms, I do not want you as a reader to become so dependent upon terms that coming across one you have read before, you instantly categorize it. For another thing, each time I reintroduce such information I do so from another direction, so to speak, so that you as a reader are meant to approach it from a different angle also. In that way, you become familiar with certain knowledge from a variety of viewpoints.

As you read those passages the question itself—"Are these after all the units of consciousness referred to earlier?"—should have triggered your intellect and your intuition to work together, even if only slightly, in another way. In other words, of course, I hope to inspire both your imagination and your intelligence in this chapter and in this section of the book, devoted to such subject matter.

Remember, again, the manifest [universe] emerges from a subjective reality, one that is implied in the very nature of your world itself. I would like you, then, to think of those units of consciousness from an entirely different scale of events.

Imagine, now, as far as you are able, the existence of All That Is, a consciousness *(pause)* so magnificently complex that what we may call its own psychological compartments are, literally now, infinite. All appearances of time, and all experience of it, must be psychological. The "speed" of electrons, for example, would reflect their psychological motion.

(9:32. With many pauses:) All That Is, as the source of all realities and experience, is so psychologically complex, so multidimensionally creative, that it constantly surprises itself. It is, itself, the invisible universe that is everywhere implied within your world, but that becomes manifest to your perception only through historic time. All That Is disperses itself, therefore, so that it is on the one hand "a massive" subjective entity, a psychological structure—and on the other hand, it also disperses itself into the phenomenal world. It is, in all meanings of the word, divine, yet it disperses even that divinity so that in your terms *(long pause),* each unit of consciousness contains within itself those properties of divinity. All That Is has no one image, but is within all images—and in parentheses: (whether or not they are manifest). Your thoughts are the invisible partners of your words, and the vast unstated subjectivity of All That Is is in the same way behind all stated or manifest phenomena.

(9:44.) In those terms, it is basically (underlined) impossible for any given species to become extinct. It can disappear for a time (underlined), become unmanifest for a while in historic events. The genetic patterns for any given species reside, of course, primarily in that species' genetic bank—but that genetic bank does not exist in isolation, but [is] invisibly connected with the genetic makeup of each other species *(all very intently).*

There are countless relationships between species that go unrecognized. The generations of all species interact. The genetic cues are not triggered on the proposition, obviously, that a species exists alone on the planet, but also in response to genetic sequences that operate in all of the species combined. The genetic system, again, is not closed nearly as much as supposed. That is, again, because the basic units of consciousness that build up matter—that form matter—are themselves endowed with a subjective acuteness. This also accounts for my earlier statement, that in usually understood terms the environment and its creatures "evolve" together. *(Long pause.)* Your position on the scale of awareness inclines you to categorize consciousnesses so that only your own familiar brand seems to fit the definition—so again here I remind you that consciousness is everywhere in the deepest terms, because All That Is disperses itself throughout physical reality. All portions of that reality have their own rights to existence, and purposes within it. So of course do all peoples, and the races.

(9:55.) Your imaginations help you bring elements of that inner implied universe into actuality. Your imaginations obviously are not limited by time. You can imagine past and future events. Your imaginations have always helped you form your civilizations, your arts and your sciences, and when they are united with your reasoning processes they can bring you knowledge about the universe and your places in it that you can receive in no other fashion.

End of dictation.

(Pause at 9:59.) A small note: Congratulations. The notes *(for Mass Events)* as usual are superb. *(I laughed.)* Enjoy the rest of the evening, as indeed I hope you have enjoyed this segment of it *(humorously.)*

("I have, very much. What are you *going to do for the rest of the evening?")*

I am going to refresh myself by diving into some new concepts, for there are new concepts for me also, of course, and I dive into them from many positions all the time as well.

A fond good evening.

("Thank you, Seth. The same to you. Good night."

10:01 P.M. Near the close of Monday evening's session, Seth had given us an insight into the nature of his own reality. I told Jane now that he'd offered us another hint tonight. His statement is particularly intriguing because Seth indicated that in his nonphysical reality, "wherever that is," he's still developing, just as we are "here on earth." I added that I'd certainly like him to comment sometime on those "new concepts" he's about to explore.)

NOTES. Session 916

1. I also kept track of Jane's progress as she wrote the Introduction for *Mass Events*. She finished that excellent piece of work seven months ago—a few days before she delivered the first formal session for the Preface to *Dreams*, the 881st, on September 25, 1979. See the opening notes for that session, in Volume 1.

2. Here are the sessions and notes for Volume 1 of *Dreams*, in which Seth and I discussed or referred to his EE (or electromagnetic energy) units, and his CU's (or units of consciousness).

Chapter 2: I cited both concepts in Note 1 for Session 884. In Session 886 Seth mentioned "units of consciousness" without being more specific.

Chapter 3: Seth discussed CU's much more extensively in Session 889. In Session 890 see his material on both EE units and CU's. While reading tonight's material, the reader might keep these brief passages from that session in mind: "Each unit of consciousness *(or CU)* intensifies, magnifies its own intents to be—and, you might say, works up from within itself an explosive spark of primal desire that "explodes" into a process that causes physical materialization. It turns into what I have called [an] EE unit, in which case it is embarked upon its own kind of physical experience." And: "Units of consciousness *(CU's)*, transforming themselves into EE units, formed the environment and all of its inhabitants in the same process, in what you might call a circular manner rather than a serial one."

In Note 1 for the 890th session I gave references to Seth's earliest material on EE units.

3. In a note like this I can only touch upon the theme of repetition. All of Jane's books, as well as my own notes for her Seth books, obviously contain repetitious material, and/or material based upon variations of certain basic concepts. It's inevitable and necessary that they do. Individually and *en masse*, and to the extent that our human systems of perception make it possible, our species has created a world and universe built upon a very limited, repetitious creation and interpretation of internal and external data. We could hardly survive without our particular communicative repetition, nor could any other species without its own.

I've often thought that the repetition in the Seth books, say, is nothing compared to the repeated barrages of suggestion—much of it negative—that our species has chosen to subject itself to daily. I constantly search for balances between the positive and the negative. Indeed, however, Jane and I think that in ordinary terms, and for many reasons, our species long ago began creating a great deal of negative thinking and action—so much so that those qualities came to range throughout all facets of our world culture. As far as I know, we humans are the only ones to indulge in such behavior. I can't imagine animals doing so, for instance—they have no *need* to!

I'm sure that in much larger terms even negativity is creative, and often in ways we cannot comprehend in our temporal reality, but I do believe that Jane's work offers more penetrating and redeeming insights into many of those challenges we create. Once again, then, on world scales ranging from the very small to the very large—and with all of them seamlessly "interlocked"— consciousness seeks to both know and surprise itself.

SESSION 917——May 21, 1980
8:49 P.M. WEDNESDAY

(No session was held Monday night so we could rest. Jane had also been doing very well on God of Jane, *and chose not to be distracted by working on anything else—even Seth material. However, this evening she thought of having a short session.*

At noon she'd received another upsetting letter. I was most interested tonight as Seth discussed the implications of the letter, along with two thoughts Jane had picked up from him a week ago Monday, on the day she held the 915th session: "Alone, reason finally becomes unreasonable. Alone, imagination becomes less imaginative over time." I wrote in the closing note for the session that I was disappointed because Seth hadn't brought up those two points in the session itself.)

Good evening.

("Good evening, Seth.")

Dictation *(with elaborate humor)*. Now: Remember that these units of consciousness of which I have been speaking are not neutral, mathematical, or mechanistic.

They are the smallest imaginable "packages" of consciousness that you can imagine, and despite any ideas to the contrary, basically consciousness has nothing to do with size. If that were the case, it would take more than a world-sized globe to contain the consciousness of simply one cell.

So your physical life is the result of a spectacular spontaneous order—the order of the body spontaneously formed by the units of consciousness. Your experience of the world is largely determined by your imaginations and your reasoning abilities. These did not develop through time, as per usual evolutionary beliefs. Both imagination and reason belonged to the species from the beginning, but the species has used these qualities in different ways throughout what you think of as historic time. There is great leeway in that direction, so that the two can be combined in many many alternate fashions, each particular combination giving you its own unique picture of reality, and determining your experience in the world.

(Pause.) Your many civilizations, historically speaking, each with its own fields of activity, its own sciences, religions, politics and art—these all represent various ways that man has used imagination and reason to form a framework through which (underlined) a more or less cohesive reality is experienced.

(9:02.) Man, then, has sometimes stressed the power of the imagination and let its great dramatic light illuminate the physical events about him, so that they were largely seen through its cast. Exterior events in those circumstances become magnets attracting the dramatic force of the imagination. Inner events are stressed over exterior ones. The objects of the world then become important not only for what they are but because of their standing in an inner world of meaning. In such cases, of course, it becomes quite possible to go so far in that direction that the events of nature almost seem to disappear amid the weight of their symbolic content.

In recent times the trend has been in the opposite direction, so that the abilities of the imagination were considered highly suspect, while exterior events were considered the only aspects of reality. You ended up with a true-or-false kind of world, in which it seemed that the answers to the deepest questions about life could be answered quite correctly and adequately by some multiple-choice test. Man's imagination seemed then to be allied with falsehood, unless its products could be turned to advantage in the materialistic existence. In that context, the imagination was tolerated at all only because it sometimes offered new technological inventions.

I have taken two contrasting examples of the many ways in which the powers of the imagination and those of the reasoning abilities can be used, There are endless varieties, however—each subjectively and genetically possible, and many, of course, that you have not yet developed as a species.

Ruburt (*Jane*) today received a letter from a man who would certainly be labeled a schizophrenic. Ruburt was distressed—not only by the individual's situation, but by the philosophic implications. Why on earth, he thought, should someone form such a reality?

(*Both of us—but Jane particularly—had been struck by the unique and original way the writer had put together his selection of words to reflect his chosen reality. Most unusual.*)

Now on the question of "mental disorders," it is highly important that individual integrity be stressed, rather than the blanket definitions that are usually accorded to any group of symptoms. In many such circumstances, however, such individuals are combining the imagination and the reasoning abilities in ways that are not in keeping with their historic periods. (*With some irony:*) It would not be entirely out of keeping, though somewhat exaggerated a statement, to claim that men who stockpile nuclear weapons in order to preserve peace are insane. In your society, such activities are, in a way that completely escapes me, somehow under the label of humanitarianism!

Such plans are not considered insane ones—though in the deepest meaning of that word, they are indeed. There are many reasons for such actions, but an overemphasis upon what you think of (underlined) as the reasoning abilities, as opposed to what you think of as the imaginative abilities, is at least partially to blame.

(*9:23.*) In the case of the man who wrote Ruburt, we have a mixture of those characteristics in which interior events—the events of the imagination—cast too strong a light upon physical events as far as the socially accepted blend is concerned. Again, I am not speaking about all cases of mental disorder here. I do, however, want to make the point that your prized psychological norm as a species means that you must also be allowed a great leeway in the use of the imagination and the intellect. Otherwise, you could become locked into a rigid conscious stance, one in which both the imagination and the intellect could advance no further. It is vitally important that you realize the great psychological diversity that is present within your psychological behavior—and those varieties of psychological experience are necessary. They give you vital psychological feedback, and they exercise the reaches of your abilities in ways that are overall most advantageous.

The man who wrote wants to live largely in his own world. He hurts no one. He supports himself a good deal of the time. His view of reality is eccentric from most viewpoints. He adds a flavor to the world that would be missing otherwise, and through his very eccentricity, to some extent he shows other people that their rigid views of reality may indeed have chinks in them here and there.

I do not mean to idealize him either, or others of his kind, but to point out that you can use your imaginations and intellects in other fashions than you do. In fact, such fashions are not only genetically possible, but genetically probable—a matter I will discuss later in the book. The imagination, of course, deals with the implied universe, those vast areas of reality that are not physically manifest, while reason usually deals with the evidence of the world that is before it. That statement is generally true, but specifically, of course, any act of the imagination involves reasoning, and any [act] of reason involves the imagination.

End of dictation.

(9:35. Now Jane delivered some material for us, then ended the session at 9:57 P.M.)

SESSION 918——June 2, 1980
9:15 P.M. MONDAY

(In Chapter 5 of Dreams, *in Volume 1, see Note 2 for the 899th session, of February 6, 1980. I wrote that in April engineers were scheduled to enter the contaminated containment building housing the damaged reactor [Unit No. 2] at the Three Mile Island nuclear power generating plant in southeastern Pennsylvania. The engineers were to gather radiological data to be used in decontaminating the crippled facility. To insure the safety of all workers, however, the plan is that over a period of several weeks a large quantity of radioactive krypton gas must first be vented into the atmosphere from the containment building. This proposed venting is still arousing much strong opposition.*[1]

Jane and I haven't had any sessions for the last 12 days, while we worked on God of Jane *and* Mass Events *respectively. "I feel like having a short session tonight," she said, "but it won't be for* Dreams. *I have a few ideas he'll discuss. . . ." Yet when Seth came through his material certainly sounded like book work to me.)*

Good evening.

("Good evening, Seth.")

Now: There are sometimes almost insurmountable difficulties involved on my part in trying to explain the origin of your world.

You think of your universe as having certain dimensions, and you want an explanation based more or less upon the proposition that those dimensions themselves made possible the origin—which must, however, have emerged from other larger dimensions of actuality than those contained in your universe itself. The terms of reality within your universe cannot hold or contain that vaster context in which such master events happen. Therefore, I must follow to some extent (underlined) the traditional references that you use to define events to begin with.

While I am doing that I am also trying to introduce you, intuitively at least, to a larger framework, in which events straddle the reality that you know. Nevertheless, we will begin with issues in which it is very possible that contradictions may seem to occur, since your own definitions of an event are so simple that they ignore larger ramifications—ramifications that would reconcile any seeming contradictions in an overall greater unity of structure and action. Your imaginations will be of high value here, for they can often perceive unities that are not evident to the intellect—which you have trained to deal specifically with the evidence of the here and now.

(Long pause at 9:28.) There are phases of relatedness, rhythms and harmonies of consciousness from whose infinite swells the molecular "music" of your universe is sounded. Your place in those rhythms is highly vital. *(Long pause.)* You exist in a kind of original interval—though, if you can, think of the word "interval" without the connotations of continuing time. It is as if an infinite number of orchestras were playing simultaneously *(long pause),* and each note sounded was also played in all of its probable positions with each other note possible, and in combination with all of the probable versions of the entire piece being played.

Between the notes sounded there would be intervals, and those unsounded intervals would also be part of a massive un-stated rhythm upon which the development of the entire sounded production was dependent. The unsounded intervals would also be events, of course, cues for action, triggers for response.

Your stated universe emerged out of that kind of interval, emerging from a master event whose true nature remains un-captured by your definitions—so there will be places in our book where I may say that an event known to you is true and untrue at the same time, or that it is both myth and fact. And in so doing I hope to lead you toward some psychic comprehension of a kind of event far too large for your usual categories of true and false. [Perhaps], then, you will let your imaginations play upon the usual events of your world, and glimpse at least in part that greater brilliance that illuminates them, so that it leads you intui-tively to a feeling for the source of events and the source of your world. The units of consciousness that I have mentioned are (underlined) that, and they do behave as I have said. They are also in other terms entities, fragments of All That Is, if you prefer—divine fragments of power and majesty, containing (pause) all of the powers of consciousness as you think of it, concentrations without substance in your terms.

There are many other universes besides your own, each fol-lowing its own intervals, its own harmony. Your ideas of historic time impede my explanations. In those terms (pause), your world's reality stretches back far further than you imagine, and in those terms—you need the qualifications—your ancestors have visited other stars, as your planet has been visited by others. Some such encounters intersected in space and time, but some did not. There are endless versions of life. There are, then, other species like (underlined) your own, and in the vast spec-trums of existence that your reality cannot contain, there have been galactic civilizations that came together when the condi-tions were right.

(9:54.) Time's framework does not exist as you think it does. Intervals of existence are obviously not the same. In ways impos-sible to explain, there are what I can only call inner passageways throughout the universe. You know how one association can suddenly in your minds connect you with a past event so clearly that it almost seems to occur in the present—and indeed, a strong-enough memory is like a ghost event. So there are processes that work like associations, that can provide passageways through the universe's otherwise time-structured ways. These passageways are simply a part of the greater nature of events that you do not perceive.

(Pause.) At times your species has traveled those passageways, and many of your myths represent ghost memories of those events. There is a rhythm, again, to all existence, and so in your terms your species returned to its home planet, to renew its roots, refresh its natural stock, to return to nature, to find solace again amid the sweet ancient heritage of dusk and dawn.

The planet has seen many changes. It has appeared and disappeared many times. It flickers off and on—but because of the intervals of your attention, each "on" period seems to last for millions of years, of course, while at other levels the earth is like a firefly, flickering off and on.

I do not mean by such a description to minimize the importance of physical life, for All That Is endows each portion of its own transformed reality with a unique existence that is duplicated nowhere else, and each spark of consciousness is endowed with a divine heritage that is never extinguished—a spark that is apparent in all other corners of the universe.

End of session.

The session was also partially in response to some questions that Ruburt had in mind. I bid you a fond good evening—unless you have a question.

("No.")

Then my heartiest regards.

("Thank you, Seth. Good night.")

10:10 P.M. "He slips it in on me, that's what he does," Jane remarked, when I kidded her about saying the session couldn't be for Dreams. *I also told her that it's one of her best. She recalled that back in her 20s—some 15 years before she initiated the Seth material—she'd written a series of poems about our species returning to the earth from space. "And here's Seth saying that it's actually happened that way—at least in some probable realities," she said. "It's an old science-fiction idea."*

The session had been one of those in which Jane thought a great deal of time was passing. She was surprised to learn that it had lasted only 55 minutes, yet she felt that she'd come through with a good amount of interesting information.[2])

NOTES. Session 918

1. I also wrote in my note for Session 899 that in relation to TMI, "once again consciousness proliferates and explores itself in new ways." Last March, a year after the accident, Pennsylvania's governor asked a respected scientific organization to propose alternatives to the krypton-venting plan. In May the group recommended scientifically acceptable alternatives, but it now appears unlikely that either the company owning TMI or the federal Nuclear Regulatory Commission will adopt any of them—and so the arguments continue. Evidently the psychological factors associated with the venting idea *will be ignored* as long as there's no foreseeable chance that physical harm will be done to the population surrounding TMI. This conclusion is, of course, extremely unsatisfactory to many people.

The planned April (1980) entry into the containment building was postponed until May for several other reasons, however. One was a lack of federal certification of the breathing equipment engineers will have to wear inside the building. Indeed, that first entry *still* hasn't been made. It's been rescheduled again—this time for late July, upon completion of the venting, and 16 months after the near-meltdown of radioactive fuel in the reactor's core.

Following the accident at TMI, and aside from the great fears "generated" by it, a host of problems began accumulating for the nuclear power industry—involving everything from poor plant design (as Seth commented in the 914th session for Chapter 7 of *Dreams*), to enormous cost overruns and the fear of default on bond issues, shoddy construction and quality control, human and mechanical error, the disposal of radioactive waste, conflicts with antinuclear and environmental groups, arguments over evacuation plans at various nuclear-plant sites, a greatly expanded list of steps (numbering in the thousands) that the NRC is compiling for utilities to take in order to increase the safety of their plants, and even governmental concern over the possible manipulation and falsification of plant safety records. The last nuclear plant was ordered in 1978. So far this year our country's consumption of electricity has increased less than 2 percent, and it is now expected to actually *decrease* next year. Unheard of, in view of all of those predictions that we must continue to build nuclear power generating plants to meet projected demands!

However, let us remember that when creating and experiencing a challenge, on any scale, consciousness may choose a predominantly positive or negative focus, or it may seek to achieve a balance. While some utility companies in the United States are in trouble with their nuclear plants, then, other companies do own plants that perform very well and very economically. They have excellent safety records. Those companies are to be congratulated. There's talk that the nuclear power industry will fail in our country, but Jane and I don't think it will. What haunts many people, especially those living downwind from nuclear facilities, are the horrifying consequences that could result from an accident that released unchecked radioactivity into the environment. This chance, no matter how remote it may be, exists in every country in the world that has even one nuclear establishment. It's just as real for those nations that are even *thinking* of going the nuclear way. So consciousness is really exploring the nuclear question in global terms, even though here in *Dreams* I usually deal with its "local" aspects.

2. After the session I wanted to tie in Seth's material on infinity with mathematical ideas of that concept, but my reading soon convinced me that such an idea was too involved a task for a simple note like this. However, I told Jane, in his own way Seth *had* incorporated mathematical ideas in his material: I saw correlations between his probable realities, his intervals, and the concept of an infinite number of points on a line—and that some mathematical definitions of infinity are considered to be more basic, or of a greater order, than others. Actually, in various branches of mathematics, from the works of Euclid (the Greek mathematician who flourished around 300 B.C.) to modern information theory, I found many relationships with Seth's ideas. I do think that Seth's material on the "origin" of our universe can be termed an "ideal point," embracing our mathematical systems, and that his concept of All That Is has no "limits" in

mathematical terms. I do not know whether my comments here will make sense to mathematicians.

My tentative inquiries led me to ask Jane if she thought the axioms of Euclidean geometry, say, are innately valid in describing the mind's *inner* reaches, or whether, in ordinary terms, those propositions represent conscious acquired interpretations of our visual experience. She hadn't thought about it. When I asked her where she might have obtained her intuitive mathematical knowledge, she just laughed.

"In high school, I flunked algebra twice, then passed, and I think the same for geometry," she said. "Most of it I couldn't get—the teachers just went too fast. When I did understand something I'd get real excited. Sometimes I'd work out the correct answer to a problem, but do it the wrong way, so the teacher would mark it wrong—and that always made me furious. I even had trouble figuring out the cost of ounces of candy when I had that job in the five-and-dime store. I don't know how many free pounds of candy I must have given out. . . ."

Jane was born in a hospital in Albany, New York, on May 8, 1929, but grew up in nearby Saratoga Springs. She began working at the variety store in the summer of 1945, when she was 16 years old. It was her first job; she had to get working papers and a Social Security number. She was always nervous in the store. "I remember when the war ended that summer," she said, meaning Japan's surrender to end World War II on August 14. "They closed the store to celebrate." That fall she continued on the job after school hours, and on an occasional Saturday.

CHAPTER 9

Master Events and Reality Overlays

SESSION 919——June 9, 1980
9:15 P.M. MONDAY

(We skipped last Wednesday night's regularly scheduled session. Jane was especially interested in trying for a short session now, however, and I brought her red wine on ice.

She's been most intrigued by Seth's referrals to the concept of "master events" ever since he gave them in the final session for Chapter 8— preparations, she hoped, for his material this evening. She came to play her own conscious part in those preparations, too: Yesterday she'd received many insights from Seth on "master overlays," and made notes. She typed some of her information after supper tonight, and I'm presenting this in Note 1, just to show how closely at times the body of the Seth material lies to her "ordinary" consciousness.)

Now: Dictation. New chapter *(9)*: "Master Events and Reality Overlays" *(all with much humorous emphasis)*.

Give us a moment. . . . Master events are those *(long pause)* whose main activity takes place in inner dimensions. *(Long pause.)* Such events are t-o-o *(spelled)* multidimensional to appear clearly in your reality, so that you see or experience only parts of them. They are source events. Their main thrust is in what you can call the vaster dimension of dreams, the unknown territory of inner reality. The terms you use make no difference. The original action, however, of such events is unmanifest—not physical. Those events then "subsequently" show themselves in time and space, with extraordinary results.

They shed their light upon the "facts" of historical time, and influence those events. Master events may end up translated through mythology, or religion or art, or the effects may actually serve to give a framework to an entire civilization. *(With much amusement:)* In parentheses or brackets or whatever you use: (As indeed occurred in the case of Christianity, as I will explain later.) End of brackets or parentheses.

Now the origin of the universe that you know, as I have described it, was of course a master event. The initial action did not occur in space or time, but formed space and time.

In your terms other universes, with all of their own space and time structures, were created simultaneously, and exist simultaneously. The effect of looking outward into space, and therefore backward into time, is a kind of built-in convention that appears within your own space-time picture. You must remember, then, when you think in terms of origins, that the very word, "origin," is dependent upon time conventions, and a belief in beginnings and endings. Beginnings and endings are themselves effects that seem to be facts to your perceptions. In a fashion they simply represent beginnings and endings, the boundaries, the reaches and the limitations of your own span of attention.

(Pause at 9:31.) I said that in your terms (underlined) all universes were created (underlined) simultaneously—at the same time. The very sentence structure has time built in, you see, so you are bound to think that I am speaking of an almost indescribable past. Also, I use time terms, since you are so used yourselves to that kind of categorizing, so here we will certainly run into our first seeming contradiction *(see the last session)* — when I say that in the higher order of events all universes, including your own, have their original creations occurring now, with all of their pasts and futures built in, and with all of their scales of time winding ever outward, and all of their appearances of space, galaxies and nebulae, and all of their seeming changes, being instantly and originally created in what you think of as this moment.

Your universe cannot be its own source. Its inner mysteries—which are indeed the mysteries of consciousness, not matter—cannot be explained, and must remain incomprehensible, if you try to study them from the viewpoint of your objective experience alone. You must look to the source of that experience. You must look not to space but to the source of space, not to time but to the source of time—and most of all, you must look to the kind of consciousness that experiences space and time. You must look, therefore, to events that show themselves through historical action, but whose origins are elsewhere. None of this is really beyond your capabilities, as long as you try to enlarge your framework.

(Long pause in an intent delivery.) The entire idea of evolution, of course, requires strict adherence to the concept of continuing time, and the changes that time brings, and such concepts can at best provide the most surface kind of explanation for the existence of your species or any other.

I hope, again, to stretch the reaches of both your imaginations and intellects in this book, to give you a feeling for events larger than your usual true-or-false, fact-or-fancy categories. Your existence as a species is characterized far more by your unique use of your imaginations than it is by any physical attributes. Your connections with that unmanifest universe have always helped direct your imaginations, made you aware of the rich veins of probabilities possible in physical existence, so that you could then use your intellects to decide which of the alternate routes you wanted as a species to follow.

(9:46.) In that regard, it is true that in the other species innate knowledge is more clearly, brilliantly, and directly translated into action. I am not speaking of some dumb instinct, but instead of an intuitive knowing, a high intelligence different from your own, but amazingly complex, with which other species are equipped.[2]

Man, however, deals with probabilities and with creativity in a unique fashion—a fashion that is made possible because of the far more dependable behavior of the other species.[3]

In a fashion man also is equipped with the ability to initiate actions on a nonphysical level that then become physical and continue to wind in and out of *(pause)* both realities, entwining dream events with historic ones, in such a fashion that the original nonphysical origins [are] often forgotten. Man overlays (underlined) the true reality quite spontaneously. He often reacts to dream events as if they were physical, and to physical events as if they were dreams. This applies individually and collectively, but man is often unaware of that interplay.

In the terms of evolution as you like to think of it, ideas are more important than genes *(quietly),* for we are again dealing with more than the surfaces of events. We are dealing with more than some physical mechanics of being. For one thing, the genes themselves are conscious, though in different terms than yours. Your cultures—your civilizations—obviously affect the well-being of your species, and those cultures are formed by your ideas, and forged through the use of your imaginations and your intellects.

Certain bloodlines, in your terms, were extinguished because of your beliefs in Christianity, as people were killed in your holy wars. *(Pause.)* Your beliefs have directed who should go to war and who should not, who should live and who should die, who should be educated and who should not, who should be isolated from society and who should not—all matters directly touching upon the survival of certain families throughout history, and therefore affecting the species as a whole.

I am not here specifically blaming Christianity, for far before its emergence, your ideas (underlined) and beliefs about good and evil [were] far more important in all matters regarding the species than any simple questions of genetic variances, natural selection, or environmental influence. In man's case, at least, the selection of who should live or die was often anything but natural. If you are to understand the characteristics of the species, then you cannot avoid the study of man's consciousness.

(10:05.) End of dictation. *(Louder, with amusement:)* You are a master notetaker. I bid you a fond good evening.

(Seth stared at me, so I asked: "What do you think of my dreams of the last two nights?")

I will go into your dreams another time. They were master productions. I bid you both a fond good evening.

("Okay. Thank you, Seth. Good night."

10:06 P.M. I'd asked my question half jokingly, to see if Seth would discuss my dreams, but obviously he didn't take the bait. I told Jane that I hadn't really expected him to.

"He didn't go into all the stuff I got yesterday," she said, *"but then he went into other stuff I* didn't *get. I feel like he was about to lead the*

*reader over some important material. . . . And very vaguely, I should
say this would be about session thirty—halfway through the book."*

Neither of us had counted the sessions we have for Dreams, *but when
I made a quick check the next day I was surprised to discover that Jane's
estimate is only two short of the 32 sessions Seth has called book dictation.
I'm still busy typing the final manuscript for* Mass Events, *but we've
already planned that I'll be adding several "nonbook" sessions, and
excerpts from others, to* Dreams *when finally I get to concentrate on the
production work for it And my own opinion, I explained to Jane, is that
Seth is considerably more than halfway through this book, even if we add
more extra sessions to it.)*

NOTES. Session 919

1. Jane wrote about her activities yesterday:

"Sunday, June 8, 1980: As I went about the day, showering,
doing my hair, reading the paper, doing my exercises and so
forth, I kept getting stuff from Seth on. . . the next chapter of
his book, I think to be called 'Master Events and Overlays.'
There can be overlays of one civilization onto another, so that a
'real' civilization in one sphere of existence can appear as myth
in another. . . . Our civilization appears as myth in other
worlds; that kind of thing represents only one kind of overlay.

"I got unclear glimpses of material on Atlantis that I didn't
really get well enough to note down, and about Christianity, as
both representing certain (other?) kinds of overlays and as examples of master events.

"I got a definition of master events but forgot some of it . . .
to the effect that master events are spectacular events whose
main thrusts are outside of time, but whose actions on or in time
[are] extravagant—out of proportion to their actual historical
connections. The physical part of [such an] event in history is
actually minimal in contrast to its effects . . . and something
about master events touching the worlds of imagination and
reason in different ways.

"And that, though Seth spoke about some matters being almost impossible to explain, he enjoyed the challenge, and felt a
sense of achievement rather than frustration. . . ."

In ordinary terms that challenge, that achievement, are Jane's
own, as she seeks to bring to consciousness information from the

creative Seth portion (whatever *its* source may be) of her psyche, and unite it with her "usual" creative accomplishments. An exhilarating quest indeed, even given the limitations imposed by words, with "some matters being almost impossible to explain."

"Master events are actually other wrinkles in probabilities," Jane said as we talked about this note. "They explain why Christianity has had such far-reaching effects, for almost 2,000 years, when its original experiences were so small in time and space— why we attach so much significance to those desert countries over there even now. . . ."

2. This paragraph of Seth's at once reminded me of some of his most evocative earlier material on animal consciousness. He gave it in the 832nd session for Chapter 5 of *Mass Events* (on January 29, 1979), and I quoted it in the Preliminary Notes to the Preface for *Dreams:* "Nature in all of its varieties is so richly encountered by the animals. . . ."

3. I think that Seth's insight here—regarding "the far more dependable behavior of the other species"—is excellent indeed. In an original way he stressed the interdependence of all life forms on earth. I like to keep such penetrating remarks before me, and wish the reader would too, for I often fear they'll become lost from conscious view within his material. (As an example, I doubt if this one will be referred to in the index for *Dreams.*) But I also think that intuitively *we know* the truth Seth so briefly expressed here, and that it never has been or ever will be really lost.

One of the poems Jane wrote for me a year ago, when I became 60 years old (in June 1979), fits in well here also. In Chapter 2 for Volume 1 of *Dreams,* see Note 3 for Session 885:

> There seems *to be*
> *no unexpressed self*
> *in animals. . . .*

SESSION 920——October 6, 1980
9:14 P.M. MONDAY

(This is Jane's first "regular" session in four months. It's a nonbook one, and I'll comment later on why I'm presenting it in Dreams. *Right now, I*

just want to note that since she gave the last session for this book, the 919th on June 9, Jane has come through with a series of 15 private, or deleted, sessions—13 of them on what Seth calls "the magical approach to reality."

I plan to mention certain secular affairs that I've kept track of while Jane has been producing Dreams, *but mainly these notes will deal with personal and professional events in our own lives. I've organized most of the material in a roughly chronological order. Some of it I took from Jane's daily journal for 1980, some from my own notes and files, and some from private sessions. Portions of it came from* Dreams *itself. And we put some of it together simply through our conversations.[1] I also remind the reader that everything described took place within the overall context of an extended presidential campaign in this country.*

See the opening notes for Session 918, which Jane held on June 2 for Chapter 8 of Dreams. *I referred to the strong local opposition to venting radioactive krypton gas from the contaminated containment building at Three Mile Island. An estimated several thousand people, not trusting the credibility of statements about safety that had been made by federal and private officials, left the area before company technicians finally began the long-delayed venting on June 29. All went well: The radiation released into the atmosphere was far below permissible limits. Surprisingly, the procedure was completed in only 13 days—considerably less than the estimated three to four weeks required for the job. The still-wary populace returned. Twelve days after the venting was completed, two engineers from TMI entered the enormous containment building on the first brief inspection trip to gather photographic, radiation, and other data.*

I'll skip ahead a bit here by noting that on August 15 four nuclear technicians made the second entry into the containment building— again, to acquire more information for future entries. [Two of the men were so strongly affected by the heat inside their heavy protective clothing that they decided to cut short their trip.] The reactor reclamation task is now projected to cost more than $760 million, and to take at least five years.

Jane doesn't often refer to such world events in her notes and journals, but we often talk about them. In fact, she made no notes of any kind in her 1980 journal from the middle of June to July 20, for a span of five weeks, but those two months were busy times for us professionally. In June, I started experimenting with paintings of my dream images, for use in a possible book—and this endeavor, I discovered, presented me with a whole set of challenges all by itself. I mailed the finished manuscripts for Mass Events *and* God of Jane *to our publisher on July 2 and 18 respectively. During those times, however, I was extremely sorry to note that Jane's physical symptoms—her difficulties "walking" and performing other routine tasks—were obviously becoming much worse.*

By then, my wife was almost always uncomfortable to some degree, and sometimes in outright pain. She had to sit on a high stool to do the dishes. She still walked by leaning on her typing table and pushing it forward step by step—but she did this much less frequently, perhaps only once or twice a day. Instead, it became routine for her to get around the house by using her feet to draw herself along as she sat in her wheeled office chair. She seldom left the house; she could barely maneuver down the two steps into the garage off her writing room, and into our car. Jane had a lot of trouble getting into the shower. She had much difficulty sitting for the long hours she spent at her desk. Her fingers didn't work easily when she typed, or wrote with pen and pencil, or held a paintbrush.

Jane resisted lying down a couple of times a day to get some relief, although usually I was able to talk her into doing so. For many complex reasons she refused to go the conventional medical route, as she always had—and I felt [and still do] that my own hang-ups in that area prevented me from helping her as much as I should have. Instead, Jane insisted upon trying to use her abilities to help herself. I grieved to see my wife in such distress, but ultimately could do little beyond helping her get as comfortable as possible. Among other things, I bought her a water-filled cushion for her chair. It gave her some relief, but she needed much more help than that.[2]

By the fourth week in July, a few days after finishing God of Jane, *Jane was reading over the 17 chapters she'd done on her third* Seven *novel,* Oversoul Seven and the Museum of Time.[3] *She made notes for* Seven Three, *as she called it. Then she wrote in her journal on the 24th: "I was looking over* Seven Three *for the first time in 14 months when sub rights called about the movie contract for the first* Seven—*so that's no coincidence! May finish the* third Seven *next. Pleased with what I've read so far!"*

The head of the Subsidiary Rights department at Prentice-Hall had informed Jane that four copies of the film option contract were in the mail.[4] *By the first of August we'd had our attorney check, sign, and notarize the contracts, Jane and I had signed them, and I'd returned them to our publisher. It has been an extremely slow-moving project, but* The Education of Oversoul Seven *may yet be a movie.*

Jane's worsening situation through June and July, then, prepared her to accept my suggestion that Seth could help her. She put aside the first session for Chapter 9 of Dreams, *and began Seth's sessions on the magical approach to reality. As Seth remarked on August 6, when he gave his first session on the subject:* "When Ruburt finished his project [God of Jane], *he found himself with all of that time that was supposed to be* used. *He also became aware of his limitations, physically speaking: There was not much, it seemed, he could do but work, so he took the rational approach—and* it *says that to solve the problem you worry about it."*

I was delighted when Jane began to show physical improvements almost at once during those early August days, and so was she. It's not contradictory to note that during August and September, following his regular schedule of twice-weekly sessions, Seth methodically presented some very exciting concepts. So closely do those 13 sessions fit together that it's most difficult to give excerpts.[5] *Seth's magical-approach material represents one of his best efforts to help us, as well as others. Jane's difficulties certainly inspired them, but their creativity also goes beyond our own needs. And as soon as I realized she was going to continue the series for a while, I jokingly asked her what was going on:* "What do you think you're up to, hon? Are you doing a book within a book, or what?" *My wife didn't answer yes or no, but I could see that she was pleased, and that she was thinking about it. The title of the new book would be automatic:* The Magical Approach to Reality: A Seth Book.

In the meantime, early in August Jane had laid Seven Three *aside once more and returned to the book of poetry she'd had in progress for a year.*[6] *And on August 15 she happily announced that she'd come up with the complete title she had been searching for all that time:* If We Live Again: Or, Public Magic and Private Love. *Her editor, Tam Mossman, enthusiastically agreed with her choice. Two days later, Jane began writing the first of the three essays she had planned for the book:* "Poetry and the Magical Approach to Life." *Her choice of subject matter there was quite natural: She'd given her third session in that series two days earlier.*

Besides enabling Jane to help herself physically, Seth's magical-approach material had other beneficial aspects for her. Some of those lay in her poetry, both for her book and outside of it. On August 25, for example, on the day she delivered the sixth session for Seth on his new theme, Jane wrote the following untitled poem. I urged her to give it a title and include it in If We Live Again. *Within its deceptive simplicity her poem carries profound meaning; I haven't seen that meaning expressed any better elsewhere. If she were to sum up the results of her life's work so far in a few lines, this poem would do the job the best of all:*

> It's not that my mind knows less
> than it did before, but that
> its reason finally deduced
> the magic of its source, and
> sensed beneath the logic of its
> ways the deeper spontaneous order
> that powers its own thought.

See Note 7, in which I used Jane's poem as a focus around which to offer certain pieces. Indeed, more and more as I worked on these notes for Chapter 9 of Dreams, *I saw how necessary it was that I write an Introduction for the book itself—to create a framework for the presentation of all of the material in it from our private and professional lives. Of course, I couldn't yet know everything that such a project ought to contain. Jane had mentioned a number of times that she'd help me with it. And she was playing around with the idea of a Seth book on the magical approach.*

Early in September Tam mailed back to us, for our approval, the copy-edited 484-page manuscript for Mass Events. *An independent reader had gone over our labors line by line, checking for everything from grammar and contradictions to philosophy, "flagging" questions for us by noting them on slips of pink paper taped to the appropriate manuscript pages. Along with our other projects—including answering a steady flow of letters—Jane and I spent the month going over* Mass Events, *accepting some suggestions but rejecting many others. On the 13th we received from Sue Watkins our first copy of Volume 1 of* Conversations With Seth, *Sue's excellent account of the ESP classes Jane used to hold in one of the two apartments we rented in downtown Elmira, before we moved to the hill house outside of town in 1975. Sue was now working on the last two chapters of the second and last volume of* Conversations. *Early in October I returned* Mass Events *to our publisher once more; it was ready to be set in type. Jane kept at her poetry and essays right into that first week in October, while her physical improvements continued to show in a modest way. Her walking especially was better, and I was able to take her on an occasional drive in the beautiful country.*

*That first, July 23rd entry at Three Mile Island took place on day
263 of the seizing of the American hostages in Iran. See Note 1 for
Session 919, in Chapter 7 of* Dreams, *wherein I reviewed not only
Iran's concern over the Russian invasion of its eastern neighbor, Afghanistan, in late December 1979, but also Iran's border clashes with its
western neighbor, Iraq, during the past year. Finally, on September 23
[day 325 of the hostage situation], the inevitable happened in the very
unstable Middle East: Amid that explosive mixture of secular and religious national consciousnesses "at work" there, Iraq launched an outright invasion of Iran. Quickly Iraq began to gobble up large portions of
Iranian territory. The whole Western world became alarmed, for economic reasons as well as others.*

*One of the tactics leaders in the West are still pursuing is to organize
world opinion against the Soviet stay in Afghanistan and the war between Iraq and Iran. Jane and I think that both situations, furnishing as
they do large-scale frameworks for the almost endless convolutions of
consciousness, may persist for many years, with no formal resolutions
materializing. Russia may simply annex Afghanistan as the years pass.
Perhaps the Iraqi-Iranian war will subside because of the exhaustion of
those countries. I speculated that the overall revolutionary and fundamentalistic consciousness of Iran is like a creative vortex, surrounded by
other great national consciousnesses that are strongly resisting its policies
for their own creative religious and political reasons. A look at a map
will show what I mean: Iran has Iraq and Turkey on its western border,
with Russia to its north and Afghanistan on its east; Pakistan lies on
Iran's eastern border also; south of Iran, across the narrow Persian
Gulf, cluster the mix of large and small wealthy states on the Arabian
peninsula. The Moslem Kurds of Iran and Iraq, minority peoples with
strong roots in eastern Turkey, are rebelling against the military forces of
their respective countries; and Pakistan has become a place of shelter for
refugees from Afghanistan. That whole area in the Middle East, then, is
a stew of emotions, actions, and consciousnesses.*

*And yet the embattled consciousness of Iran persists, and will, I think,
survive for a long while. Many consciousnesses in the Middle East have
much to work out yet.*

*At the beginning of the notes for this 920th session I wrote that the
session isn't dictation for* Dreams. *Yet it is, of course, since in it Seth
illuminates from still another perspective his concept of value fulfillment.[8] The session grew out of the encounter we had yesterday afternoon
with an unexpected visitor from out of state. Seth hardly mentions the*

individual involved, however, but instead goes into the subject of mental illness in more inclusive terms. I see many correlations between this evening's material and that in Session 917 for Chapter 8; there, among other things, Seth had discussed the reasoning mind, the imaginative mind, and schizophrenia. That session had been triggered, at least in part, by a letter Jane had found to be quite upsetting.

I admit that for some mysterious reason of my own I let Bill Baker, as I'll call that youngish individual, fool me when he knocked on our back-porch door yesterday afternoon. He was very well dressed and very well spoken, and I didn't pay enough attention to the doubts I sensed when he told me about hearing voices in his head, and asked if Jane did the same thing with Seth. I said no. After introducing him to my wife, I went back to my writing room. I could understand what they were saying by concentrating upon the murmur of their voices from the living room, but I seldom did so. She almost called me, Jane said later, when she realized that Bill Baker is a disturbed[9] person. He told her he'd been hospitalized several times for mental problems, and demonstrated his ability to speak very fluently a "nonsense" language he cannot decipher. [Later I remembered hearing a bit of that.] Our caller had received a number of pages of information from Jesus Christ. He described how he's relating the Seth material to his sexual fantasies involving young girls, and detailed other instances in which he'd been strongly rebuffed when trying to physically actualize some of Seth's ideas. There was more. Jane caught him in a number of contradictory statements.

Bill Baker left soon after learning that Jane no longer holds her ESP classes. The episode reminded us once again that many of our visitors are seeking help of one kind or another, and that we hadn't had the remotest idea that this would be the case when Jane began her psychic development late in 1963. Sometimes we're not sure whether the people are simply rebelling against the help offered by establishment disciplines [especially when that "help" is partially or wholly ineffective], or are more aware than most that some individuals, like Jane, have other "psychic" dimensions of personality that can be asked for information. Yet, I told Jane, look at the excellent letters we've recently received from psychiatrists, mathematicians, and "ordinary" folk engaged in a variety of endeavors.

And Bill Baker has benefited from reading the Seth material, I said, since now he reasons that some of his ideas are "core beliefs" that he's created—and so can change. "Where would I be without the Seth material?" he'd asked Jane.

As we sat for the session, Jane said that Seth would discuss schizophre-

nia in general—so certainly our visitor's appearance led to information on a subject we wouldn't have asked about otherwise. Jane's delivery as Seth varied from being fast to one with many pauses.)

Good evening.

("Good evening, Seth.")

I will use your yesterday's visitor as the point around which to build a discussion.

First of all, the term "schizophrenia" is of basically little value. Many people tabbed with that label should not be. There are so-called classic cases of schizophrenia—and borderline ones, so-called—but in any case the label is highly misleading and negatively suggestive.

What you are dealing with in many instances are exhibitions of various, sometime quite diverse personality patterns of behavior—patterns that are, however, not as assimilated, or as smoothly operative as they are in the person you call normal. The patterns are seen in an exaggerated fashion, so that in some such cases at least you can gain glimpses of mental, emotional, and psychic processes that usually remain psychologically invisible beneath the more polished or "finished" social personality of the usual individual.

The person labeled schizophrenic, momentarily or for varying periods of time, lacks a certain kind of psychological veneer. This is not so much a basic lack of psychological finish as it is the adoption of a certain kind of *(pause)* psychological camouflage.

Such people—in a fashion, now—play a game of quite serious hide-and-seek with themselves and with the world. They believe in the dictum: "Divide and conquer." It is as if, for reasons I hope to discuss, they refuse to put themselves together properly, refuse to form one fairly united self. The idea behind this is: "If you cannot find me, then I cannot be held accountable for my actions—actions which are bound in one way or another to betray me."

The self becomes operationally scattered or divided, so that if one portion of it is attacked, the other portions can rise up in defense. Such persons use the various elements of the personality as spies or soldiers, scattering their forces *(pause)*, and forced under those conditions to set up elaborate communication systems to keep those portions of the self in contact with each other. In times of stress, they set up an even greater isolation of one part of the self from another, which puts stress upon the system of communication, of course, so that it must be used constantly.

The communications themselves are often a kind of psychological or symbolic code, such as might indeed be used in military intelligence. If the messages were to be clearly deciphered and understood, then of course the game would be over, for the one to understand the message would be the united self who [had] felt the need of such camouflaged self-troops (hyphen) to begin with.

(*Slower at 9:36:*) Such a person does feel under seige. Often such people are highly creative, with good reserves of energy, but caught between highly contrasting beliefs, either of good and evil, or power and weakness. They are usually extremely idealistic, but for various reasons they do not feel that the abilities of the idealized self can be actualized.

I am making generalizations here, but each individual case should be looked at in its own light. Such people as a rule, however, have an exaggerated version of the self *(pause),* so idealized *(long pause)* that its very existence intimidates practical action. They are afraid of making mistakes, terrified of betraying this sensed inner psychological superior. Usually, such an idealized inner self comes from the acceptance of highly distorted beliefs—again, concerning good and evil. You end up with what can amount to two main inner antagonists: a superior self and a debased self. The qualities considered good are attracted to the superior self as if it were a magnet. The qualities that seem bad (underlined) are in the same fashion attracted to the debased self. Both of them, relatively isolated psychological polarities, hold about equal sway. All other psychological evidences that are ambiguous, or not clearly understood by either side, group together under their own psychological banners. This is a kind of circular rather than linear arrangement, however, psychologically speaking.

(*Long pause at 9:44.*) Such people are afraid of their own energy. It becomes assigned on the one hand as a possession of the superior self—in which case it must be used for great adventures, heroic deeds. On the other hand, the person feels unable to use energy in a normal fashion, since in the ordinary world no venture could live up to the superior self's exaggerated ideals. The person then becomes frightened of pitting himself against the world, or committing himself to ordinary actions, since he feels that in the light of such comparisons he can only debase himself.

He requires undue amounts of praise and attention from others, since he obviously will get little from himself. In a fashion, to an extent he will refuse to be accountable for his actions—therefore taking them out of the frame of judgment within which other people must operate. He then can avoid putting his "talents and superior abilities" to the test, where he feels he would certainly fail. He half realizes that the superior self and the debased self are both of psychological manufacture. His abilities are not really that grand. His failures are not nearly that disastrous. The belief in these highly contrasting elements of personality keep him in a state of turmoil, however, so that he feels powerless to act in any concerted fashion.

The term "schizophrenia," however, covers multitudinous experiences—some such people are quite satisfied with their condition, find their own niches, are able to support themselves, or have means of support. Others live in an atmosphere of constant fear of their own condition, while at the same time they are excited, as soldiers might be in combat. Some can be quite functional in society, and the condition in any case is highly variable, covering people who are simply social misfits to those who are in deep psychological trouble.

(10:03.) With most people *(long pause)*, there is a kind of psychological paved road upon which impulses travel before they meet *(pause)* an intersection with the conscious mind, which then determines whether or not the impulse will be followed or acted upon. *(Long pause.)* In the kinds of cases we are discussing, however, instead of a paved road you have a dangerous, rocky field that might be filled with mines ready to explode at any time.

(Long pause at 10:08.) Give us a moment. . . . Remember, we are dealing with a scattered force, various elements of the personality sent out to do different tasks—and in a fashion they are caught between the superior self and the debased self. There is, then, no clear line for action to follow. It must also be camouflaged. Instead of clear impulses toward action that intersect directly with consciousness, you have bursts of impulses that emerge as orders to act, coming from another source, or from other sources. These may appear as voices telling an individual

to do this or that, as "automatic" commands through writing, or as perceptions that would be called hallucinatory. In this way the individual need not take responsibility for such actions. They do not seem to be coming from himself or from herself. The terrible possibility of failure is there to that extent, in that situation, momentarily relieved.

There is always an overall order to the personality, even though it is in the background, so that in any given case all of the separate "selves," or other sources with whom the individual feels in contact, would together point toward the totality, or unity, that lies beneath. The outstanding mental phenomena, therefore, show in isolated fashions those elements of the personality that are not to be assimilated in the usual smooth fashion.

There are countless instances where "schizophrenic episodes" occur in otherwise normal personalities, where for learning purposes and periods of growth the personality sorts its parts out, and helps them enlarge their frameworks.

The personality can indeed put itself together in multitudinous fashions. There is great leeway in the use of inner and outer perceptions, and the manners in which these are mixed and matched to form an acceptable picture of reality at any given time.

(Long pause at 10:24.) Physical perception gives you a necessary kind of feedback, but it is also based upon learning processes, so that from a young age you learn to put the pieces of the world together in acceptable fashions. In a way, under certain conditions, some schizophrenic situations can give you righter glimpses of inner psychological mobility, a mobility that was focused and directed as you grew through childhood. Schizophrenia represents a kind of learning disability in that particular respect.

("Can I ask a question?")

You may.

("I heard Bill Baker speak a very fluent—uh, foreign—language, one that he said he couldn't decipher.")

The language is an excellent example of the coded messages I mentioned earlier (as I'd thought). It is supposed to remain secret, you see, yet becomes the symbol of the all-powerful knowledge of the exaggerated superior self, while making the knowledge impossible to act upon. To translate the information would mean a more serious commitment to physical communication than that young man was willing to make.

(Pause.) I will have more to say about such communications, and the ways in which they can point out the greater psychological mobility that is a more or less natural element in children. When you are a child, you are not held accountable for your actions in the same way that adults are, and schizophrenia often begins around puberty, or young adulthood, when people feel that their youthful promise is expected to bear fruit. If they have been considerably gifted, for example, they are now supposed to show the results of schooling through adult accomplishments. If they are nearly convinced, however, that the self is also dangerous or evil, then they become afraid of using their abilities, and indeed become more frightened of the self—which, again, they then try to conquer by dividing. They feel cut off from value fulfillment. In a fashion they begin to act opaquely in the world, showing a divided face.

(10:35.) End of session. I will continue the subject, tying it more securely to value fulfillment, and stressing the importance of positive action in the physical world, so that ideals can be expressed rather than feared, and so that the doors between impulses and their activations can be left open with some confidence.

A note. . . .

(Seth added a few sentences of personal material for Jane, then ended the session at 10:40 P.M. Jane's delivery had often been very animated and forceful, and I told her she'd done well. I was going to joke with her by asking if this was a "fill-in" session, but decided not to. I felt that except for our own time limitations, Seth could have given much more material on the whole subject of mental illness.)

NOTES. Session 920

1. I don't mean to imply that it was particularly easy to assemble these notes. It took me days. Sometimes over the years, in my frustration at being unable to find a certain line or passage in a session, or in something Jane or I have written, I've ended up thinking that I merely *imagined* its being: "It doesn't really exist at all," I've told myself, "so why am I wasting my time looking for

it?" Yet once I start hunting, it's difficult to stop until I've exhausted all reasonable chances of finding what I want. Even a thorough indexing of every paper we have in the house, including each page of the Seth material, often wouldn't locate the kinds of references I need. To suit me, I've told Jane more than once, the index would have to be practically as long as our lifework itself. I've gone through those episodes a number of times. (So have others, according to their letters, even though the books are indexed.)

2. When Jane and I married on December 27, 1954, we promised each other that neither one of us would interfere with the other's creative approach to life, no matter what resulted from the actions we individually chose. We have kept those promises for the 26 years we've been together. Of course, we couldn't possibly have foreseen the great variety of challenges that lay before us. Nine years were to pass before Jane began coming through with the Seth material. She's certainly given me the complete freedom to be myself, and I've floundered often. So has she. Yet as the years passed I still had to learn the obvious—that Jane's creative powers are inextricably a part of her whole approach to life, including her symptoms. How could it be otherwise? That doesn't stop me from desperately wanting to help her. I've tried, in many ways. She's helped me often. Jane even agrees with me that she's a very stubborn lady—albeit an extremely creative one—who's determined to go her own way.

When they're published the reader will be able to see that she touched upon her physical hassles in Chapter 17 of *God of Jane*, for example, and referred to them in her Introduction for *Mass Events*. She didn't actively object when I began to mention them more extensively in the notes for *Dreams*. But as Seth said in Volume 2 of *"Unknown" Reality*, while discussing her goals in life: "The power of his *(Ruburt's)* will is indeed awesome, and he is just beginning to feel it." In that volume, see Session 713 for October 21, 1974. And in larger terms, if Jane is at all correct in her expression of the Seth material, then each action we've taken in connection with her symptoms has been valid and creative, just as each action we have yet to take will be.

3. In Chapter 6 for Volume 1 of *Dreams,* see Session 907.

4. In Chapter 2 for Volume 1 of *Dreams,* see the opening notes for Session 885.

5. Seth hardly flattered us in this first session. He also gave us a clue as to how Jane delivers certain sessions for him. To begin with, however, his magical-approach information reminded me at once of the two thoughts Jane had picked up from him back on May 12, the day she held the 915th session for Chapter 8. I'm stressing these points because I think they're important: "Alone, reason finally becomes unreasonable. Alone, imagination finally becomes less imaginative over time." Nine days later, Seth finally gave a little information relevant to Jane's insights; see the 917th session after 9:23.

Now from the private session for Wednesday evening, August 6, 1980 (and with some occasional paraphrasing):

"The natural person is indeed the magical person, and you have both to some extent had very recent *(telepathic)* examples of such activity. . . . Framework 2 has been a rather fascinating but mainly (underlined) hypothetical framework, in that neither of you have really been able to put it to any perceivable use in your terms. This is not to say that it has not been operating. You have not had the kind of feedback, however, that you want.

"When you were both intensely involved in your projects *(Mass Events* and *God of Jane),* just finished, you let much of your inner experience slide, relatively speaking. Since then, however, you have each been struck by the magical ease with which you seemed, certainly, to perceive and act upon information that you did not even realize you possessed.

"Some of Ruburt's notes that you have not seen have further important insights as to such activity. The main point is the importance of accepting (underlined) a different kind of overall orientation—one that is indeed a basic part of human nature. This involves an entirely different relationship of the self you know with time.

"Important misunderstandings involving time have been in a large measure responsible for many of Ruburt's difficulties, and also of your own, though of a lesser nature. All of this involves relating to reality in a more natural, and therefore magical, fashion. There is certainly a kind of natural physical time in your experience, and in the experience of any creature. It involves the rhythm of the seasons—the days and nights and tides and so forth. In the light of that kind of physical time, there is no basic cultural time . . . which you have transposed upon nature's rhythms.

"Such a cultural time works well overall for the civilization that concentrates upon partialities, bits and pieces, assembly lines, promptness of appointments, and so forth.

"Ruburt culturally has felt that each moment must be devoted to work. You have to some extent felt the same. Natural time is far different than you suppose. Far richer, and it turns inward and outward and backward and forward upon itself.

"Being your own natural and magical self when you dream, you utilize information that is outside of the time context experienced by the so-called rational mind. The creative abilities operate in the same fashion, appearing within consecutive time, but with the main work done outside of it entirely. . . . When you were both working on your projects, your cultural time was taken up in a way you found acceptable. When the projects were done, particularly with Ruburt, there was still the cultural belief that time should be so used (underlined), that creativity must be directed and disciplined to fall into the proper assembly-line time slots.

"There is much material here that I will give you, because it is important that you understand the different ways of relating to reality, and how those ways create the experienced events.

"You have not really, either of you, been ready to drastically alter your orientations, but you are approaching that threshold. As Ruburt's notes also mention, the 'magical approach' means that you actually change your methods of dealing with problems, achieving goals, and satisfying means. You change over to the methods of the natural person. They are indeed, then, a part of your private experience. They are not esoteric methods, but you must be convinced that they are the natural methods by which man is meant to handle his problems and approach his challenges.

"I use the word 'methods' because you understand it, but actually we are speaking about an approach to life, a magical or natural approach that is man's version of the animal's natural instinctive behavior in the universe. That approach does indeed fly in direct contradiction to the learned methods you have been taught.

"It certainly seems that the best way to get specific answers is to ask specific questions, and the rational mind thinks first of all of something like a list of questions. In that regard, Ruburt's response before such a session is natural, and to an extent magical, because he knows that no matter what he has been taught, he must to some degree (underlined) forget the questions and the mood that accompanies them with one level of his consciousness, in order to create the proper kind of atmosphere at another level of consciousness—one that allows the answers to come even though they may be presented in a different way than that expected by the rational mind.

"What we will be discussing for several sessions, with your permission jointly—and, I hope, with your joint enthusiasm—will be the magical approach to reality, and to your private lives specifically, in order to create that kind of atmosphere in which the answers become experienced (underlined.)"

6. In Chapter 8 of *Dreams*, see the opening notes for Session 915.

7. At first some of these excerpts might seem quite diverse in content from one another, but with Jane's poem in mind I intuitively chose each one for inclusion here. I'd wanted to show the first two items for several years, and surely the reader can divine how they're related to the poem and to Seth's material on the magical approach to reality. The next three excerpts are either from, or are directly related to, later sessions in the "magical" series.

A. From Jane's journal for 1975. She doesn't recall the month in which she wrote this—only that she did so at high speed:

"Life as we know it is excitement; highly organized—excitement at all levels, microscopic, macroscopic, psychic. It is the result of the relationship between balance and imbalance, between organization and 'chaos.' It is excitement ever in a state of flux, forming psychic and material knots. It is explosive yet filled with order; it becomes so filled with itself that it explodes in the same way that a flower bursts; the same principle is acting in a hurricane or a flood or a murder or the creation of a poem, or the formation of a dream; in the birth and death of individuals and nations. We instinctively know that disasters mimic the birth and death of cells within our bodies—we instinctively know that all life survives death, that death is the bursting of life into new forms, hence our fascination with accidents and fires. The psyche itself leapfrogs our beliefs at usual conscious levels, and sees us as a part of all life, excitedly forming all kinds of complexes which then fill themselves to the brim, exploding, escaping the framework only to form another. The emotions themselves can sense this when we let them, and grasping that sense of excitement can show us a glimpse of the even greater freedom of our own psychic existence, which flows into us as individuals and then bursts apart that short-lived form into another, as the excitement of individuation leaps from life to life."

B. From Jane's journal for 1976. She wrote these notes on March 6, when she was 47 years old:

"My own ideas must be colored to some extent by my place in time also, and middle age seems to be an excellent spot for such a study because theoretically time stretches as far ahead as it does behind. That is, there is as much anticipated time as there is remembered time.

"In childhood we have little past time to remember. We seem to come from darkness, taking our parents' memories on faith for proof that there was time before our birth. As we grow toward old age, we have past time to play with—we know where we came from in usual terms—and the darkness that once seemed to stretch behind our source or origin seems to be our destination. Certainly an examination of the mind and reality from the standpoint of old age will be invaluable."

And: "Today now I feel that acceleration that tells me that my intent is traveling out into the unknown, or out into the universe to bring in answers to my questions, even questions I'm not consciously aware of. And from experience I know that enough energy is generated to do this though the results will come to me in time. I know I get them from outside of time in some unknown way."

C. From the second session on the magical approach; Jane held it on Monday evening, August 11, 1980:

"Ruburt's state of mind was in *(telepathic)* correspondence with your own state of mind, even as you are in some kind of correspondence with your old *(childhood)* environment, so in these cases you have a free flow of information at other levels.

"Now when you understand that intellectually, then the intellect can take it for granted that its own information is not all the information you possess. It can realize that its own knowledge represents the tip of the iceberg. As you apply that realization to your life, you begin to realize furthermore that in practical terms you are indeed supported by a greater body of knowledge than you realize, and by the magical, spontaneous fountain of action that forms your existence. The intellect can then realize that it does not have to go it all alone: Everything does not have to be reasoned out, even to be understood."

D. From the third session on the magical approach, Wednesday evening, August 13, 1980. Seth made certain comments that led to my writing this note:

"Seth, of course, not only dictates his material—the session—but must keep the *whole* session in mind while doing so, so that each sentence as he delivers it makes sense compared to its predecessors *and those to follow.* Quite a feat on his part, and Jane's, when one stops to think about it. How is this possible? Seth has no script to go by, nor can he refer during the session to my own notes to check up on what he's already said.

"I believe a great memory must be involved here, one that on deeper levels is coupled with a shortening of time as we think of it. Seth-Jane's abilities remind me of material I wrote recently on how certain portions of the psyche must very shrewdly and carefully construct dreams *in advance,* so when the dreams are played back they render just the right messages to the other part or parts of the psyche that need them. I'm not being contradictory here when I write that dreams are also spontaneous productions."

E. From my opening notes for the 13th and last session in the private series on the magical approach to reality. Jane gave the session on Wednesday evening, October 1, 1980—just five days ago:

(*I was curious as to why Seth had devoted two other private sessions in late September to different subjects. When I asked Jane about this tonight, at first she rather matter-of-factly said that she didn't know. Then: "Well, I don't tell you everything, but for some time now I've known that Seth gives what I call* fill-in *sessions. I've labeled them that way in my mind. They cover* floating material—*stuff he could give any time. They aren't book sessions or really personal ones. They keep the sessions going over periods of time—usually by discussing past material—connecting it to the present, while not necessarily adding new stuff. And* not *specifically given on one subject. Originally I think the Christ sessions got started that way."*

"*So after all these years I find that out,*" I said. "*What else haven't you told me? How come the big secret?*"

"You never asked me." Jane's reply had a familiar sound. Checking later, I learned that she'd given me the same answer about Seth's material on Jonestown. We used that information in Mass Events. *[When that book is published, see Note 3 for Session 835, dated February 7, 1979.]*

"I think the fill-in sessions happen between book sessions, for a change of pace—where the material doesn't have to fit a more concentrated overall book focus," Jane added. She agreed to write a short account of what she'd just told me, for the record.)

Our exchange had quickly reminded me of a note I'd written a couple of weeks ago, and hadn't placed yet in *Dreams:*

"Of course, I thought, in ordinary terms the vast potential of the Seth material is fated never to be developed. No matter what Jane and I do in our joint reality, this is so. She could hold sessions 24 hours a day for the rest of her life, and still not exhaust Seth's potential store of information. We've had many indications that his material is multichanneled, as when Jane has felt him ready to discuss any one of a number of subjects on any given occasion. I call that feeling, that awareness, a pale indication of what Seth means with his theory of probable realities—for like probable personalities, the unspoken channels he has available are certainly *real* whether or not they're actualized in our physical reality.

"I can envision Seth's material expanding almost endlessly just on a day-to-day basis, as he deals with events in the lives of Jane and me—and this idea conveys nothing about news of his reactions to and interactions with events on various levels of his own reality, plus other realities he may be able to reach. In Chapter 8 of *Dreams,* when I asked Seth what he was going to do for the rest of the evening (in our terms), he replied: 'I am going to refresh myself by diving into some new concepts, for there are new concepts for me also, of course, and I dive into them from many positions all the time as well.' (See the conclusion of Session 916 for May 4, 1980.) Think of the questions one could ask him relative to just this one statement! Such provocative assertions leave behind them unsatisfied voids of curiosity. Actually, most of his information does, regardless of subject matter. But obviously, if Seth *did* take up every moment of our temporal lives with personal material, all else would be probable."

8. In the unpublished 842nd session for March 21, 1979, which he gave in the middle of producing the sessions for Chapter 6 of *Mass Events,* Seth had this to say:

"First of all, however, a note primarily to Ruburt: I often quite purposefully *(with amusement)* break off book dictation to discuss other matters that come into your experience. This allows me to cover material from several different viewpoints, and to organize it in different fashions. Actually, however, there are several self-formed books in your material already. Do you follow me?"

(I nodded yes.)

"He need not feel that all sessions must be book dictation, nor feel that he is in any way negatively responsible, as he sometimes does."

9. I do not mean the word "disturbed" to be derogatory in any sense at all. Instead I refer only to a behavioral departure from the generally accepted "norm." As Seth said in Session 917, which was held last May 21 for Chapter 8 of *Dreams:*

"Now on the question of 'mental disorders,' it is highly important that individual integrity be stressed, rather than the blanket definitions that are usually accorded to any group of symptoms."

SESSION 921——October 8, 1980
9:05 P.M. WEDNESDAY

(Jane's arms and legs have been sore today, off and on, but she feels that beneficial changes are taking place in them as a result of the sessions on the magical approach to reality. She's "real pleased" with her progress on the poetry and essays for If We Live Again.

After supper Jane said that Seth might talk about reincarnation, schizophrenia, and possession, tying those subjects together. Right away I could see how they might be related at times, yet I wasn't able to spontaneously verbalize the connections. Here are three points:

1. Seth's material on schizophrenia is an extension of his discussion on Monday evening, which is why this session is given here.

2. Jane's mention of reincarnation came from my idle speculations at our evening meal, after we'd been told about how a local man and

woman had embarked upon a radically new joint life-style, to the conster-
nation of many in our area. I'd wondered whether aroused reincarna-
tional ties might have played a part in the couple's actions. Such factors
simply aren't usually considered in "modern" social analyses of people's
behavior—yet sometimes they might actually play a very important role.
However, I certainly don't mean that supposed reincarnational relation-
ships can or should be used to justify present-life behavior, Many other
psychological elements are involved in any human situation.

3. Jane's mention of possession came about because today I'd read her
an article in a scholarly journal we subscribe to. The piece contained
public information with which we were already familiar. Briefly, most
authorities in the Roman Catholic Church realize that almost all of those
who are supposed to be "possessed" by malevolent forces are in actuality
mentally ill people who need treatment. Yet the church must admit the
separate reality of the devil and numerous demons, because their exis-
tences are given in the Gospels. This contradiction was reinforced in
1972, when Pope Paul VI declared before several thousand people that
the devil is a distinct, actual being.)

(Whispering:) Good evening.

(Whispering: "Good evening, Seth.")

Now: For our psychology lesson *(with gentle amusement)*, continued from before.

(Pause.) Communications between various scattered portions
of the self often appear, again, in such situations as automatic
writing, speaking, the hearing of voices, or through what the
person believes to be telepathic messages from others.

The supposedly telepathic messages can be attributed to contemporaries—enemies, gods, devils, or what have you. Spacemen are a recent addition. In most cases, what you have here are
expressions of strong portions of the self that are more or less
purposefully kept in isolation. They may appear or disappear,
psychologically speaking. They present a kind of chain of command—one that is not usually permanent for any long period,
however.

Particularly when the voices or communications give orders to
be obeyed, they represent powerful, otherwise repressed, images and desires, strong enough to form about themselves their
own personifications. Some may seem relatively genuine in
terms of presenting a fairly well-rounded representation of a
normal personality. That is a fairly rare occurrence, however.

Usually you are presented with, say, semi-personalities, or even with lesser versions (dash)—fragmentary expressions of impulses and desires that are dramatically presented only in snatches, heard by the person as a voice, or perceived as a presence.

In many situations, the main personifications are instead of a ritual nature, taking advantage of psychological patterns already present in the culture's art or religion or science. You end up with Christs, spacemen, various saints or spirits, or other personality fabrications whose characteristics and abilities are already known.

(9:19.) You have schizophrenic models, in other words, and the particular model chosen in any case, at any given time—for the models change—gives indications quite clearly of the person's basic problems and dilemmas. Such cultural models are present in society to begin with, because in one way or another they express in an exaggerated form certain portions of man's psychological reality that he does not as yet understand. This applies to the "good" schizophrenic models and to the "bad" ones—that is, to the gods as well as to the demons.

Such *(pause)* "communications" with the gods or demons, St. Pauls or Hitlers, represent in such instances dramatized, exaggerated personifications of the portion of the personality that is at the head of the chain of command at the moment.

(Long pause at 9:25.) In the first place, reality is primarily a mental phenomenon, in which the perceptions of the senses are organized and put together in ways that perfectly "mimic" in physical terms a primary *(long pause)* nonphysical experience. This is tricky to express, because the application of a psychological awareness through the auspices of the flesh automatically makes certain transformations of data necessary.

(A one-minute pause at 9:29.) Devils and demons have no objective existence. They have always represented, again, portions of mankind's own psychological reality that to some extent he had not assimilated—but in a schizophrenic kind of expression, projected instead outward from himself. Therefore, it does not seem he must be held accountable for acts that he considers debasing, or cruel. He isolates himself from that responsibility by imagining the existence of other forces—the devils or demons of the nether world.

(9:35.) On an individual basis, the schizophrenic carries through those cultural patterns. The contrasts between, say, the superior self or the idealized self, and the debased self, may vary, They may be brilliantly apparent or somewhat blurred. In many such instances there will also be at least a short spurt of intense but scrambled, perhaps garbled, creative activity, in which the individual tries to recognize these various elements, as mankind himself has attempted many times in the creative, sometimes garbled creation of his own religions *(with soft irony).*

Here you can have anything from banal rubbish to the most excellent creative product, but in the schizophrenic framework it will be of brief duration, experienced outside of the framework of usual day-to-day living, concentrated. Period.

The Christ image is often used because it so perfectly represents the combination of the grandiose self, as per the all-knowing son of God, and the martyred victim who is crucified precisely because of his lofty position.

The Christ figure represents the exaggerated, idealized version of the inner self that the individual feels incapable of living up to. He feels he is being crucified by his own abilities. He may—or of course she may—on other occasions receive messages from the devil, or demons, which on their part represent the person's feelings about the physical self that seems to be so evil and contradictory in contrast to the idealistic image. Again, there is great variety of behavior here.

Such people, however, in their fashion refuse to accept standardized versions of reality. Even though they are so uncertain of themselves that their psychological patterns do follow those of culture, religion, science, or whatever, they try to use those patterns in their own individual ways. They are actually in the process of putting their own personalities together long after most people have settled upon one official version or another—and so their behavior gives glimpses of the ever-changing give-and-take among the various elements of human personality.

Most of the declared instances of telepathy or clairvoyance that happen in schizophrenic situations are instead the individual's attempts to prove to himself or herself that the idealized qualities of omnipotence or power are indeed within grasp—this, of course, to compensate for the basic feeling of powerlessness in more ordinary endeavors. In some situations, however,

there are definite, quite valid instances of telepathy or clairvoyance, vivid out-of-body experiences, and other excursions beyond the officially accepted realm of reality.

(Pause as 9:54.) These are often complicated, however, since
the individuals' belief patterns are of such an exaggerated blend
to begin with, so that such episodes are usually accompanied by
phantom figures from religion or mythology. The individuals
may feel forced to have such experiences, simply because, again,
they do not want to face responsibility for action, for the reasons
given earlier.

In your terms of time, man has always projected unassimilated
psychological elements of his own personality outward, but in
much earlier times he did this using a multitudinous variety of
images, personifications, gods, goddesses, demons and devils,
good spirits and bad. Before the Roman gods were fully formalized, there was a spectacular range of good and bad deities, with
all gradations [among them], that more or less "democratically"
represented the unknown but sensed, splendid and tumultuous
characteristics of the human soul, and have stood for those
sensed but unknown glimpses of his own reality that man was in
one way or another determined to explore.

It was understood that all of these "forces" had their parts to
play in human events. Some stood for forces of nature that could
very well be at times advantageous, and at times disadvantageous—as, for example, the god of storms might be very wel-
come at one time, in periods of drought, while his powers might
be quite dreaded if he overly satisfied his people. There was no
chasm of polarity between the "good gods and the bad ones."

Jehovah and the Christian version of God brought about a
direct conflict between the so-called forces of good and the so-
called forces of evil by largely cutting out all of the intermediary
gods, and therefore destroying the subtle psychological give-
and-take that occurred between them—among them—and po-
larizing man's own view of his inner psychological reality.

There were no schizophrenics in the time of the pagans, for
the belief systems did not support that kind of interpretation.
This does not mean that certain behavior did not occur that you
would now call schizophrenic. It means that generally speaking
such behavior fit within the psychological picture of reality. It
[did so] because many of the behavior patterns associated, now,

with schizophrenia, are "distorted and debased" remnants of behavior patterns that are part and parcel of man's heritage, and that harken back to activities and abilities that at one time had precise social meaning, and served definite purposes.

(10:14.) These include man's ability to identify with the forces of nature, to project portions of his own psychological reality outward from himself, and then to perceive those portions in a revitalized transformation—a transformation that then indeed can alter physical reality.

The next natural step would be to reassimilate those portions of the self, to acknowledge their ancient origins and abilities, to return them so that they form a new coating, as it were, or a new version of selfhood. It is as if *(pause)* man could not understand his own potentials unless he projected them outward into a godhead, where he could see them in a kind of isolated pure form, recognize them for what they are, and then accept them—the potentials—as a part of his own psychological reality *(all very intently)*. As a species, however, you have not taken the last step. Your idea of the devil represents the same kind of process, except that it stands for your idea of evil or darkness, or abilities that you are afraid of. They also stand for elements of your own potential. I am not speaking of evil possibilities, but that man must realize that he is responsible for his acts, whether they are called good or evil.

You make your own reality, Man's "evil" exists because of his misunderstanding of his own ideals, because of the gap that seems to exist between the ideal and its actualization. Evil actions, in other words, are the result of ignorance and misunderstanding. Evil is not a force in itself.

End of session.

("Very good.")

Tell Ruburt to relax, and to encourage and trust his body when it is undergoing so many changes, for the changes are all for the better. *(Pause, as Seth stared at me with some amusement.)* A fond good evening.

("Good night, Seth.")

10:26 P.M. I told Jane that the session is another excellent one, "I do believe he's going to go on with that material," she said. I hope so, for it appears that Seth is far from carrying his discussion through to the subject of reincarnation. I'm most interested that he do so.)

SESSION 922——October 13, 1980
9:14 P.M. MONDAY

(Late last week Tam Mossman called Jane to tell her that he's begun work on her contract for the publication of If We Live Again. *I wrote Tam this morning, asking questions about what long-range plans Prentice-Hall may have for the 15 books Jane and I have sold the company. [That total includes* Mass Events, God of Jane, *and the poetry book, all of which are yet to be issued.] In the private session for September 22—one of his series on the magical approach to life—Seth had told us that our work is "protected." I've been curious about that statement ever since, and mentioned it to Jane today in connection with my letter to Tam.*

She was quite upset after our nap this afternoon because we'd over-slept; she regretted the lost time. We had to eat supper later than usual. This evening, however, Seth used my interest in the question of protection beautifully as he discussed a facet of Jane's abilities that's strongly related to his concept of value fulfillment. Because of that relationship, this session fits very well into Dreams *even though it's not book dictation.)*

Now—

("Good evening, Seth.")

—you are protected. Your work is protected.

(Pause.) Some years ago, Ruburt had an experience in which he glimpsed in the center of the living room a strange form. He sensed that the form was composed of energy that was definitely predisposed to come to his assistance, or to do his bidding.

He also realized that at least to some extent this energy had accumulated as a result of his own good intentions, and his desire to help others. He called this "Helper,"[1] and he never saw the form clearly again. The form represented *(long pause)* the personified, accumulated positive energies that were working to his advantage at that time, that provided him protection, but that also automatically worked to the benefit of his life and projects.

The very idea of protection, however, as you know, implies a threat—so if you believe in threats you had better have protection. It was not necessary for Ruburt to see the form again—merely to sense the reality of that powerful energy, and realize that it worked on his behalf. In a fashion the form also represented the innocent and powerful inner self, or spontaneous self, or naturally magical self—the terms are synonymous.

Ruburt knew that Helper could be sent out to others, to their advantage, and in that regard the form stood for the great power of natural, positive desire and thought patterns. *(To me:)* You have the same kind of "form." These represent the greater source-selves out of which your present persons spring. I told you that you possessed far more knowledge about your own lives, and the lives of others, than you were intellectually aware of.[2] You act on that knowledge, for one thing, when you are born physically, when you grow. The squirrel acts on that kind of knowledge when it buries nuts—as you saw, again, on a recent TV program—and the squirrel's greater knowledge includes the knowledge of its species as well.

(9:30.) Helper represents the part that possesses such knowledge. In practical terms, it is very important to understand that such knowledge and protection do exist, that all of your problems need not be solved through conscious reasoning alone—and, indeed, few problems can be solved exclusively (underlined) in that fashion.

Your work is protected, not only because it is one of your projects, but also because in a fashion it becomes its own kind of entity—a well-intended one that exists in a rather concentrated form, distilled from your own best aspirations. Hence it is also filled with energy, and also becomes a collector of it.

(Long pause, one of many in a much slower delivery.) I do not want to become involved in a confusion of terms. The mind's powers are far greater than those generally assigned to rational thought alone, as per our last *(private)* sessions. Rational reasoning, overdone, can for example actually limit practical use of the intellect's faculties, and therefore serve to dim some of the mind's scope. In a fashion, again, Helper represents the true capacity of the mind's functioning, the kind of instant comprehension that is behind both the intuitions and the intellect's activities. You are dealing, then, with the spacious intellect, the knower.

(9:40.) That k-n-o-w-e-r *(spelled)* is instantly aware of all your needs, and is the portion of the universe that is personally disposed in your direction, because its energies form your own person. That protection always couches your existence. It means that you live "in a state of grace."[3] You can be unaware of that state. You can deny it or refuse it, but you are within it regardless. It forms the very fabric of your individual beings. Value

fulfillment means that each individual, each entity, of whatever nature, spontaneously, automatically seeks those conditions that are suited to its own fulfillment, and to the fulfillment of others.

In the most basic of terms, no one's fulfillment can (underlined) be achieved at the expense of another's. Fulfillment does not happen that way. Your very lives seek the best directions for fulfillment. Our work seeks its own best directions for fulfillment.

When you realize this, then you can accept seeming setbacks, or seeming contradictions, with a calm detached air, realizing that such factors appear as they do only in the light of your present intellectual knowledge—a knowledge that must be limited to current events—and that in the larger picture known to you at other levels, such seeming contradictions, or seemingly unfortunate situations, or whatever, will be seen to be to your advantage. You do not have all the facts, you see, at that intellectual level, so if you base all of your judgments—all of your judgments—at that level alone, then you can be quite short-sighted.

We are dealing with the psychology of experience, however, so you yourselves alter the situation according to your own reactions. If you feel threatened by certain situations, and lacking protection, then you will take certain steps that might not be taken otherwise, so your actions are vastly different according to whether or not you realize that you are indeed being protected.

If you build up feelings of threat, then at your level you also react to those. The protection exists, but in such cases you do not allow yourselves to take full advantage of it.

Take a break.

(9:50. I was surprised that Seth suggested a break—a rarity in the sessions these days. Then Jane said that she had called for the break because she was out of cigarettes. She was giving the session while sitting in her wheeled office chair. At that time of night she wasn't about to use her typing table as a support while she "walked" from the living room, where we were having the session, around the room divider and out into the kitchen to get her smokes; instead she remained in her chair and maneuvered herself along with her feet. I told her the session is excellent. "I see it led to something after all," she called out.

All of our discourses were related to tonight's material, if only intuitively. Jane got herself back into position across the coffee table from me while I described what I'd learned lately about Cro-Magnon man, who had lived in Europe some 35,000 years ago. The Cro-Magnon are of the same species, Homo sapiens, *as modern man. They displayed an exquisite artistry in their toolmaking, painting, and religion—indeed, in their whole culutre. Next we talked about early man in Palestine, before 3000* B.C.

Then somehow our conversation led me to wonder whether our cat, Billy, is color-blind, as we've heard most animals are. So far Billy had spent the session beside me on the couch, alternately napping and preening himself. I'd been admiring the loving care with which he'd addressed himself to each portion of his body. In the light from the lamp above and behind my right shoulder on the room divider, his greenish eyes were so beautifully colored, yet mysterious, that I found it hard to believe he can't see color. I also asked Jane about what use the gorgeous colors of Billy's luxurious fur are to him if he can't appreciate those patches and stripes of sienna, black, warm gray, and pure white. Or do his colors serve other purposes for him that we're unaware of? Intuitively, I felt that more is involved here than questions of camouflage and protection—that at the very least there must be connections between Billy and his colors in this reality and his source in a nonphysical one.[4]

Jane was interested in our talk—mine, mostly—but finally she revealed that it was better for her when Seth didn't take a break: "I like it when he zooms right through to the end." I replied that my questions carried no hints for material from Seth. "Yes," she said, "I guess if no one had anything to say, we'd sit here like dummies."

And yet, my talk did *bring about a change in the session's material. Resume at 10:09.)*

Apropos of one of your brief discussions.

(Long pause.) The ideas for inventions, tools or products exist mentally, to be brought into activation whenever they are required, say, by circumstances, or by the environment.

Various tribes in different parts of the earth would suddenly begin using new tools, say, not because there might be any physical communication among them, or cultural exchanges, but because separate conditions in their own environments triggered mental processes that activated the particular images of the tools required for a given job at hand. The information, which was nonphysical, was then transformed into practical knowledge either from inner visual imagery by itself, or through the state of dreaming.

Dreams have always served as such a connective. You know more about your life than you think you do—and far more about your life and society than you are intellectually aware of. Early man was in that same position, and his inventions—his tools, his artistry, and so forth—came into being from the inner, ever-present realm of the mind, triggered by his unconscious but quite real estimation of his position within the universe at large, and in regard to his own environment.

(Long pause at 10:18.) In a fashion—and forgive me for using one of my favorite qualifications again—but in a fashion, cultures do not evolve in the kind of straightforward manner that is usually supposed. Of course, cultures change, but man instantly began to fashion culture, as for example beavers instantly began to form dams. They did not learn how to form dams through trial and error *(humorously).* They did not for untold centuries build faulty dams, for example. They were born, or created, dam makers.

Man automatically began to form culture. He did not start with the rudiments of culture, as is thought. He did not learn *(pause)* through trial and error to think clear thoughts. He thought quite clearly from the beginning. He did learn through trial and error various ways of best translating those thoughts into physical action. The first cultures were as rich as your own. In your terms, reading and writing are great advantages, but it is also true that in the past the mind was also used to record information, and transmit it with an artistry that you do not now use.

Memory was so perfected that men at one time were indeed living histories, and carried within their minds their genealogies and backgrounds and the knowledge of their peoples, which were then passed on to their children. It is true that reading and writing have certain advantages over such procedures, but it is also true that knowledge possessed in that old fashion became a part of a man, and a society, in a much more personal, meaningful manner. It was, of course, a different kind of knowing. At its best it did not lead to rote renditions of remembered material, but to dramatic renderings of it through music, poetry, dancing. In other words, its rendition was accompanied by creative physical expression. It is true that, practically speaking, a man's mind, or a woman's, could not hold all of the information available now in your world—but much of that information does not deal with basic knowledge about the universe or man's place within it. It is a kind of secondary information—interesting, but not life-giving.

(Long pause at 10:34.) Man did not have to learn by trial and error what plants were beneficial to eat, and what herbs were good for healing. The knower in him knew that, and he acted on the information spontaneously. The knower is of course always present, but the part of your culture that is built upon the notion that no such inner knowledge exists, and those foolish ideas of rational thought as the only provider of answers, therefore often limit your own use of inner abilities.

You will end up with, if all goes well, a kind of "new" illuminated consciousness, an intellect who realizes that the source of its own light is not itself, but comes from the spontaneous power that provides the fuel for its thoughts.

End of session.

("It's very good,")

A fond good evening. Tell Ruburt to change his pillows more frequently.

("Okay. Good night, Seth."

10:40 P.M. "Well," Jane laughed, as soon as she was out of trance, "you did get something out of break. . . ."

I told her the material is fascinating in its implications. It's an excellent point, I said, that in her ability to tap into a seemingly endless amount of Seth material, she strikes a parallel with early man and his capacity to carry all personal, cultural, and historical information within himself. As early man functioned on his own, without writing or any of the other modern conveniences of communication that we have, so does Jane function through Seth. I speculated about what reincarnational connections might exist involving Jane and ancient men and women. Seth has never discussed the subject, nor have we asked him to. His potential for oral history appears to be unlimited.

Seth didn't return to the material on reincarnation, schizophrenia, and possession that he began discussing last Wednesday evening in the 921st session.)

NOTES. Session 922

1. See Chapter 6 of *Adventures in Consciousness* for Jane's description of how she became aware of "Helper" early in November

1971—a little over nine years ago. She's sent Helper on journeys to many who have requested aid of various kinds. She still does. Numerous people have written of beneficial events taking place in their lives when Jane did her thing for them, but she's kept no formal records. We've often speculated that just knowing Jane cared enough to send out an emissary like Helper was (and is) of psychological benefit to at least some of those in need, helping them generate positive actions on their own.

2. In this chapter, see Section C of Note 7 for Session 920.

3. Among others in *The Nature of Personal Reality: A Seth Book*, see Chapter 9: Seth discusses the state of grace, natural guilt, artificial guilt, and related subjects.

4. Checking after the session, I learned that cats are believed to have weak color vision. That is more than I'd expected, I told Jane, yet I still find it hard to believe that Billy, for example, doesn't have a much keener sense than that of his own colors.

SESSION 928——November 12, 1980
9:19 P.M. WEDNESDAY

(Since Jane held the 922nd session a month ago, she's given five more nonbook regular sessions. Small portions of three of them contain Seth material for herself.

In the middle of October, five technicians carried out the third entry into the radioactive containment building at Three Mile Island. A fourth trip, with a larger crew, is planned for next month.

On October 30 Sue Watkins called to tell us that she's finished writing Volume 2 of Conversations With Seth. *Prentice-Hall will publish the book late next year.*

On November 4 our country's president lost his bid for a second term. On that same day—day 367 of the hostage crisis—Iran demanded a quick reply from the United States to its latest set of conditions for the release of the 52 American hostages. For a number of complicated reasons, our State Department refused to give the Iranians a speedy answer. Evidently Iran wants to bring the hostage crisis to an end because of the economic boycott the Western world has imposed upon it, because in January it will have to deal with a new United States president, and because of the military pressure being exerted against it by Iraq. Iraq invaded Iran on September 23; on November 4 also, the president of Iraq proclaimed that his country is prepared to fight a long war for the recognition of its "rights" by Iran.

As for Jane: So many physical changes had taken place in her body today, she was so "out of it" by suppertime, that she didn't know whether or not she could even have a session. She'd mentioned this morning that Seth might resume work on Dreams, *and because of that feeling spent part of the day reviewing sessions for the book. After supper I got her iced wine—at her request—and started these notes while we waited to see what happened.*

Actually, my wife has become pretty much housebound. She's spending her time with the sessions, working on her book of poetry, and painting. For a long time now I've been doing it all in the outside world. I'll summarize the central challenge of Jane's life, and of my own, by presenting in Note 1 the private, or deleted, portion of the session she held last Monday night. We've been quite discouraged at times lately, yet Seth has had a different story to tell. Our struggle, our challenge, and one that's most difficult for us, is to understand *his material as much as possible.*

"Well, at least I feel him around." Jane said at 9:16, after she'd sipped some wine. She used many pauses in her delivery.)

Now—

("Good evening.")

—master events, then, involve "work" or action whose main thrust exists outside of time, yet whose effects are felt within time.

Such effects <u>may</u> (underlined) appear suddenly within time's context, rather than slowly emerge, say, into that framework. It is, of course, that kind of outside-of-time activity that in your terms explains the origin of your universe. There are dimensions of activity, then, that do not appear within time's structure, and developments that happen quite naturally, following different laws of development than those you recognize. It is not just that <u>highly accelerated</u> versions of time can occur at other levels of actuality *(long pause)*, but that there are dimensions in which those [versions] are no impediments to the natural "flow" *(pause)* of events into expression.

Your closest approximation will be, again, your experience with time in the dream state—or instances in which complicated problems are suddenly solved for you in dreams or in other states of consciousness, so that the answers appear full-blown before you.

There are "durations," then, that have nothing to do with time as you understand it: psychological motions that manipulate time but are apart from it. Any sudden emergence of a completed universe would then imply an unimaginable and a spectacular development of organization—that it did not just appear from nowhere, but as the "completed physical version" of an inner highly concentrated endeavor, the physical manifestation of an inspiration that then suddenly emerges into physical actuality.[2]

(9:32.) That kind of activity, that kind of "work," exists behind all of the structures and organizations and experiences with which you are familiar.

(A one-minute pause at 9:34.) Give us a moment. . . . The world of ideas everywhere permeates physical reality, but ideas, even when they are unexpressed, possess their own organizations, correspondences,[3] their own spheres of motion and development. Master events emerge from that reality of idea, now, from which all ideas originate, uniting these through the use of natural correspondences. Every physical manifestation that you know has its nonphysical counterpart, in which it is always couched, from which it came, and to which it will return.

(9:40.) Your historical time is, say, but one species of time that dwells upon the earth. There are many others. Time itself emerges from idea, which is itself timeless *(long pause),* so in those terms there was no point where time began, though such a reference becomes necessary from your own viewpoint.

(Long pause at 9:44.) It is probably almost impossible for man to see that he forms the idea of historical context through his own associations and focuses. The heavy, specialized use of so-called rational thought has often caused him to narrow even his neurological recognition of other kinds of experience that might enlarge his view. In dreams there is greater leeway in that regard. Consciousness becomes more familiar with its own inner motion, and even with the kinds of work and actions it performs outside of its usual waking prejudices. The story of the Creation, as Biblically stated, is the symbolic representation of a master event—a legend that became its own event, of course, forming about it whole arts and cultures, religions and disciplines. The

same applies to Christianity itself, for all of the seemingly historical events connected with the official (underlined) Christ did not
happen in physical reality. They happened at another level of
actuality, and were inserted into your time framework—touching a character here, a definitely known historical event there,
mixing and merging with the events of the time, until the two
lines of activity were so entwined that you could not unravel one
without unraveling the other *(all very intently)*.

History happened in certain definite forms because of a belief
in events that did not, in your world of facts, occur. The main,
brilliant thrust of those inner events, therefore, splashed out
upon the human landscape, propelling peoples and civilizations.

(Long pause at 9:55.) The Christ story in the beginning was not
nearly as singular and neat as it might now seem, for the finally
established official Christ figure was one settled upon from endless versions of a god-man, with which man's psyche has long
been involved: He was the psychic composite, the official Christ,
carrying within his psychological personage echoes of old and
new gods alike—a figure barely begun, comma, to be filled out
in time, although originating outside of it *(again, all very intently)*.

Such master events cause (underlined) physical events, but
they do not emerge originally from them *(all repeated as given,
and once more very intently.*

(10:02.) Paul *(Saul of Tarsus)* had his vision. Now the vision *(in
which Paul not only saw the light of Christ, but heard his voice)* happened in the world of fact. It occurred—but Paul did not see, or
communicate with *(long pause)*, a person of divine heritage, sent
by his father to earth, who lived the life of the official Christ, and
who was crucified. Paul had a vision in response to the needs,
desires, and dictates of his own psyche as it was connected to the
world of his time, following the patterns of stories about Christ
that he had heard that had begun to release within him a great
yearning that was, in that vision, then, expressed.[4]

Christianity for many centuries served as an amazingly creative organizational framework, that expressed the vast complexity of the soul's reality. It also in its way managed to even focus
some of man's less handsome attributes toward ends that were
less reprehensible than in the past. Master events of that particular nature bring about a completely new interpretation of historic events. Their intensity, power, and seemingly impelling

nature exist precisely <u>because</u> their origins are not physical, but are drawn from the <u>psyche's</u> deepest resources.

All of that was book dictation.

(10:13. After expressing a couple of reassuring thoughts for Jane, in line with his private material for Monday night's session, Seth said good night at 10:15 P.M. "Listen, I came so close to not having this session," Jane said. Her delivery had been very slow but more intent than usual, and she was surprised and pleased: "How about that? I'll be damned. I looked the book over today, but I didn't expect anything on it before next week. I didn't know I'd get anything to do with Christ. I'll bet that's why he didn't say it was book dictation until the end of the session. . . ."

"I thought it was [book] dictation right away," I laughed, "but I didn't ask." Jane hadn't sensed any nervousness before the session, as she often does when knowing she's about to resume work on a book project. She felt much better now.)

NOTES. Session 928

1. Here are my notes for the private portion of Monday evening's 927th session:

(Jane has been very uncomfortable for much of the last month. She's still bothered considerably in her arms, legs, knees, and back—especially when trying to sleep at night. I haven't been calling her in the mornings, for they have seemed to be the most peaceful resting times for her.

We realize that all of those bodily changes are positive things. I told Jane before the session that her arms are definitely straighter, for example. This afternoon, "off and on for almost an hour," as she put it, her eyesight had improved remarkably as she sat working at her desk. She's missed walking with her typing table lately, yet her steps from her chair to the couch often have been much steadier and better balanced, even though she's still bent way over. When I suggested that tonight's session be about her, she replied: "He'll just say the same things.")

"Now," Seth said when he resumed the session at 10:13, "Ruburt's body is trying to right itself. When he lies down, it is trying to straighten out. Nerve patterns are being reactivated, circulation patterns reinforced, muscles contracting and expanding in their own exercises, right now, in a concentrated, rather intensified bodily commotion. You are used to thinking of any bodily commotion as disruptive, and put it in the worst possible light because your backgrounds have given you little experience in such situations—you, Ruburt, or anyone else—largely in your culture.

"Afterward, however, Ruburt does sense certain releases. His steps by the couch are (underlined) firmer. His back begins to arch more naturally. It is very important that he understand and trust such occurrences. He does feel isolated and frightened sometimes under those conditions. You can be of help in just talking to him, or massaging. He can help himself by remembering what I am saying, by exercising gently at such times, and by remembering the miraculous processes within the body that are indeed supporting him.

"He is also on to some excellent ideas on his own."

"End of session. A fond good evening."

("Jesus, I ought to go in trance more often," Jane laughed after she'd ended the session at 10:20 P.M. "I wasn't aware of how I was sitting or anything. I was the most comfortable I've been all day. . . .")

2. I suggest a rereading of Chapter 2 for *Dreams*, in Volume 1.

3. In this Chapter 9 of *Dreams*, once again see Section C of Note 7 for Session 920.

4. In the New Testament, see Acts 9:1–9, wherein Luke the Evangelist describes the conversion of Paul on the road to Damascus. Jane had told me earlier in the week that she didn't think Paul had received a vision or communication from Jesus Christ.

SESSION 931——July 15, 1981
8:37 P.M. WEDNESDAY

(I have difficulty believing it even when I write it—but eight months have passed since Jane held her last session for Dreams, *the 928th, on November 12, 1980. The time has passed so quickly, it has been so filled with all kinds of personal, professional, and worldly events for us, that its motion is hard to visualize. During this period Jane gave two regular nonbook sessions [on November 26, 1980, and on January 5, 1981], plus 48 private sessions, so we've been busy! Out of that private total, Seth devoted 25 sessions, either completely or in part, to her "sinful-self"*

material. Jane delivered the introductory session on that subject on March 11 of this year, and I'll be quoting from it in a note. The next 24 sessions on the sinful-self material came through in a concentrated block from April 14 to July 13. I also plan to excerpt several of those sessions for notes, and to quote a number of times from Jane's personal journals for 1980 and 1981. In other words, these opening notes for the 931st session are going to be long ones.

Following Session 928, Jane, even with Seth's obvious attempts to help, and with her obvious willingness to obtain and accept that help, remained housebound, as I came to think of her condition. She gave up walking with the aid of her typing table on November 16, according to my notes for the private session of that date.

The very next day we were distracted: We received back from our publisher the film option contracts for The Education of Oversoul Seven. *The filmmaker required certain additions for legal reasons; we had to have our attorney renotarize the contracts. On the same day I returned them to Prentice-Hall, I also sent in Jane's signed contract for* If We Live Again—*and the mail brought us the copy-edited manuscript for* God of Jane.

Even though she wasn't walking, Jane continued taking her steps between her office chair and the living-room couch, from which she was giving most of her sessions those days. As December came she stopped getting into the shower because of the trouble she had maneuvering in the bathroom, so I began helping her take sponge baths instead. Her physical condition was obviously intimately related to her creative condition. Even the simple act of writing was becoming increasingly difficult for her.[1] On December 4 I sent back to our publisher the corrected copy-edited manuscript for God of Jane. *And late that month, and for the very first time, Jane allowed me to push her in her chair in front of company—a Friday-night group of friends, one reminiscent of the free, exuberant gatherings we used to have every weekend in our downtown apartments. Not that all of our friends hadn't known of Jane's physical symptoms for some time, but that Jane, with her innocence and determination—and yes, her mystical view of temporal reality[2]—had for the most part refused to put herself on display, as she termed it: She felt that she should offer something better to herself and to others, even with all of the intensely creative work she'd done for herself and for others over the last 17 years.*

A fourth entry had been made at Three Mile Island in November, and a fifth, with a 14-man crew, was projected for December 11. We followed the news accounts of the negotiations between the United States and Iran for the release of the hostages, and of the war between Iran and Iraq. Since Jane couldn't leave the house by herself, let alone go holiday shopping, she had a close friend buy the Christmas presents she had in mind for me. My wife did her own wrapping, though, working at it in her writing room after warning me to stay away until she was through. [With eyes averted, I had to carry my own presents to a closet, where I deposited them until Christmas Eve.] Then late in December the page proofs for Mass Events *arrived for our checking. This is the last major stage we're concerned with before a book is printed, other than okaying routine components like frontmatter proofs—meaning the table of contents, dedications, quotations from Seth and Jane, and so forth—and the index.*

Mass Events had been a particularly troubling book for Jane to produce; she'd experienced many long delays in giving the sessions for it. While reading those proofs Jane opened up new insights into her reactions to herself and her work. She summarized those conflicts in the note she wrote on our 26th wedding anniversary.[3] *I saw that same pattern of delay at work in her holding the sessions for* Dreams—*and to me that meant the same psychic and psychological forces were still operating. We finished correcting the proofs for* Mass Events *during our very quiet celebration of the year-end holidays, and early in January I mailed the book to Tam.*

Jane did feel considerably better by the time the page proofs for God of Jane *reached us in mid-January. We corrected those over the time our new president was sworn into office on the 20th, and the 52 American hostages were simultaneously released after 444 days of captivity. We found the workings of our national consciousness to be both mightily creative and terribly frustrating in numerous ways. I thought the simple services in which our President and Vice-President were sworn into office were extremely moving: Unable to speak because of my emotion, I sat beside Jane on the couch while we watched the ceremonies on television, and had soup and crackers for lunch. At the same time, the hostages were "almost free" in Iran, aboard their plane taxiing into takeoff position at Iran's Tehran airport. When our national anthem was sung I sat as though mesmerized, my eyes wet, hoping and praying [trite words!] for our country, for our defeated President, for his successor, and for the hostages. Then the hostages' plane was in the air, flying toward Algiers, in North Africa.*

"Oh God, I hope it all works out," Jane said.

"Well," I said, groping a bit, "what we're seeing is the best the country can offer at this time. It's always this way—you know, the collective expression of our national consciousness—uh, cooperating in whatever way with Iran's, and with that of every other country on earth. . . ."

As if manufacturing tiny, intensely personal counterparts to those large events, Jane and I finished checking the proofs for God of Jane; *she resumed work on her essays, and some new poetry, for* If We Live Again; *I painted, answered a lot of mail, and helped her continue our private sessions. And those acts of ours, I thought, while so small compared to the national dramas being enacted, actually were our contribution to those great plays. Even the fact that by January 26 my wife hadn't walked with her typing table for ten weeks played its part. I felt that connection, but couldn't describe very well what I meant. On that same day back went* God of Jane *to the publisher, for the last time.*

Jane, again, dreamed often of walking, running, dancing, moving normally. To me those dreams were messages of encouragement not only from her own psyche, but from that certain other version of herself that I referred to in Note 2 for this session. In that reality [as well as in some others], she did *have all of her motive powers. In* this *one, she was physically uncomfortable much of the time. Early in February she wrote an essay on Seth as a "master event."[4] That piece was inspired by her material in an old journal; Jane elaborated upon it in an effort to fit events from our own lives into our national consciousness. If Seth truly is a master event, I told her, the implications of her creative work are great: What she has to offer does count, it helps others in a significant way. . . .*

"I plan to begin typing my poetry book final draft shortly," she wrote in her journal on February 11. "The poetry itself doesn't need a final draft—just the essays."

Amid her incessant questioning as to who or what Seth is—even if he is a master event!*—and amid her concerns about leading others astray, Jane added to her journal four days later: "The* worst *explanation for Seth that I can imagine is that he is the part of me that I can't express otherwise—making a psychological statement. Since his material is so terrific, why would this be bad? Because I'd be pretending to be better than I was—better than others? Or leading others to believe in life after death, because the material is so convincing?"*

When I asked her if she'd consider giving up the sessions for a while, to rest, to let her creative self give her answers to such questions, she said no.[5] She had embarked upon a surge of private sessions, and wasn't going to stop. Two days later, on February 17, Seth had some things to say that were quite revealing, both from his standpoint and from ours:

"Now: Generally speaking, Ruburt enjoys our sessions, and considers them with a natural zest.

"This applies—again, generally speaking—whether or not actual book dictation is involved. Difficulties arise, however, in book dictation on those occasions when he becomes too heavy-handed and worries about the responsibility of helping to solve the world's problems—about his or my capacities in that regard—and when he considers the possible and various objections that any given subject might activate on the part of any given group of people. So if the area becomes too sensitive we let dictation go for a while. Sometimes I insert the particular material in your private sessions first of all, so that he becomes somewhat acclimated to it."[6]

Two weeks later, on March 3, Jane and I really received a surprise through a friend who lives on the California coast: news of a Spanish-language translation of Jane's first book, How to Develop Your ESP Power. The edition was printed in Mexico and is on sale in that country and on our West Coast. Our friend has a Mexican friend who showed him a copy of the book. Jane and I didn't know what to think, since the American publisher of ESP Power, Frederick Fell Publishers, Inc., hadn't advised us that a translation into Spanish had been authorized. The almost wordless quality of our surprise reminded me of our feelings of a year and a half ago, when we'd learned that the Dutch firm, Ankh-Hermes, had published an abridged edition of Seth Speaks in that language, without our permission.[7]

While she contended with her physical difficulties and related questions, having to do with who and what Seth may or may not be, Jane continued to paint for relief. [See the opening notes for Session 928, in this chapter.] Her options had become several steps more limited once she no longer left the house. She could read and write, paint, have sessions, watch television, do a little simple housework, call or see a few close friends, and answer some of the mail. She seldom saw visitors. She no longer washed dishes or cooked at the stove. I became very uneasy at her struggling to get up on the high stool she needed to sit on at the kitchen sink. Like the sink, the stove was too high for her to reach while sitting in her chair, and, because she had to stretch across hot burners, too awkward and possibly dangerous for her to operate from the stool. She did do *some cooking on a hot plate I placed on the kitchen table, where we often ate lunch and supper, but I also cautioned her to be careful while using that appliance.*

Painting is really unalloyed fun for Jane. Not that she doesn't have her failures, but her work has greatly improved since we met in 1954, and in ways that I hadn't foreseen for her. Indeed, I now think that my wife is a better painter in her way than I am in mine. This doesn't mean that I'm knocking my own abilities in any way. Jane is freer. *She works in oils, acrylics, and watercolors. When painting she knows a release from time, care, and responsibility that she doesn't experience otherwise—and surely that pleasure emphasizes qualities of living that Seth has always stressed. Her painting is her unhampered creative translation of the Seth material into pigments instead of words. Because of her defective vision Jane sees perspective differently than I do, yet achieves her own kind of depth with her "instinctive" designs and color choices. Her art contains a charming, innocent,* mystical *freedom that I envy. She's produced many more paintings than I have in my own more conventional, more plodding way [although now I'm working faster than I used to]. I think that any assessment of her writing and psychic abilities will have to include a close study of her painting. To me, the lessening of Jane's physical mobility has resulted in a strong compensating growth in her painting mobility. I also think her painting reflects her free physical motion in her dreams. Hardly accidental, any of that. I've seen her turn almost automatically to the relief that only painting can give her.*

Jane laughed when she read what I'd written. "No, that's not it, honey," she said. "I paint like I do because I don't have any depth perception. I can't do anything else. . . ."

Those first days in March were mentally crowded ones for Jane. During the early morning hours of the 6th she had a very vivid and joyful reincarnational dream involving herself, and a dream in which she returned to her own past in this life. "I rarely have reincarnation-type dreams, but awakened around 2:00 A.M. with this and the following dream," she wrote the next day. The first one gave her information about a life she'd lived as a nun in the former province of Normandy, France, in the 16th century. The second dream concerned her strong reaction to the death of her maternal grandfather, Joseph Burdo: "Little Daddy," as Jane had affectionately called him, died in 1948 in the family's hometown of Saratoga Springs, New York.

Jane's connections and challenges with religion across lifetimes are obvious among her dream of being a nun, the "nightmarish experience"[8] *she had two nights later, and the subject matter of the private session she gave on the evening of March 11. In that session Seth used her night-mare as the basis for a discussion of her life as a nun, mentioned her grandfather, and began the "sinful-self" material I referred to at the beginning of the notes for this 931st session. His information on the sinful self opened up a very important development in Jane's [and my own] search for an understanding of her symptoms, and I'm presenting excerpts from that session in Note 9. [Before long, I realized that I could use notes to carry portions of several more sessions on the sinful self.]*

The day after that session for March 11 was held we received a jolt: Eleanor Friede, Jane's editor at Delacorte Press, informed us that Jane's book, Emir's Education in the Proper Use of Magical Powers, *was being remaindered—taken off the market because in the publisher's view it wasn't selling enough copies. Eleanor's protests at the action had done no good. We were given the chance to buy as many copies as we wanted to, at a very low price per book. We'd known that* Emir *hadn't been setting any records since its publication in September 1979, but we'd also thought the book's sales were respectable enough that the people at Dela-corte Press would keep it in print until it became better known. Perhaps our shock came about because we'd become spoiled without realizing it, but of Jane's 14 books* Emir[10] *is the first one to be withdrawn—and, ironically, the last one she'd had published. That status would soon change, however, when* Mass Events *and* God of Jane *reached the marketplace.*

On Monday, March 30, 1981, Jane happily finished typing her manuscript for If We Live Again—*and in our nation's capital that same afternoon our President was wounded in an assassination attempt. We watched television replays of the shooting over and over again dur-ing the rest of the afternoon and into the evening, as for the second time within a generation the overall consciousness of the United States strug-gled, through our leaders, to meet one of the great challenges to our democratic way of life.*

On the screen we saw a parade of citizens expressing shock, sadness, and outrage, frustrated by the knowledge that it had all happened be-fore—not only in our country but around the world—and that it would happen again many times more. It became almost a cliché for people to wonder what was wrong with people: Why do those who attain promi-nence often attract those who want to destroy them? I think the Seth material contains some penetrating insights into such questions, but those ideas aren't nearly well-enough known to help on a national scale. Seth didn't comment upon the shooting, It wasn't that he couldn't, or wouldn't—but that Jane herself is basically so innocent, so repelled by the violence involved in such episodes, that she often chooses not to go into the subject. I thought she might later in connection with other material, however; this had been the case when Seth discussed the mass suicide at Jonestown, Guyana, in November 1978.[11]

Three days later, after a final checking, I mailed Jane's book of poetry to Tam Mossman at Prentice-Hall. Since she wouldn't be working with that project for some little time now, Jane's restless creative mind began to play with other ideas. Even though she often didn't feel well, a portion of her creativity led her to have dreams of walking and dancing, of being completely healed physically. She wrote more poetry. She painted. And once again she considered a book featuring Seth's sessions on the magical approach to reality, the series he'd given through August and September of last year.[12]

On April 12 the space shuttle Columbia *was launched into orbit around the earth, and I thought that Jane was complementing that obvious exploration of outside space by exploring inner space with the only vehicle she had available—her own mind. That same day, Seth agreed that her new book idea was a good one. Somewhere in here we received from our friend in California the photocopies I'd asked him to obtain, of the frontmatter for the Spanish-language edition of* ESP Power. *So the book* was *out in Spanish, we saw—but we were so preoccupied with Jane's symptoms and related matters that we let the photocopies lie on a shelf. During this time, we had been often rereading Seth's information on the sinful self as he'd given it on March 11. [See Note 9 for this session.] That material had deeply touched us. The result was that on April 14, the day* Columbia *landed, Seth initiated a long series of sessions on both Jane's own sinful self, and that quality in general. The very next evening Jane allowed him to come through with some extremely important material.*[13]

As he progressed with the series, Seth delved into Jane's sinful self from a number of viewpoints: its birth and growth during her intense relationship with the Roman Catholic Church throughout her early years; the development of her very stubborn core beliefs; her creative dilemmas after she left the church in her late teens; the conflicts she began to experience after our marriage, involving on the one hand her sinful self and the religion she thought she'd left behind, and on the other hand science, art, writing, and the unconventional direction she discovered her natural, mystical abilities were taking via the Seth material; her growing fears of leading others astray; and the very real necessity for her—and for each individual—to achieve value fulfillment.

Seth also discussed Jane's persistent psychological abuse and mistreatment by her mother, Marie, over the years, and the young girl's resultant deep fear of abandonment. Jane never lost that fear, and needed frequent reassurances that she was a worthy person. She'd seldom found that reinforcement while living with a parent who had been divorced and become bedridden by the time Jane was three years old, and who had a host of problems—challenges—of her own to meet.

During her early years Jane had naturally and deeply loved her mother, and tried in every way a child could to please her—yet she became ashamed at the treatment she was receiving from Marie, and for the most part kept it a secret while growing up; we'd been married for some years before I really began to understand the depth of her feelings on that score. Why, Jane's sinful self even felt guilty, *Seth told us, because of her abusive treatment by Marie—assuming that it must have been bad, that it* deserved *all those years of psychological assault!*

We had a hard time believing him when Seth told us the very next evening, on April 23, that Jane's sinful self thinks her physical symptoms are necessary *"for the personality's own good"; that that self has no conception that its policies have become self-defeating; that, following Catholic and non-Catholic Christianity, it believes that suffering is good for the soul; that the idea of the flesh itself being graced is, to it, blasphemous.*

And yet, Seth told us, in spite of everything Jane's sinful self could begin to change once it was reached. We had *reached it to some degree, and more than once, but the emotional upsets involved had left Jane feeling worse during this time. Her sinful self, according to Seth, no longer identifies with the Church. That self itself has become frightened, in conflict within itself over its early training and Jane's great creativity, which it regards as wrong: The creative self is guilty. Jane had panic attacks while sleeping.*

Through April and into May, I had problems controlling my own anger and hurt feelings toward Jane's sinful self as I came to better understand its mechanisms of operation. Obviously. of course, my feelings reflected upon the workings of my *sinful self, or upon some similar psychological quality—for how could I be so involved with my wife's challenges, for almost 26 years, without complementing them within deep portions of my own personality? My anger, Seth told me, was just the way* not *to react, and even amid the welter of my emotions I had to agree.*

Jane had refused to listen to that self of hers in earlier years. "The idea is in no way to accuse the sinful self," Seth said on April 28. "It is instead to understand it, its needs and motives, and to communicate the idea that it was sold a bad bill of goods in childhood—scared out of its wits, maligned. . . . Ruburt's entire group of symptoms do not follow any established pattern. They are the result of applied stress, exaggerated finally by feelings of hopelessness, and by some relative feelings of isolation." And I was so struck by his reference to Jane's hopelessness that once more I returned to the private session for April 15. See Note 13, in which I quoted Seth's material on her search for value fulfillment—how, without the psychic breakthrough of the sessions, "Ruburt would have felt unable to continue the particular brand of his existence."

During the first week in May, Jane received from Tam the copy-edited manuscript for If We Live Again. *As she checked that book she listed several areas of her body where beneficial changes had begun to appear, as well as others that hadn't shown any improvement. Her difficulties maneuvering in the bathroom were especially bothersome. She was both encouraged and discouraged, then—but did have more energy. I returned the poetry to our publisher on May 13.*

By now it must be plain to the reader that Seth's material on the sinful self—any sinful self, or all of them—could very well be considered the other side of his information on the magical approach to reality. I was all too aware of an uncomfortable dichotomy. Indeed, how irritating it was, I thought, that for Jane and me at least the magical self seemed to be so far removed from daily reality, while the sinful self was so close! Reaching out to the magical self could be thought of as some theoretically attainable goal—but the sinful self was right there, functioning within the most intimate areas of personal life. For how many others is the same situation true? Seth, I knew, would simply say that the magical self is just as real and close as any other self. The challenge for the individual is to know and to believe that, to clear unwanted growth from around the magical self so that it can bloom unimpeded. . . .

Late in May we received from Prentice-Hall our first copy of Mass Events. *We were both delighted and bemused that the book was published at last, especially when we considered that Jane had given the first session for it over three years ago [the 801st for April 18, 1977]. We felt that lifetimes had passed since then.*

Jane's overall symptoms worsened, and I sensed connections between her situation and the arrival of Mass Events. *As of June 2 she hadn't walked for six and a half months, even with the aid of her typing table. That very day a crisis appeared: In the bathroom, and for the first time in all the years of her physical troubles, she couldn't manipulate well enough on her feet to get back into her wheeled office chair over by the sink. I carried her—and that act was a deep blow to the stubborn self-reliance that is so characteristic of each one of us. I was dismayed, as Jane was. As if to atone for my own frustration at a deteriorating situation, when typing that evening's session [the next day] I inserted a statement of my love for my wife. I was to learn that that simple reinforcement greatly affected her, as it had me when I wrote it.*[14]

Within a few days, after I'd taken certain measurements from Jane while she was sitting down, our friend Floyd Waterman [who is a contractor] helped me cut down an old-fashioned straight chair and equip it with small wheels. This one was narrower than later-model chairs, and it fit well in the bathroom and some other spots in the hill house. Jane could easily hoist herself onto it from her office chair, the couch, or the bed; she could either move on it around the house by herself, or have me push her. There was only one small problem: She couldn't tolerate sitting on the bare wooden seat for more than a few minutes at a time. So while she slept late the next morning, I rebuilt the chair by myself and padded its seat. Then she found it very useful.

On succeeding days Jane made several attempts to get on her feet so that she could try to walk by leaning upon her typing table and pushing it before her, but each time she couldn't quite make it. Her feet began to swell. She worked on a long poem about Stonehenge, the great megalithic monument of standing stones in southern England. She did little typing because her arms were so sore, but she did do some painting. We held a session on the evening of June 15, and here's the key paragraph from my opening notes for it:

"After supper I discussed with Jane the question I've been keeping in mind for Seth, concerning what her sinful self may have learned since we began this series of sessions. I said it was essential to communicate to her sinful self [so named by Seth for convenience's sake only] that its performance has been very destructive to Jane, and that it must release its hold. I want to know that self's attitude toward the fact that Jane is now helpless as far as her physical survival is concerned—she can no longer take care of herself without my help, and this obviously implies that if her condition continues to worsen to the point of death, her sinful self will die also. I want to know what it 'thinks' about such a contradictory situation.

No matter how it must reason or react, that self has to be concerned about its own survival—but in what ways, and based upon what knowledge and reasons? Of course we have some answers now, but I want more."

In the session itself, Seth barely began an answer to my question. Instead he went into considerable detail as to how Jane could write a "psychic statement of intentions," so that her sinful self would know exactly what she wanted out of life. She started work on it the next day. That same day, I congratulated her when our first published copy of God of Jane *reached us; that excellent book had followed* Mass Events *all the way through the publishing process. I told Jane that* God of Jane *is her best book yet, and that I hope it does well in the marketplace.*[15] *Yet I sadly noticed that the book's appearance led to another intensification of her symptoms—the same reaction she'd had when we received our first copy of* Mass Events *25 days ago. We were to discover very soon that her sinful self had put together the publication of the two books, my question of last night, and Seth's own suggestion, to form an emotional trigger.*

That June 15th session was Seth's 20th on Jane's sinful self, and the concept in general. Yet, as if they weren't enough, on the 17th that trigger was released: Jane suddenly began writing down material directly from her own sinful self. It seemed that that self had been at last goaded into rising to its own defense; for five days she wrote in periods of excited strain as it gave forth its contentions and defenses through 36 handwritten pages. Jane also began work on several poems to accompany her prose, and had several relevant dreams.

If we had been appalled when Seth began giving his version of the beliefs her sinful self held, we were even more so when that self began to express itself "personally." And once more I had to guard my own expressions of frustration and anger; those emotions were so mixed up with my love for my wife that I even developed a perverse, almost black humor about the entire situation. Then Seth came through with another session on the same subject while Jane's sinful self was in the midst of its own revelations! But she simply had to get that final, direct message from that portion of herself by herself; except for that one session, she even made Seth figuratively stand aside while she did so. But Seth himself was delighted with her breakthrough.[16]

Along with our shock came elation. Here, we congratulated ourselves, lay bared all of those beliefs and motivations that for years had been hidden and operative beneath Jane's symptoms: Here were the real reasons—now we could eradicate her physical hassles! Jane's own sinful-

self revelations certainly complemented Seth's, which in turn, we thought, were the other side of his material on the magical approach to reality.

She was tired out when the flow of her material finally ended. "Wow," she said, her eyes red and baffled, "I never knew—I never dreamed— that I had all of that inside me. . . ."

How fortunate she'd been able to dig it all out, we said. And how sad, we said, that others who needed such help might not be able to do the same. . . . Jane's material from her sinful self is obviously too long and complicated to present here, but I stress that one of its main concerns is its genuine and ironic puzzlement as to why man has for so long— probably from even before he started recording his history—persisted in the creation of and reliance upon entities like the sinful self! Surely that concern is creative, I told Jane; her sinful self is really questioning why she's maintained it within such narrow confines.

Once again, we had no guidelines on how to use Jane's material, except to trust that we'd do the best we could. Achieving results could take a while. "If you do that book on the magical approach," I asked her, "are you going to use all this stuff on the sinful self, or what?" Jane didn't know. She did know that she'd been considering an outline for a book on the magical approach. In the meantime, the plan that spontaneously came to me on that last day of her own effort, on June 22, was to present a page or two of her sinful-self material here, then repeat it, along with other excerpts, in the Introduction I've already mentioned that I must write for Dreams.[17]

Jane had begun writing for her sinful self this way [with my insertions bracketed]:

"I resent the designation unjustly given me, for if I have believed in the phenomenon of sin and sought—apparently too rigidly—to avoid it, my intentions and interests always were not the avoidance of sin so much as the pursuit of eternal truths; the alliance with universal goals, the unity in spirit at least of self, whole self, and universal mind. Those goals ignite your creative powers and have (and still do) propelled you to explore all categories of existence possible, seeking to express those divine mysteries that lie within and behind each existence—yours, and mine as well.

"Our explorations involved no second-handed evidence handed down by others, but the direct personal encounter of our consciousness and being with the vast elements of the unknown—a meeting of the self

(human and vulnerable) with the psychological realms of gods and eternities; giant realms of mind that our *nature felt attracted to . . . and [was] uniquely equipped to perceive.*

"I believed in the soul's survival first of all, and inspired the 'creative self' to step out as freely as possible even while in my heart I [also] believed in the existence of sin and devil. I felt upon my heart the heavy unkind mark of Cain, sensing that humanity carries (unfairly) the almost indelible strain—the tragic flaw—[of] being tinged by sin and ancient iniquities. Thusly I reasoned: If I am flawed I must automatically distort even those experiences of the soul that seem clearest. I must unwittingly fall into error when I trust myself the most, since I share that sinful propensity. Yet despite those feelings did I (did we) unswervingly set forward."

There was no doubt about it, though: As if they had a collective life of their own, Jane's symptoms continued to clamp down after the publication of Mass Events *and* God of Jane. *Her feet became more and more swollen, for instance; she could take the few steps between her chair and the couch only with much difficulty. A number of times she refused my offers—and those of others—to get her medical help. The reason I don't write more in these notes about doctors and the medical profession is that I have nothing to write about. Jane, with that exquisite stubbornness she can display, simply wouldn't cooperate in that fashion. We studied her own sinful-self material as she typed it. Again and again we scrutinized all of those elements that we thought were bound up in her symptoms: choice, fear of abandonment and the need for self-protection, penance, and the controversial nature of her gifts. July 1981 came. On the evening of the 4th—yes, we "worked" on the holiday because Jane felt like having a session, and because "time" had become so precious to us—Seth came through with some very interesting new material as a result of our questioning.*[18]

By July 8 we'd accumulated 61 fully private sessions since Jane had given the first session for this chapter of Dreams, *the 919th, on June 9, 1980. [During that 13-month period we also held 10 regular nonbook sessions and one more book session.] As she began to study that mass of private material on the 8th, Jane abruptly laid it aside to spontaneously write a complete outline for a book on Seth's magical approach to reality. She'd had many such impulses since giving the first session on that subject 11 months ago, and I'd been hoping she would try the venture. Seth had announced as recently as four days ago that he's heartily in favor of the*

*project. He repeated his approval in our 63rd private session, held on
July 13.*

Jane's last session for this chapter of Dreams *is the 928th; she came
through with it eight months ago. Since then I've packed full these notes
for Session 931, in order to round out our personal, professional, and
secular situations—yet, looking back, I wonder if I've properly put everything in perspective: There are other sessions I could have quoted instead
of the ones chosen, other notes I could have written; there are other
questions Jane and I could have asked, and, perhaps, other conclusions
we could have drawn.*

*Recently, for example, I reread this passage of Seth's from Session
915, for Chapter 8 of* Dreams, *Jane gave the session in May 1980, a
year before the publication of* Mass Events:

*"Now Ruburt is undergoing some profound therapeutic changes.
Probabilities at each point intersect with your time, and those probabilities are psychologically directed so that, in your terms once again, he is at
an excellent intersection point, where the prognosis is excellent. Tell him
I said this. And you are both responsible, for both of your lives merge in
their fashions."*

*Now why didn't I orient all of this introductory material around that
session, instead of following the course I did? Why has Jane's physical
condition deteriorated so much since then, and why haven't we been able
to prevent that slide? The possibilities for having helped her seem bound-
less in retrospect, with at least some of them certainly being better than the
way we chose.*

*Jane doesn't agree with my doubts. As always, she's been letting me
put this book together the way I think best—and inevitably that way has
followed how we've been trying to understand our joint long-term situation. She innocently accepts my labors as they come out. And that trust
always reflects, I'm sure, Seth's own larger view of reality, as I just
quoted him from Session 915. Our challenges echo throughout all of our
probable realities simultaneously, and through all of them together the
largest picture of Jane and myself is presented. In this probable reality
we work with what we can pick up from that great whole. We keep trying
to learn to ask better questions.*

*Now that we're up to date, let's begin the 931st session, which we sat
for at 8:37 P.M. on Wednesday, July 15, 1981, as usual:*

*Just before the session Jane reminded me that she was most interested
in Seth commenting upon the reincarnation-type dream experience she'd*

had early this morning. This is the second time in four months that she's had such an experience—most unusual for her—and this one even caused her to reflect upon her sinful self in a new way. After breakfast she wrote a very rough account of what she can remember.[19] *She thinks the experience was triggered by a television movie she watched last night. I saw only the end of the program, but it involved, Jane told me, a person's traveling from a present life into a past life. She finds some of the story's concepts to be quite intriguing.*

It developed, however, that Jane's reincarnational adventure might end up doing double duty: Not only had it given her insights concerning her sinful self, but now she picked up from Seth that his remarks about it could result in dictation for Dreams. *She'd been looking over sessions for the book at various times lately, so perhaps I shouldn't have been so surprised. She asked if I'd mind work on* Dreams *this evening, and I said of course not—that she and Seth have the absolute freedom to talk about anything at all. If Seth did discuss her experience, Jane replied, it would be in connection with "time overlays." She wasn't nervous about going back to* Dreams. *She said that dictation for it wouldn't mean she was giving up on private material, or on her projected book on the magical approach, either.*

Slowly, with many long pauses:)
Now, good evening.
("Good evening, Seth.")
Time overlays are versions of master events, in that they occur in such a fashion that one "face" of an overall event may appear in one time, one in another, and so forth.

Time overlays are the time versions of certain events, then. These time overlays always exist. *(Pause.)* They may become activated, however, by certain associations made in your present, and therefore draw into your present time some glimpses either from the future or the past. So-called present time is thickened, then, by a psychological realization on deep levels of the psyche that all events are interrelated, and that the reincarnational experiences of any given individual provide a rich source of experience from which each person at least unconsciously draws.

Such usually unconscious knowledge is of great benefit to the species itself, so that at certain levels, at least, the knowledge of the species is not imprisoned within any given generation at once, but flows or circulates within the overall larger reincarnational picture. Probabilities are very much involved here, of course, and it is easier for particular events to fall within one time sequence than another.

I do not want you to feel that you are fated to experience certain events, however, for that is not the case. There will be "offshoots" of the events of your own lives, however, that may appear as overlays in your other reincarnational existences. There are certain points where such events are closer to you than others, in which mental associations at any given time may put you in correspondence[20] with other events of a similar nature in some future or past incarnation, however. It is truer to say that those similar events are instead time versions of one larger event. As a rule you experience only one time version of any given action. Certainly it is easy to see how a birthday or anniversary, or particular symbol or object, might serve as an associative connection, rousing within you memories of issues or actions that might have happened under similar circumstances in other times.

(8:54.) Actually, that kind of psychological behavior represents the backbone of social organization as far as the species is concerned, and it is the usually hidden but definite past and future memories of reincarnational relationships that cement social organizations, from small tribes to large governments.

To a certain extent, of course, you have been or will be each related to the other. In that light all of the events of time rub elbows together. You brush against the elbow of a future or past event every moment of your lives.

In the culture that you know, such information remains hidden from you. Your main belief systems lead you to feel that your present life is singular, unsupported by any knowledge of prior experience with existence, and fated to be cut off or deadended without a future. Instead, you always carry the inner knowledge of innumerable available futures *(emphatically)*. Your emotional life at certain levels is enriched by the unconscious realization that those who love you from past or future are connected to you by special ties that add to your emotional heritage and support.

As many have supposed, particularly in fiction, love relationships do indeed survive time, and they put you in a special correspondence. Even if you were aware of reincarnational existences, your present psychological behavior would not be threatened but retain its prominence—for only within certain space and time intersections can physical actions occur. The more or less general acceptance of the theory of reincarnation, however, would automatically alter your social systems, add to the richness of experience, and in particular insert a fresh feeling for the future, so that you did not feel your lives dead-ended.

Earlier I mentioned several times that we must reach a point at which you are able to see around the corner of seemingly contradictory material,[21] and this is one of those occasions. *(Long pause.)* Time overlays present you with a picture in which you have free will—yet each event that you choose will have its own time version. Now those time versions may be entirely different one from the others, and while you certainly initiate your own time version, in terms of usual understanding there is no true place or time in which that version can be said to actually originate *(again with emphasis)*.

(9:14.) Such a time version suggests an occurrence in time, of course, and yet the event may leave only a ghostly track, so to speak, being hardly manifest, while in another life the time version may be of considerable prominence—while in your own experience it represents a fairly trivial incident of an ordinary afternoon.

The inner core of events, however, is held together by just that kind of activity. You are at every hand provided an unending source of probable events from past and future, from which to compose the events of your lives and society. Again, let me remind you that all time exists simultaneously.

In an experience last evening in the dream state, Ruburt received fresh evidence by viewing for himself portions of two other lives—merely snatches of environment, but so dearly filled with precious belongings and loved ones, so alive with immediacy–that he was shocked to realize that the full dimensions of existence could continue so completely in such detail and depth at the same time as his present life.

It seemed that he could step from any one such existence to the other as you might walk from one room to the other, and he knew that at other levels of the psyche this was indeed possible—and, of course, at other levels of the psyche those psychological doors are open.

(9:25. With many pauses, but all intently:) Ruburt has had partic-

ular difficulty, however, with "the theory of reincarnation,"[22] because as it is usually described, it seemed that people used it to blame as the source of current misfortune, or as an excuse for personal behavior whose nature they did not otherwise understand, and it has been so maligned. Its reality, however, serves to generate activity throughout time's framework as you understand it, to unite the species, to reinforce structures of knowledge, to transmit information, and perhaps most of all to reinforce relationships involving love, brotherhood, and cooperation between generations of men and women that would otherwise be quite separate and apart from each other.

Through such relationships, for example, say, the cavemen and the people of the 22nd century rub elbows, where in strict terms of time the species would seem to be quite disconnected from its "earlier" or "later" counterparts.

Through such behavior the overall value fulfillment purposes and intents of the species are kept in focus, and those necessary requirements then planted in whatever space or time [is] required. Again, free will still operates in all such ventures.

Now while it seems that your world contains more and more information all the time, your particular brand of science is a relatively narrow one, in that it accepts as valid only certain specific areas of speculation. The areas outside of its boundaries become taboo, so that the realm of the unknown is no longer the material universe or the mysteries of space, but the interior universe and the mysteries of the mind as these are experienced or suspected to exist outside of those official areas. To that degree, the unknown is more feared by science than it ever was by religion.

Religion was hampered—and is—by its own interpretation of good and evil, but it did not deny the existence of other versions of consciousness, or differing kinds of psychological activity and life. (Long pause.) Reincarnation suggests, of course, the extension of personal existence beyond one time period, independently of one bodily form, the translation or transmission of intelligence through nonphysical frameworks, and implies psychological behavior, memory and desire as purposeful action without the substance of any physical mechanism—propositions that science at its present stage of development simply could not buy, and for which it could find no evidence, for its methods would automatically preclude the type of experience that such evidence would require.

People can become quite frightened, then, of any kind of experiences of a personal nature that imply reincarnational life, for they are then faced with the taboos of science, or perhaps by the distorted explanations of some religions or cults. You therefore protect yourselves from many quite natural upthrusts that would on their own give you experience with your own reincarnational existences, and you are often denied psychological comfort in times of stress that you might otherwise receive.

I do not necessarily mean that full-blown pictures of other existences would necessarily come into your mind, but that in one way or another you would receive a support or change of mood as those loved by you in other lives [in] one way or another sensed your need and responded.

The entire nature of events, then, exists in a different way than you have supposed, only small portions slicing into the reality that you recognize—yet all underneath connected to a vast psychological activity. You might compare events to psychological consonants that underlay or underlie the more unusual features of physical psychological environment.

That was dictation.

(9:57. After giving a few lines of personal material for Jane, Seth said good night at 10:01 P.M.)

NOTES. Session 931

1. On the evening of December 2, 1980, Jane typed this material for insertion into her loose-leaf journal:

"Finish checking copy-edited manuscript of *God of Jane* this afternoon. Feel this important. . . . As I finish, I realize how much physical activity and energy is required for even that seemingly sedentary task, for I've been uncomfortable, sitting, switching my weight, body soreish, eyes not seeing properly and so forth. . . . But in some newish way I seemed to understand how much seemingly mental work is dependent upon physical vigor, flexibility and so forth; and then rather strongly—emotionally it came to me that I'd thought it my duty to clamp down physically, to cut down mobility in order to . . . have mobility as a writer; that is, to sit down, cut down on impulses, distractions, to make sure I'd 'do my work,' pursue my goal undeviatingly; that new [book] contracts instantly led me to that kind of behavior and that I really see that such behavior carried to its extremes would end up smothering my writing, defeating the purposes it (seemingly) meant to protect. But I did fear that impulses and body motion were . . . distractions to work. . . . Now I see how much impulses are conducive . . . to just typing, for God's sake; imagine typing and seeing with ease, just thinking about what I'm thinking about, instead of trying to get my fingers on the proper keys. I feel as if I'm on to something here . . . feel some relaxation. If this is the case, the entire process could be changed around quite quickly, of course, toward mobility. I'm not writing here tonight about the reasons behind such behavior—many ideas—but did want to get something down now. . . ."

2. At times after Jane began to really show her physical symptoms, my awareness of the fact that basically she's a mystic became submerged beneath many other more "practical" matters. Perhaps I should have stressed her nature more throughout *Dreams*. I never took that essential quality of hers for granted during those times, but instead accepted it so easily that I lost conscious stress upon it. She doesn't use the word in connection with herself, yet I think that Jane's mystical nature, which is so at odds with the realities most people create for themselves, actually offers the only real framework for understanding her physical condition, her *choices*, in our probable reality.

To those of us who are rooted in more conventional approaches to our probability, Jane's course may at times seem incomprehensible—but as far as she's concerned that only shows our lack of comprehension of her viewpoint. As a mystic she can have motivations toward exploring certain avenues of the human condition that most of us don't have. Her view of basic reality is her view, and even I must still grope at times to understand her chosen role. To actually *carry out* her way, as she's doing, is something I cannot do. Her sacrifice of physical motion in order to have greater creative motion is a "bargain" I shrink from making. Jane used to say to me: "I told myself that if I let myself do that, then I'll do this in return," One can say that that kind of equation hardly represents a mystical view, yet I know that in her case it does. I don't believe those kinds of bargains are necessary in life to begin with, but what's real for Jane can be quite different than it is for me, and for most other people. She does have her reasons.

Jane's nature has even led me to speculate more than once that in most basic terms she may be visiting our probable reality from one that's actually far more native to her nonphysical entity, or whole self. I don't mean that as a physical creature she has magically switched temporal realities, but that she's closely allied with that version of herself in that other reality. When I mention this to her, she nods but says little. Jane's "mission" (a term she wouldn't use) would be to give us not only greater insight into what our species has done within our historical context, both for better and for worse, but to signal what we *can* do—to open up unexpected vistas before us, to encourage us to explore those realms far more actively than we have so far.

(All of the above is only a portion of the tale, of course—for according to Seth other versions of Jane exist in numerous probable realities. This is the case for each of us.)

3. We married on December 27, 1954—and certainly we had no idea at all that exactly 26 years later Jane would write a piece like the following. Slightly abridged from her journal for 1980, with my interpolations in brackets:

"Yesterday while checking the page proofs for *Mass Events* I got the feeling that that book really bothered me, served as a focal point. My eye troubles started the same spring that Seth started dictating it [in 1977]; I was doing [my world-view book on William] James; and those people were picketing Prentice-Hall's offices in New York City because of the Seth material. The fact had escaped me earlier that *Mass Events* represented Seth's and my direct attack on official dictums—or so it seemed to me. Before, we sort of did it by inference.

"I accept everything in the book, but I think I felt that if I was going to tell it like it was—and I was, was determined to—then I also needed more protection from the world, and began cutting down mobility again. My idea is that the eyes get bad after the muscular strain reaches a certain point. The idea [of protection] also came back after reading a book on William James that a friend gave us for Christmas. [James's] attitudes and mine so often seem similar—that he was determined to be daring, press ahead no matter what, explore consciousness—while at the same time being attracted to safety, disliking controversy, wanting peace, etc. I think I am that way. The long breaks when Seth didn't dictate [book work] may have come when I got particularly concerned about the material, the wisdom of presenting it to the world.

"In fact, Seth gave us Framework 1 and 2 stuff in there, to help me. I did grab hold several times, and with the *God of Jane* book, the new inspiration there and the material on following impulses, made some very good improvements. [Rob's emphasis:] But far more than Rob from the beginning, I was nervous and anxious about directly coming out with many of the ideas— which at the same time I fervently and even passionately believe in. . . . I may fear that if you go too far . . . telling it like it is . . . that the establishment will just cut off your platform . . . or that people will stop buying the books . . . something like . . . biting the hand that feeds you. You can only go so far. Yet I've always known that these ideas conflicted with official ones. It's just that [earlier our] 'attack' was less direct.

"Lately I've been working with ideas of safety, saying and believing that I AM safe, secure and supported and that I DO trust my natural spontaneous motion. NOW as I write some old dumb stuff comes emotionally to mind—my mother saying that I'd destroy those I loved or some such nonsense. But it's as if I always felt that spontaneously, left alone, I'd end up taking away people's comfort blankets, and I felt bad about that, even while I knew that those philosophic blankets were wormy, had to go. And I do see that I'm offering something far better. . . .

"But you're doing great, hon," I told Jane after I'd read her journal entry. I was glad to reassure her, for I believed what I said. If she has hassles, I added, they're quite understandable: Not only is she offering our world creative new ways by which to understand reality, but in her uncertainty about what she's doing, she feels that she must *prove* her ideas to the world all by herself—something that few people have to do in such an all-encompassing manner. At the same time she has to protect herself, for both of us are caught in the uneasy notion that every time Jane gets too close to any sort of basic truth, she automatically threatens many of the deeply entrenched, rigid belief systems people have built up in our reality. Obviously Jane thinks her contemporaries often reject her—and sometimes I also think they do. Consciousness exploring itself once again, I said, more than a little ironically. . . .

One of those periods of delay in Jane's delivering the sessions for *Mass Events* lasted for 42 weeks, or 9½ months; in that book see the opening notes for Session 831, in Chapter 5. This hiatus in Chapter 9 of *Dreams* lasted for eight months, between sessions 928 and 931.

4. Jane wrote the material I quoted in Note 3 some six weeks ago. In this spontaneous essay for her new journal she attempted to move beyond that thinking not only by searching through her own past, but by incorporating some of Seth's latest ideas. Here are excerpts:

"Copy of inspirational-type material received Friday, February 6, after reading portions of my 1973 notebook:

"Seth as a 'master event.' As the *Mona Lisa* is 'more real' than, say, a normal object or the [materials] that compose it, so is all good or great art more than its own physical manifestation. Consider art as a natural phenomenon constructed by the psyche, a transspecies of perception and consciousness that changes, enlarges and expands life's experiences and casts them in a different light, offering new opportunities for creating action and new solutions to problems by inserting new, original data.

"To confine such creativity to solve life's problems *primarily*, or to direct it primarily in that fashion, limits it and holds it in an improper focus; shackles it.

"We have to go beyond that—back to stressing the creative larger-than-life aspects. Otherwise all we have is a better problem-solving framework. . . . I've rejected all that kind of hash projected onto Seth's books by others or myself—the assumptions that Seth must prove himself as a problem-solver—or the importance of functionalism over art. The larger view is that art, by being itself, is bigger than life while springing from it; that Seth's and my books go beyond that simply by being themselves. They automatically put people in a different, vaster psychological space, another frame of reference, in which a good number of problems vanish or simply do not apply. . . .

"To [achieve] that, I have to drop those old feelings of responsibility as a primary focus, because they strain the Seth-book framework, particularly when I demand that in each book Seth answer all questions and so forth.

"Again as with master events, we're dealing with a different framework of action entirely, where the *Mona Lisa* is 'more real' than the physical properties that compose it. This is not to deny the validity of its [materials]. But to discuss Seth and his ideas primarily from the true-or-false framework is the same thing as considering the *Mona Lisa* only from the validity of the physical properties of its paint and panel: very very limiting. . . . I don't have to 'live up' to anything. I don't have to 'make the material work,' or prove through my actions that it does, because it proves itself in the way that creativity does, by being beyond levels of true-false references. Otherwise I'm at cross-purposes with myself."

5. For that matter, I've often told my wife that it would be all right with me if she decided to give up the sessions entirely—for good—period. Anything to help, I always thought at such times. More than once I've asked her if she keeps the sessions going just for me. *Jane* comes first with me—not the sessions, or anything else she might do. Her *being* is what I want to spend the rest of my life with. Once again I recalled Seth's statement in Chapter 5 of *Dreams*, in Volume 1. See Session 899 for February 6, 1980: "But the purpose of your life, and each life, is in its being *(intently)*. That being may include certain actions, but the acts themselves are only important in that they spring out of the essence of your life, which simply by being is bound to fulfill its purposes."

6. Seth went on to say in that session for February 17, 1980: "The only other times there are any such difficulties also involve responsibility, when he concentrates upon his responsibility to hold the sessions—that is, when he focuses upon need, function, or utility as separate from other issues involved. Such feelings can then for a while override his natural inclinations, his natural enjoyment and excitement with which he otherwise views our sessions.

(Intently:) "To begin with, he would not have had the sessions over this period of time *(more than 17 years)* for your sake alone, or even for your sake primarily: They simply would have petered out. You do have a large role to play, however, and I will

go into that more clearly, along with the way that you might have sometimes misread some of your own attitudes. Nothing, however, would have kept him at the sessions for this amount of time unless he wanted them."

Seth's comments of February 17 also reflect upon Jane's own ideas as she described them just 11 days ago; see the excerpts in Note 4. Then in this Chapter 9 of *Dreams*, see Note 8 for Session 920.

7. In Chapter 2 of *Dreams*, in Volume 1, see my account of the Ankh-Hermes affair, as given in Note 1 for Session 885. We didn't know whether *ESP Power* had been published without our American publisher's consent—but there we were, confronted by another puzzling development involving a foreign-language edition of one of Jane's books. At once I wrote to our California friend, asking him to obtain from *his* friend photocopies of three pages in the frontmatter of *ESP Power*: the title page, the table of contents, and the page that nobody reads, containing the information on copyright, permission for translation, and the name of the Mexican publishing firm.

8. Jane woke me up often while she was having this very revealing experience, and each time I tried to comfort her. Note how she expressed from another perspective the power of her early religious training, as well as religion's fear of the power of the unknown—and how even now she still has to deal with those factors in her search for knowledge.

"Sunday morning, March 8, 1981.

"Part of me doesn't want to contend with this material at all," Jane wrote for her journal, "but last night I had one of the strangest, quite frightening experiences—all the odder because there are so few real events to hang on to. Very early after we went to bed I realized I was in the middle of a nightmarish experience, one terribly vivid emotionally yet with no real story line. I only know that the following were involved: a childhood nursery tale and a toy like the cuddly cat doll I had as a child, named Susie, and thought the world of. Anyway, the point is that the story . . . and there I lose it; I don't get the connections. All I know is that I awakened myself crying, my body very sore, sat on the side of the bed and made the following connections from my feelings at the time.

"They were these: that the entire world with its organization was kept together by certain stories, like those of the Roman Catholic Church; that it was dangerous beyond all knowing to look through the stories or examine them for the truth, and that all kinds of taboos existed to keep us from doing this, since . . . on the other side, so to speak, there was an incomprehensible frightening chaotic dimension, malevolent; powers beyond our imagining; and that to question the stories was to threaten not just personal survival but the fabric of reality as we know it. So excommunication was the punishment, or damnation . . . which meant more than mere ostracism, but the complete isolation of a person from those belief systems, with nothing between him or her and those frightening realities . . . without a framework in which to even organize meaning. This was what damnation really meant. To seek truth was the most dangerous of well-intentioned behavior, then . . . and retribution had to be swift and sure.

"I can't remember the events connected with the nightmare that gave rise to the feelings, but at the same time I was being assaulted or attacked by . . . a psychological force who wanted me to understand the danger of such a course. When I went back to sleep the entire thing would happen again. Once I think the title of a children's tale appeared in the air in large block letters, the idea also being that outside of the known order provided by these stories, there were raging forces working against man's existence. (The old idea of Pandora's box comes to mind.)

"I equate all of this with three events: a movie I saw on TV the night before last in which the hero finally saw through the god of his people; a Raggedy Ann doll Rob found in the backyard the other day and brought in (it was probably dragged there by a dog, its right arm is missing)—but it reminded me of my old Susie; and part of a review I read yesterday of a book about death.

"The book was based on the idea that nature was against man; and that religion was man's attempt to operate within that unsafe context. The feelings I was getting went even further, that religion or science or whatever weren't attempts to discover truth—but to escape from doing so, to substitute some satisfying tale or story instead. And I suppose that if someone persisted long enough, he or she would find the holes in the stories . . .

and undo the whole works, The idea of the stories was to save each man from having to encounter reality in such a frightening fashion. . . . The characters in the stories did this for him in their own fashion, and if you kept [searching] . . . you threatened the fine framework of organization that alone made life possible. . . ."

9. Seth, in the private session for Wednesday evening, March 11, 1981:

"Ruburt's nightmare experience *(three nights ago)* is a beautiful example of the kind of explosive emotional content that many people carry, fairly hidden, representing certain taboos, translated of course in individualistic terms.

"I do not want to go into a history of culture here, but your organizations historically have largely been built upon your religious concepts, which have indeed been extremely rigid. The repressive nature of Christian thought in the Middle Ages, for example, is well known. Artistic expression itself was considered highly suspect if it traveled outside of the accepted precepts, and particularly of course if it led others to take action against those precepts. To some extent the same type of policy is still reflected in your current societies, though science or the state itself may serve instead of the church as the voice of authority.

"Behind such ideas is the central point of Christianity, or one of them at least: that earthly man is a sinful creature. He is given to sin. In that regard his natural expression must be closely guarded. It must be directed toward officialdom, and outside of that boundary lay, particularly in the past, the very uncomfortable realm of the heretic.

"In medieval times, to be excommunicated was no trivial incident, but an event harkening severance that touched both the soul and the body, and all political, religious and economic conditions by which the two were tied together.

"Many people were dependent upon the church for their well-being, and in reincarnational terms many millions of people alive today were familiar then with such conditions. The nunneries and monasteries were long-term social and religious institutions, some extremely rigorous, while others were religiously oriented in name only. But there is a long history of the conflicts between creative thought, heresy, excommunication—or worse, death. All of those factors were involved in one way or another in the fabric of Ruburt's nightmare material.

"The church was quite real to Ruburt as a child, through the priests who came *(to the house)* regularly, and through direct contact with the religious *(grade)* school, and the support offered to the *(fatherless)* family. Ruburt's very early poetry offended Father *(Boyle)*, who burned his books on the fall of Rome, so he had more than a hypothetical feeling about such issues. Many of his fears originated long before the sessions, of course, and before he realized that there was any alternative at all between, say, conventional religious beliefs and complete disbelief in any nature of divinity.

"Ruburt became afraid that if he went too far he would discover that he had catapulted himself into a realm where both questions and answers were meaningless. To do that is one thing, but to take others with you would be, he felt, unforgivable—and in the framework of those fears, as his work became better known he became even more cautious.

"The entire structure of fears, of course, is based upon a belief in the sinful self and the sinful nature of the self's expression.

"Outside of that context, none of those fears make any sense at all. In a large regard the church through the centuries ruled through the use of fear far more than the use of love. It was precisely in the area of artistic expression that the inspirations might quickest leap through the applied dogmatic framework. The political nature of inspirational material of any kind was well understood by the church. Ruburt well knew even as a child that such religious structures had served their time, and his poetry provided a channel through which he could express his own views as he matured.

"He did initiate a small religious order in the 16th century, in France, and he was in love for many years with the man he met in his dream *(five evenings ago)*—a cleric. The love was not consummated, but it was passionate and enduring nonetheless on both of their parts.

"Ruburt had considerable difficulty with church doctrine even then, and the rules of the order as actually practiced were later considered to hold their own seeds of heresy. As an old woman, Ruburt was forced to leave the order that he had initiated. He left with a few female companions who were also ostracized, and died finally of starvation. It was a time when unconventional patterns of thought, of unconventional expression, could have (*fateful*) consequences.

"The name Normandy comes to mind, and the name Abelard. The dream came to remind Ruburt of those connections, but also to remind him that his life even then was enriched by a long-held love relationship. The two corresponded frequently, met often, and in their ways conspired to alter many of the practices that were abhorrent yet held as proper church policy.

"The dream representing his grandfather symbolically allowed him to go back to the past in this life, to a time of severe shock—his grandfather's death—which occurred when (*Ruburt, at age 19*) was beginning to substitute scientific belief for religious belief, wondering if his grandfather's consciousness then fell back into a mindless state of being, into chaos, as science would certainly seem to suggest. In the dream his grandfather survives. His grandfather survived in a suit that was too large, which means that there was still room for him to grow. Ruburt had a small experience of hearing a voice speak in his mind (*yesterday*)—a voice of comfort, all he remembered of quite legitimate assistance he received from other personalities connected with the French life, that came as a result of the French dream.

"He still needs your reassurances, and should tell you when he feels discouraged. . . ."

I could add much material from Jane's personal past to supplement just the session excerpts given here; perhaps the two of us can explore those fascinating connections in a later work. Right now I'll make just one point: The priest, burning Jane's books in the backyard of the house she lived in, taught the growing girl in most specific terms that she had to protect her natural abilities and her inquiring mind even from the very institution—the Roman Catholic Church—that she had so strongly identified with.

10. Like each of Jane's books, *Emir* has its own life, its own place upon our planet, and resists categorization. It falls somewhere between being a book for children and one for adults. That made it difficult for its publisher to market. Tam Mossman said it best in September 1977, when Jane was writing the book and

Prentice-Hall was considering its publication: *Emir* is really a book for "readers of all ages." Jane has received many favorable comments upon it from readers, and we're sorry to see it go out of print. Being remaindered usually means the end of a book, unless it can be placed with another publisher. That's difficult to do.

11. When *Mass Events* is published, see Session 835 for February 7, 1979, in Chapter 6.

12. See the opening notes for Session 920 in this Chapter 9.

13. Seth, in the private session for Wednesday evening, April 15, 1981:

"Ruburt found great comfort in the church as a young person, for if it created within its members the image of a sinful self, it also of course provided a steady system of treatment—a series of rituals that gave the individual some sense of hope the sinful self could be redeemed, as in the framework of most of Christianity, through adherence to certain segments of Christian dogma.

"When Ruburt left the church, the concept of the sinful self was still there, but the methods that earlier served to relieve its pressures were no longer effectively present. The concept was shifted over to the flawed self of scientific vintage. Science has no sacraments. Its only methods of dealing with such guilt involve standard psychoanalytic counseling—which itself deepens the dilemma, for counseling itself is based upon the idea that the inner self is a reservoir of savage impulses. Period.

"Ruburt's creative nature early began to perceive at least that man's existence contained other realities that were deeper. Some of this is difficult to separate. To leave the church, say, meant to carry still some of the old beliefs, but without the bandaids that earlier offered some protection.

"He began to search actually from childhood in a natural fashion toward some larger framework that would offer an explanation for reality, that bore at least some resemblance to the natural vision of his best poetry. I have said before that many creative people, highly gifted, have died young in one way or the other because their great gifts of creativity could find no clear room in which to grow. They became strangled by the beliefs of the cultural times.

"In that regard, Ruburt's creativity kept struggling for its own growth and value fulfillment. His psychic recognition or initiation represented a remarkable breakthrough, meant to give him that additional psychic room that would insure the continued expansion of the abilities of the natural self. The sinful-self concept is a personal one for each who holds it, but it is also projected outward into the entire species, of course, until the whole world seems tainted.

"Ruburt's creativity broke through to provide our sessions and to release the psychic abilities that had earlier been <u>nearly</u> but not completely repressed.

"His poetry acted in some regards as a stimulator. That breakthrough, you might say, with perhaps some exaggeration, was a lifesaver, for without some such expansion Ruburt would have felt unable to continue the particular <u>brand</u> of his existence. It is not possible to say in words what one <u>person</u> or another <u>looks for</u> in life, or what unique features best promote his or her <u>growth</u> and development. Even two plants of the same kind sometimes require completely different treatments. The sessions, then, opened the door to a particular kind of value fulfillment that was natural to Ruburt's being. Now to some extent it was that poor, unhappy sinful self, a psychological structure formed by beliefs and feelings, that was also seeking its own redemption, since even it had outgrown the framework that so defined it.

"I have said that in almost every case of severe dissatisfaction or illness, the underlying reasons will not so much be found in the discovery or expression of buried hate or aggression— though these may be present—but in the search for expression of value fulfillment that is for one reason or another being denied.

"Ruburt broke through both psychically and creatively—that is, the sessions almost immediately provided him with new creative inspiration and expression, and with the expansions needed psychologically that would help fulfill his promise as a writer and as a mature personality. He was still left, however, with the beliefs in the sinful self, and carried within him many deep fears that told him that self-expression itself and spontaneity were highly dangerous.

"In that regard, you have what amounts to a creative dilemma.

"It is one thing to say that the dilemma is unfortunate, but it is also true to say that the dilemma existed because of a break-through that gave him what amounted to a new life at the time. . . ."

For the first time ever since Jane began the sessions over 17 years ago, in December 1963, I got the chills when Seth delivered a passage—for when he remarked that without some such creative psychic expansion as the sessions "Ruburt would have felt unable to continue the particular brand of his existence," I surely thought he meant that Jane could have chosen to die. I didn't mention this to her after the session, and she seemed to have no such reaction when she read the typed session the next day. We did talk about a number of highly gifted people who had died at young ages; indeed, we'd often speculated about what further contributions such individuals could have made had they chosen to continue living physically. In ordinary terms, it's easy to say that those early deaths were wasteful—but not, I said now, from the standpoints of those involved. Great variations in motivation, intent, and purpose must have been operating, but each person had done what he or she could do in this probable reality—then left it. Jane agreed that Seth had come through with excellent material. I told her I didn't see how it could be any better.

The session triggered my own associative processes several times. Almost at once I recalled a passage Seth had given in the session of the night before (on April 14), when he'd discussed my attitude toward religion in general and my own sinful self in particular:

"It is no coincidence that you have been relatively free of that concept in its traditional religious connotation—you worked that out in your Nebene existence to a large extent, and because of your own preparations for a life in which you are now involved."

(Seven and a half years ago, Seth had referred to a version of myself living in first-century Rome: "So Joseph 'was' Nebene, a scholarly man, not adventurous, obsessed with copying ancient truths, and afraid that creativity was error; authoritative and demanding. He feared sexual encounter, and he taught rich Roman children." In Volume 2 of "Unknown" Reality, see Session 721 for November 25, 1974. One might say that I'm still obsessed with truths—as I take down the Seth material, for example—only now I call them timeless rather than ancient or new.)

Next, and certainly because of my concern for Jane, I recalled a session she'd given for Chapter 7 of *Dreams*. Checking, I found that it's the 911th for April 28, 1980—which means, incredibly, that Seth gave it almost 15 months ago. Mainly he'd discussed one's choice of genetic defects before birth, but to me portions of his material are very reminiscent of Jane's situation:

"While I admit that many people will not agree with me, I know from experience that most individuals do not choose one 'happy' life after another, always ensconced in a capable body, endowed by nature or heritage with all of the gifts most people seem to think they desire.

"Each person seeks value fulfillment, and that means that they choose various lives in such a fashion that all of their abilities and capacities can be best developed, and in such a way that their world is also enriched. Some people will choose 'defective' bodies purposely in order to focus more intensely in other areas. They want a different kind of focus. . . . Such a choice demands an intensification. It is made on the part of the individual and on the parts of the parents as well. . . ."

And for me, at least, the reincarnational dimensions behind our present joint situation were heightened by a third association. It lay in the unpublished 874th session for August 22, 1979—the first one Jane held after having finished *Mass Events* a week earlier. I felt a distinct start of surprise when I came across this passage of Seth's, for I'd completely forgotten it: "Jane, for example, entered the fetus when it was about three months old, and accepted this as a new life. You waited longer." I didn't remember Jane ever referring to that bit of information; certainly she'd never asked Seth to elaborate. I hadn't either. (That was one of the few times when Seth had called her Jane instead of Ruburt, by the way.)

I took those associations to mean that no matter what her evolving focuses in her present life, Jane should be as much aware of my reactions to her situation as she is of her own—that even though I'd worked out religious questions in a previous life, still this time around I had chosen to share with her a probable reality within which her physical symptoms, bound up as they are with the subject of religion, could occur. (But at the same time, I reminded myself, her great creativity had also found its modes of expression in spite of everything.) If, as Seth said on April 15, conflicts like Jane's often stem from the gifted individual's unrequited search for value fulfillment—even resulting in an early death—then that premise is at least consciously understandable. I've suspected for quite a while that something like this is operating in Jane's case. It's not that she perversely refuses to get well, even with all of the help Seth and I have tried to give her—and that she has even *asked* for—but that the deepest portions of her being in this physical life *have other goals*, toward which her nonphysical self and her physical symptoms are traveling together. Without such thinking, I was coming to feel, there could be little comprehension of my wife's long-term challenges.

Otherwise, I thought, all too often the afflicted one is left with that great yawning "Why?" in the face of whatever drastic negative events are taking place; and those who suffer with the sufferer are as fated as the sufferer is to receive no satisfactory answers within *their* lifetimes, either. To search for answers within the narrow frames of reference offered by the conventional view of reality could be like trying to peer into the depths of personality through an opaque window. . . .

14. Seth, from the private session for June 2, 1981:

"Your love for each other is large enough to withstand any natural expression of aggression or resentment on either of your parts. As mentioned earlier, because of Ruburt's background he feared abandonment often. It seemed to him that he did not offer what most men expected of women, so that if he wanted a good lifelong companion he had to tread lightly. He felt that many of his own characteristics were considered disadvantageous in a man-woman relationship."

As Jane finished delivering that passage for Seth I felt like interrupting the session to most strongly protest her poor assessment of herself, but I didn't. Instead, later I added my rough statement to the session. Besides expressing my love for Jane, it reveals other churning emotions:

(*"I should take a moment here to note that Seth has mentioned this attitude of Jane's before, and that she has referred to it also. I haven't had any such feelings, since from the very beginning of our relationship I've always felt certain that in Jane I'd found the ideal mate—an achieve-*

ment I've considered most fortunate, one I'd hardly dared dream I'd ever manage to do. Looking back, our meeting and getting together seemed the most natural and inevitable things in the world; how could I improve upon those? I've always been intensely proud of Jane's abilities and achievements, and glad to participate in them to whatever degree. The thing that has left me distraught, nearly brokenhearted, is to see her in such a progressively poor physical situation as the years have passed. Especially devastating is this when the material explains that this isn't the only way things can be. No wonder I say to her that we've paid too high a price for our accomplishments. I want to see her able to manipulate like other people, of course, and to have her achievements also. That things haven't worked out that way so far can't but help have a profound effect upon my feelings, hers, and our relationship, which I've always taken absolutely as being as solid and enduring as the elements. It still is.")

15. I tell Jane that each book she does is her best—and I mean it each time, for each one is. The Seth books sell better, however, than do her "own" books: *How to Develop Your ESP Power, Adventures in Consciousness, Psychic Politics, Cézanne* and *James,* her Oversoul Seven novels, *Dialogues* and *Emir.* (See the opening notes for this 931st session, as well as Note 10, for my description of the demise of *Emir.*) Now Jane adds *God of Jane* to her list, with *If We Live Again* to follow in a few months.

That the Seth books outdo Jane's other works has always puzzled us. *Each one* of her books, whether produced by herself or with Seth, is an equally valid and intimate expression of her basic creativity. Seth doesn't come from some separate, more exalted portion of Jane's psyche that's off limits to her when she's writing her own books. As he's often said himself, he isn't omnipotent: Like Jane, he shrinks from being a guru—and I stress that Seth doesn't hold that attitude just because Jane does. Neither seeks to dominate the other; each tries to help the other.

One can also say that the Seth books are a step farther removed than Jane's are from the immediacy of life as we conceive of it. Even with the elimination of the Seth element from them, Jane's own books would still represent a remarkable overall achievement, and had she never given expression to the Seth material I'm sure she would have developed her abilities in ways quite unknown to us now. Within her basic creativity lies the source of Seth as we are to understand him in our temporal reality. Her expression of Seth is an adjunct to that creativity, as he is the first to acknowledge.

Interesting, to speculate upon what kind of reception Jane's work would have received all of these years, without the Seth material.

16. We held that one session on the evening of June 18, at the end of Jane's second day of recording her own sinful-self material.

"The main issues with which the sinful self was concerned were focused most clearly in *Mass Events* and *God of Jane*," Seth told us, "since more than the other books they represent a direct confrontation, 'attacking' the very legitimacy of the entire concept of sin and evil, insisting more dramatically on the good intent of man's basic impulses. . . . [Ruburt's] sinful-self explanation represents a fascinating psychological document in that regard, and also shows the self's mobility and willingness to learn and change—once the intent is made to take a stand.

"It might be of value to have Ruburt mentally ask the sinful self for a few comments on how its beliefs about the female sex were connected with its concepts of sin, and if those attitudes are changing."

17. See the opening notes for Session 920, in this Chapter 9.

18. Earlier in the opening notes for this session, I referred to the poor relationship between Jane and her mother, Marie.

"I now want to put the sinful-self material in a larger spectrum," Seth told us in part. "Ideally, infants 'bond' with their parents, particularly with the mother but with the father also, and they bond with the general ideas of their society. This offers the sense of safety in which the youngster can then feel free and curious enough to explore its world and the nature of reality.

"You are social creatures. You fear abandonment for that reason, since you are meant to develop individually while also interacting with others, that interaction giving you the peculiar quality of established civilizations.

"Now Ruburt had only one parent available most of the time, and he did not feel secure in that relationship—a situation chosen ahead of time, now. There is great leeway in the nature of such bondings. . . . With some people, they are so secure that they provide an overall, fairly permanent inner and outer framework. Ruburt's relationship with his mother left much to be desired. The bonding did not secure him that vital sense of safety, and he felt threatened by abandonment. His bonding to the cultural beliefs of religion was very strong to make up for that initial lack. The sinful-self material represents those ideas that were a strong element in his original belief structures. The 'troublesome' material remained relatively inactive until his curiosity and ability led him to actively challenge those ideas while [he was] also in a situation where the natural fear of abandonment might be suggested. At certain points, the assimilation of new information is so qualifiedly different from the original belief structure that in order to assimilate it the personality is left for a time between belief systems.

"The point at which such a situation happens is of course internal, and it may or may not have anything to do with the quality of material, but with its nature. Each society—or each system of knowledge, for that matter—has its own taboos built in, and most of these imply abandonment by the community. A firm bonding with the parent ideally implies, however, that the child will not be abandoned, despite parental anger at any given time.

"Now remember that Ruburt's mother used phrases like: 'I hereby disown you,' and: 'You are hereby disinherited,' and: 'I consider you no longer my daughter.' Such situations increased Ruburt's sense of not being safe, yet also reinforced feelings of independence, for he did not have to feel as dependent upon Marie as he might otherwise. The time would come, however, when the old bondings had to be encountered, for they simply could not hold the newer larger frameworks of understanding. The ideas of the so-called sinful self represent several layers of activity, then—troublesome aspects of belief structures that are shared by millions in your society, and by certain levels of Ruburt's personality. He is now trying to assimilate a greater framework, to become bonded to a higher sequence of knowledge.

"Once those old beliefs are understood, they will no longer be considered shameful in themselves, nor humiliating, or as attitudes to be accused of. . . ."

"His idea of a project on the magical approach now is excellent, for it suggests a new concentration or focus."

19. For material on Jane's previous reincarnation-type dream experience, see the excerpts in Note 9 from the private session for March 11, 1981. Here's what she rapidly typed today for her journal:

"Wednesday, July 15, 1981. Last night or rather this morning I had a strange strange dream experience, very vivid while happening, quite important I felt, and now I hardly remember it. The affair involved an excellent TV movie on reincarnation we saw last night. In the dream experience I think I was considering doing a book, a sequel, to the movie—but I was also seeing one or maybe two reincarnational lives of mine, seeing how a belief in reincarnation helped open a sense of the future in the present: I was learning how to visit those lives, which were still happening and for which I think I yearned—without dying in this life. There was a road and other scenes from my past I wanted to paint too; a significant green bottle; people I dearly loved, and Rob might have been involved too. Lots I've completely forgotten about people who loved you in particular lives always in some way being supportive; that we're caught up in time-to-time overlays Seth has referred to in his late book dictation; that rhythmic time overlays happened as various anniversaries or significant events from various lives overlapped, bringing them momentarily closer (like comets) when entries back and forth, and interchanges, are particularly easier.

"Part of my physical hassles come from fear of the unknown, once I realized I was gifted in that direction—that certain friends we've made here represent loved relationships of reincarnational origin, that offer support now if I accept it.

"How a belief in reincarnation and immortality added support to life, so that it didn't seem dead-ended. That I could relax now, admitting and realizing that I did have certain fears per the sinful self's document (instead of pretending that I didn't). Because brought into the light I really could handle them and see how they originated. Stuff on how society operated, whether it knew it or not, on a reincarnational basis, and how association was many-lives-thick, so to speak. Only these are thoughts I'm left with, connected to the experience while I've forgotten the events themselves, and the scenes that were extremely colorful and emotionally charged."

I told Jane after the session that her material brings up innumerable questions—that just from our side, in physical reality, the variety of connections between the living and the "dead" has to equal the number of individuals on earth. For instance, I'd wondered, as I read her paper, how often does the newly deceased person's meeting loved ones from other lifetimes "dilute" the love he or she had felt for the mate, say, who is left behind this time? How ironic, that the one still physical grieves for the departed loved one, while that newly dead individual is joyfully becoming aware of connections with other existences, other loves. . . .

One can, of course, turn the whole thing around in various ways: The freshly dead person, still carrying his or her nonmaterial emotions, can feel a grief equal to that of the one left behind; their mutual sorrow can form a bond stronger, perhaps at least temporarily, than those created by either one in other lives with other people. Or the one still "alive" can turn away from the dead partner, relative, or friend in order to be psychically and physically free for new adventures. The variety of relationships between parents and children, no matter on which side the death occurs, must be vast. Jane said that perhaps we can get some answers from Seth.

20. In this chapter, see the third section of Note 7 for Session 920. I presented Seth's comments on an example of correspondence involving Jane and me, along with his short, more generalized discussion of the phenomenon.

21. Seth discussed his "seemingly contradictory material" throughout Session 918, which is the last session for Chapter 8 of *Dreams,* and up to 9:46 in Session 919 for Chapter 9. While researching this little note, I was once again startled to realize that Jane had delivered those two sessions over 13 months ago— early in June 1980.

22. Although Jane has had "particular difficulty" with the theory of reincarnation, both through Seth and in her poetry she's always kept psychic windows open through which she can view and express reincarnational ideas and emotions. Poetically, this will be obvious when *If We Live Again* is published late this year. (Probably in December. We expect to receive from Prentice-Hall the page proofs for the book, for our review, any day now.) In her poetry the young Jane was using ideas akin to reincarnation

before she even knew the word—subject matter that was strongly disapproved of by the Catholic priests who visited Jane and her bedridden mother at home.

I've noted before that Seth himself has no reservations at all about expressing reincarnational material. Listening to some of the tapes students made in Jane's ESP class—in the early '70s, say—I hear Seth being allowed to spontaneously give regular students and first-time visitors often quite detailed and penetrating insights into their other lives; explaining how events and emotions from other existences can intermix with their counterparts in present lives. Jane still picks up such information from others, but now she seldom expresses it through Seth. I think her deep concern about leading others astray, related as it is to her early religious training, is the inhibiting force here. Then see Notes 9 and 19 for this session; their contents show that she hasn't closed a certain window into the dream state, either.

SESSION 932——August 4, 1981
8:50 P.M. TUESDAY

(Seth discussed generalized sinful-self material in only one of the five private sessions Jane has held since she came through with the 931st session for Dreams *three weeks ago.[1] In some respects lately she's felt a bit more at ease.[2]*

We received the page proofs for If We Live Again *on the last day of July. They're very easy for Jane to check, compared to those for her other books.*

This afternoon we had a long discussion about the conflicts we often feel between our natural desires for creative privacy and the fact that our works go out into the world. Each of us has a strong sense of responsibility toward those who read our books. Involved here also is Jane's sinful self and "its" attitude concerning the requests she receives to go public through radio and television interviews, lectures, records, tapes, and so forth. She turned away from media attention many years ago. It took me some time after she'd started delivering the Seth material to realize that in spite of her outgoing, friendly nature, Jane is as much a private person as I am.)

Dictation.

I will have something to say about your discussion at our next session.

Now: Again, master events are those that most significantly affect your system of reality, even though the original action was not physical but took place in the inner dimension. Most events appear both in time and out of it, their action distributed between an inner and outer field of expression. Usually you are aware only of events' exterior <u>cores</u>. The inner processes escape you.

Those inner processes, however, also give many clues as to some native abilities that you have used "in the past" as a species. Those inner processes do sometimes emerge, then. Here is an example.

One morning last weekend *(Saturday)* Ruburt found himself suddenly and vividly thinking about some *married* friends. They lived out of town, separated in time by a drive of approximately [half an hour]. Ruburt found himself wishing that the friends lived closer, and he was suddenly filled with a desire to see them. He imagined the couple at the house, and surprised himself by thinking that he might indeed call them later in the day and invite them down for the evening, even though he and Joseph had both decided against guests that weekend.

Furthermore, Ruburt did not like the idea of making an invitation on such short notice. Then he became aware that those particular thoughts were intrusive, completely out of context with his immediately previous ones, for only a moment or so earlier he had been congratulating himself precisely because he had made no plans for the day or evening at all that would involve guests or other such activities. Very shortly he forgot the entire affair. Then, however, about fifteen minutes later he found the same ideas returning, this time more insistently.

(Long pause at 9:05.) They lasted perhaps five minutes. Ruburt noticed them and forgot them once again. This time, however, he decided not to call his friends, and he went about his business. In about a half hour the same mental activity returned, and, finding himself struck by this, Ruburt mentioned the episode to Joseph and again cast it from his mind.

By this time it was somewhat later in the day. Ruburt and Joseph ate lunch, and the mail arrived. There was a letter written the morning before *(on Friday)* by the same friends that had been so much in Ruburt's mind. They mentioned going on a trip *(on Saturday)*, and specifically asked if they could visit that same afternoon. From the way the letter was written, it seemed as if the friends—call them Peter and Polly—had already started on their journey that *(Saturday)* morning, and would stop in Elmira on their return much later toward evening. There was no time to answer the letter, of course.

Peter and Polly would be on the road, it seemed, unreachable by phone, though they had included the number of their answering service, and had also written that they would call before leaving—yet no such call had been received.

It would be simple enough, of course, to ascribe Ruburt's thoughts and feelings to mere coincidence. He remembered the vividness of his feelings at the time, however. It looked as if Peter and Polly were indeed going to arrive almost as if Ruburt had in fact called and invited them. That evening the visit did take place. Actually, some work had prevented the couple from leaving when they intended. Instead, they called later from their home to say that they were just beginning their trip, and would stop on their way.

Ruburt was well prepared for the call by then, and for the visit. Now the visit and Ruburt's earlier feelings and thoughts were part of the same event, except that his subjective experience gave him clues as to the inner processes by which all events take place. More is involved than the simple question: Did he perceive the visit precognitively? More is involved than the question: Did he perceive his information directly from the minds of his friends, or from the letter itself, which had already been mailed, of course, and was on its way to Ruburt at the time?

What you have is a kind of inner backbone of perception—a backup program, so to speak, an inner perceptive mechanism with its own precise psychological tuner that in one way or another operates within the field of your intent. This is somewhat like remote sensing, or like an interior *(pause)* radar equipment that operates in a psychological field of attention, so that you are somewhat aware of the existence of certain events that concern you as they come into the closer range of probabilities with which you are connected.

In a certain fashion you "step into the event" at that level. You accept or reject it as a probability. You make certain adjustments, perhaps altering particular details, but you step into and become part of the inner processes—affecting, say, the shape or size or nature of the event before it becomes a definite physical actuality.

(9:27.) For centuries that is the main way in which man dealt with the events of his life or tribe or village.[3] Your modern methods of communication are in fact modeled after your inner ones. Ruburt's thoughts almost (underlined) blended in enough to go relatively unnoticed. They were almost (underlined) innocuous enough to be later accepted as coincidence. They did have, however, an extra intentness and vitality and peculiar insistence—qualities that he has learned are indicative *(pause)* of unusual psychological activity. The point is that in most such cases the subjective recognition of an approaching event flows so easily and transparently into your attention, and fits in so smoothly with the events of the day, as to go unnoticed. You help mold the nature and shape of events without realizing it, overlooking those occasions when the processes might show themselves.

When they do, you might question: Could it be possible that you really were perceiving an action ahead of time? Later, some people more stubborn than others might try to "prove" that some events are definitely precognitively perceived—but the point is that all events are precognitively perceived *(intently)*, and that you actually step into an event, become part of it, reject it, accept the certain version you have "picked up," or exert yourself to make certain changes that affect the nature of the event itself.

Even the conscious mind contains much more information about the structure of events than you realize you possess. The physical perceiving apparatuses of all organizations carry their own kinds of inner systems of communication, allowing events to be manipulated on a worldwide basis before they take on what appears to be their final definitive physical occurrences in time and space.

Individually and globewide, value fulfillment is in a fashion the purpose of all events. *(Long pause.)* Value fulfillment, again, is the impetus that drives the wheels of nature, so to speak. As the origin of your world did indeed emerge from the "world of dreams," so the true root of all events lie in such subjective activities, and the answers to individual challenges and problems are always within your grasp, ready to appear in physical actuality.

In the next chapter I hope to show you the importance of value fulfillment in your own life, and give you clues that will allow you to take better advantage of your own subjective and objective opportunities for such development.

End of chapter, end of dictation, end of session, and a fond good evening to you both.

(*"Thank you. Good night."*

9:48 P.M.)

NOTES. Session 932

1. For the record only: Inclusive from Session 919 (June 9, 1980) to Session 932 (August 4, 1981), almost 14 months passed while we had Chapter 9 in progress. During that time Jane held four book sessions, with small portions of three of them being deleted, or private; 10 regular nonbook sessions, with brief sections of four of those being private; and 68 completely private sessions. Of that last total, she devoted 13 sessions to material on the magical approach to reality, and 27 to the subject of the sinful self. She came through with 82 sessions, then, during the production of Chapter 9.

2. Here's an example of how far I went myself to obtain a sense of ease about an imaginary situation upon which I'd often projected negative thoughts.

Over the past year or so I'd become more and more concerned about what I could do if a nighttime emergency—like a fire—trapped Jane and me in our bedroom. Because of the conventional ranch-style floor plan of the hill house, our bedroom is isolated from the front and back doors; we reach it at the end of a hall opening off the living room. We had no door at the entrance to the hall. A blaze anywhere in the central section of the house, with its heat, gas, and smoke, could easily prevent me from reaching the front or back door as I sought to carry Jane to safety. (It would be useless to try to push her in her chair.)

The windows in our bedroom are rather small. Even if I could manage to force Jane out of one of them, in an act of desperation, she would almost certainly be injured as she fell to the ground amid the tangle of juniper shrubs growing below.

I'd told myself to forget it each time I caught myself worrying that way—but finally, more concerned than ever about Jane's physical condition, I gave up. With more than a little wry humor over what I considered to be a failure of belief on my part, I took action: Late in July I had a contractor, who is a friend of ours and well acquainted with Jane's situation, install a heavy outside door in a bedroom wall, and construct the necessary step to the ground. He also hung another heavy door at the living-room entrance to the hall; we're to keep that one closed at night. I had our friend position smoke alarms throughout the house.

Characteristically, Jane said little about the improvements once I'd explained to her why I was having them made. And—belief or no—I judged the success of the changes by the fact that my worries disappeared as soon as they were completed.

3. I see correlations between Seth's material here and my speculations at the end of the 922nd session (for this chapter), concerning his apparently unlimited capacity for oral history.

CHAPTER 10

The Pleasure Principle. Group Dreams and Value Fulfillment

SESSION 933——August 7, 1981
8:22 P.M. FRIDAY

(Because the proper detection equipment was not in place, government officials do not know just how much radiation was released into the Pennsylvania countryside 28 months ago [in March 1979], when the reactor of Unit No. 2 at Three Mile Island overheated and approached a meltdown of the uranium-packed fuel rods in its core. Federal and state agencies have announced long-term population studies to measure the effects—if any—of this radiation. Since 1925 scientists have been steadily reducing their estimates of what a "safe" dose for human beings really is, however, and many now believe that there's no such thing as a completely harmless amount of even low-level radiation. Any such dosage would be in addition to the earth's natural background radiation, which varies across our country and around the world because of altitude and other factors.

Jane and I think that the psychological effects of the accident at TMI are at least as important as the physical ones—and that eventually they will be much more so around the world. To my way of thinking, the consciousness connected with TMI is of an unknown quantity and quality.[1]

Six weeks ago in Tehran, the capital city of Iran, over 150 officials of the ruling Islamic Republican Party were killed by bomb explosions which destroyed their headquarters building. At first revolutionary zealots blamed the "Great Satan"—America—for the crime. They also accused Iraq, with whom Iran is at war, but it's almost certain that one of the dozen or more Iranian underground revolutionary groups is responsible. [The most powerful one, the Mujahedin-e Khalq, for example, is a Marxist-based guerrilla organization of "People's Crusaders" that espouses its own brand of radical Islamic republicanism.] The mass killing resulted in an immediate increase in the government's campaign to eliminate opponents of clerical [Shiite] rule in Iran. Over 70 dissidents had already been executed by the time of the blasts; many others have been arrested since.

Then yesterday I read a long newspaper account of how the members of the Bahai faith in Iran are being severely persecuted by the government and the Shiite clergy. Why, I wondered as I began to read, are Iranians harassing a whole group of other Iranians in such unpleasant ways—really seeking to exterminate them? The hatred the Shiites hold for the Bahais is based upon a century-old, primitive religious zealotry. Even though they too worship but a single God and the Koran, the Bahais are too liberal, too heretical in their peaceful and progressive ways; they are called unpatriotic and secular; some Bahais are attacked, dispossessed, lynched or executed, it seems, every day.

In all of this—the bombings and persecutions and killings—I thought of great, loose groups of consciousnesses swirling in angry revolt, with each consciousness "working" individually and collectively for and against others, each one seeking to know new creative aspects of itself within the framework of a chosen national structure.[2]

Jane finished correcting the page proofs for If We Live Again *five days after receiving them from Prentice-Hall, and yesterday I sent them back to our publisher. We'll be seeing the frontmatter proofs later this month. Tam Mossman has told us the book probably will be published before the end of the year.*

Last month, in the opening notes for Session 931, in Chapter 9, I recorded that on July 8 Jane spontaneously wrote "a complete outline for a book on Seth's magical approach to reality." Actually, we've been quite aware of the potential of such an idea ever since Seth began that material a year ago.[3] *After supper this evening we went over the loose-leaf notebook of information Jane has accumulated for* The Magical Approach to Reality: A Seth Book, *and discussed how she could follow her outline in putting all of that material—on our dreams, psychic events and insights, her poetry and our essays—together with Seth's private sessions on the magical approach. She'd had trouble doing that at various times in the past year. Such a book would involve the publication of much Seth material that could either lie in our files for a long time, or never be published. I now feel that many of those sessions aren't so private after all, and can help others. The more I talked about the idea the better I liked it. Jane seemed to pick up on my own enthusiasm.*

Then just before session time, I mentioned my question about her sinful self's reactions to our efforts to help her in recent weeks. We have yet to see the kind of physical response we want, and I wanted to know if we'd prompted her sinful self to step up its attempts to keep her "under control." I explained that I think Seth's and our own endeavors on her behalf had been negated each time because we'd alerted her sinful self's fears—making it try harder to protect her according to its own very restrictive orientation.

Jane's idea tonight was to have a session on Dreams *only: "I don't want more private stuff that'll just make me feel more stupid," she said. I reminded her that when I refer to her sinful self, I only mean certain groups of ideas that we've personified for convenience's sake.)*

To begin with, dictation.

Next chapter heading *(10)*, to be called: "The Pleasure Principle. Group Dreams and Value Fulfillment."

As I have frequently mentioned, you have a hand in forming all events to one extent or another, and at certain levels you are therefore involved in the construction of those global events that affect the world, whether they be of so-called natural or cultural nature.

Earlier, I also spoke about the importance of dreams in man's early background, and their importance to you as a species. Here, I want to stress the social aspects of dreams, and to point out the fact that dreams also show you some of the processes that are involved in the actual formation of physical events: You actually come into an event, therefore, long before the event physically happens, at other levels of consciousness, and a good deal of this prior activity takes place in the state of dreaming.

Yet (remembering what I said about seeing contradictions), your dreams are also social events of a kind, and the state of dreaming can almost be thought of as an inner public forum in which each man and woman has his or her say, and in which each opinion, however unpopular, is taken into consideration. If you want to call any one dream event a private event, then I would have to tell you that that private event actually was your personal contribution to a larger multisided dream event, many-layered, so that one level might deal with the interests of a group to which you belong—say your family, [or] your political or religious organization—reaching "outward" to the realm of national government and world affairs. *(Pause.)* As your private conscious life is lived in a community setting of one kind or another as a rule, so do your dreams take place in the same context, so that as you dream for yourself, to some extent you also dream for your own family, for your community, and for the world.

Group dreaming was at one time taken for granted as a natural human characteristic—in a tribe, for example, when new locations were being sought, perhaps in time of drought. The various tribal members would have dreams in which the problem was considered, each dreamer tackling whatever aspect of the problem that best suited his or her abilities and personal intents. The dreamers would travel out-of-body in various directions to see the extent of drought conditions, and to ascertain the best direction for the tribe to take in any needed migration.

(Pause at 8:43.) Their dreams would then be shared by the tribe in the morning, or at special meetings, when each dreamer would give a rendition of the dream or dreams that seemed to be involved. In the same way, other dreamers would simply check with the dreamers of other villages or tribes—perhaps a hundred or even more miles distant. Some such dreams were extremely direct, others were clothed in symbolism according to the style of the dreamer, but in any case the dream was understood to have a public significance as well as a private one.

The same still applies, though often dreams themselves are forgotten. Instead, for example, for news or for advice you watch your morning television news, which provides you with a kind of manufactured dream that to some extent technologically serves the same purpose. Instead of sending cameramen and newspaper people to the farthest corners of the earth, early man sent out aspects of himself to gather the news and to form it into dream dramas. Oftentimes much of the material did not need to become conscious: It was "unconsciously" acted upon, turned directly into action. Now such dreams simply act as backup systems, rising to the fore whenever they are needed. Their purpose was and is to increase the value fulfillment of the species and of the individual.

Psychologists often speak of the needs of man. Here I would like to speak instead of the pleasures of man, for one of the distinguishing characteristics of value fulfillment is its pleasurable effect. It is not so much that man or nature seeks to satisfy needs, but to exuberantly, rambunctiously seek pleasure—and through following its pleasure each organism finds and satisfies its needs as well. Far more is involved in the experience of life, however, than the satisfaction of bare needs, for life is everywhere possessed with a desire toward quality—a quality that acknowledges the affirming characteristics of pleasure itself.

In your terms, there is a great pleasure to be found in both work and play, in excitement and calm, in exertion and rest *(long pause)*, yet the word "pleasure" itself has often fallen into disrepute, and is frowned at by the virtuous.

(Long pause at 9:00.) One of the main purposes of dreaming, therefore, is to increase man's pleasure, which means to increase the quality of living itself. Dreams are mental work and play combined, psychic and emotional rich creative dramas. They also involve you in the most productive of enterprises as you begin to play with versions of events that are being considered for physical actualization, as on a personal level you "view" the probable events which your family, tribe, organization, community and country will actualize.

(Long pause at 9:06.) End of dictation.

As he'd hinted in his greeting this evening, Seth did have some material for us—regardless of my wife's announced disinterest—and that information contained some surprises. See Note 4 for the rest of the session.)

NOTES. Session 933

1. Recently I asked Jane if Seth could give us some information on the consciousness connected with nuclear energy—a fascinat-

ing question I've often speculated about—and she promised me that he'd discuss it soon. I think his material will certainly include many original insights into the whole subject of consciousness-and-energy in general, as well as into the role of consciousness in events like the accident at Three Mile Island. I reminded Jane that some time ago Seth had remarked that as physical creatures we human beings cannot bear to directly confront the basic, vast, unimaginably awesome and creative consciousness of All That Is. Since we cannot bear to face the great raw power of nuclear energy either, I've often wondered whether this situation can be an earthly, imperfect and time-ridden analog to what must be the reality of All That Is.

(A note: Six years have passed since Jane delivered the passage I was trying to recall. It's from Session 747 for May 14, 1975, and I found that I had quoted portions of the session in Volume 2 of *"Unknown" Reality:* See Note 11 for Session 742. In essence my memory had been fairly accurate—yet rereading Seth's material was like a revelation to me. I told Jane that I don't think anyone else has ever said it as well. Through Seth she expressed the heart of her mystical knowledge:

"All That Is creates its reality as it goes along. Each world has its own impetus, yet all are ultimately connected. The true dimensions of a divine creativity would be unendurable for any one consciousness of whatever import, and so that splendor is infinitely dimensionalized (*most intensely throughout*), worlds spiraling outward with each 'moment' of a cosmic breath; with the separation of worlds a necessity; and with individual and mass comprehension always growing at such a rate that All That Is multiplies itself at microseconds, building both pasts and futures and other time scales you do not recognize. Each is a reality in itself, with its own potentials, and with no individual consciousness, however minute, ever lost.")

2. Sometimes together, sometimes separately, Jane and I listen to portions of the tapes students had made of the sessions and other exciting happenings in her ESP classes. I'd hardly put into shape for Session 933 my musings about the workings of consciousness than I heard Seth come through with these two passages; at once they reminded me of what I'd just been writing about.

The first quotation is from material Seth gave class members on November 3, 1970 (almost 11 years ago):

"Violence will always be used creatively. You cannot be destructive even when you try. Beyond that, however, in the meantime the violence that you do, you do to yourself. You are a part of All That Is—of all the nature that you know and experience, of the world that you know, and even a part of the world that you know that you do not like. If you rip off the wing of a fly, you are yourself less. If you purposefully, now, or with malice, step upon an ant, then to the extent of your malice you step upon yourself all unknowing. Violence will always be used creatively, but if you do not understand this—and at your present rate of development you do not—then any violence is violence against yourself. This applies to each of you, for when you think in terms of violence you think in terms of malice or aggression. Despite all man does, he cannot really work any destruction—but while he believes in destruction, then to that extent he minimizes what he is, and must work harder to use creativity."

Most of our tapes are dated—but not the one containing the session I'm quoting from below. I estimate that Seth gave this information to a group of visitors who attended a class some time in 1974 (or seven years ago):

"All action is creative and ever-occurring—the only way I can get these ideas across to you. All energy is personified. When you look at atoms and stars you are looking at simultaneous action. You are looking into the past and into the future at the same time, as you think of it. From the landscape of the brain you are trying to look at the landscape of the mind.

"You do not perceive the consciousness within the self. You do not perceive the consciousness within a star, either—yet the star is the physical materialization in your reality of another kind of consciousness, and all you perceive of it."

3. In Chapter 9 of *Dreams*, see the opening notes for Session 920 at superscript number 5.

4. *(Seth at 9:07:)* "Your earlier comment *(about Jane's sinful self)* is pertinent. Remember, again, that the sinful-self designation is a method of identifying certain attitudes. Those attitudes are indeed changing.

"In the case of our book *(Dreams)*, however, Ruburt himself was worried about your attitude. His overall concerns of course to some extent blocked his creative processes, which further alarmed him. The main issue here is that feeling of responsibility again, so that he writes or whatever because he loves to do it, not because he should or must, and that involves my book as well as his own.

"He becomes overly serious, overstressing the entire picture, as you can at times, so that the affair *(of the symptoms)* seems hopeless: the evidence before your eyes, and so forth.

"That kind of projection continues that kind of situation. You do get what you concentrate upon. I try to break up blocks of your concentration, and at various times have indeed succeeded, so that creative changes show in all areas, including Ruburt's condition.

"Thus far, however, the old habits have returned, and for all of your joint good intents the idea of bringing things to a crisis point is still far less beneficial than it might appear. This does not mean such a method cannot work at times. It does mean that on the whole it is a difficult method, and in utmost honesty and clarity in that regard, I can only tell you what I have said before: Regardless of how ill-founded it may seem on certain occasions, basically speaking the situation becomes less as you pare it down in your mind, rid it of significance in your mind, say things like: 'Well, after all it is not that bad yet,' or in other ways turn your attention otherwise.

"The main issue of course is not to project negatively into the future, for there you are borrowing trouble. With physical conditions already apparent in the present, you can at least realize that while these [confront] you with a certain evidence, the evidence will indeed change—and can change, and is changing the minute you realize that the evidence, while present, is not inevitably all the evidence available.

"The body is at each and every stage also filled with health and vitality. Those rules do not change. Ruburt is safe and protected. Those reassurances are highly important here now.

"End of session, end of lecture *(heartily)*—and a fond good evening."

("Thank you, Seth."

End at 9:25 P.M. The "crisis point" Seth referred to revolved around the continuous efforts Jane and I had been making to help her; see the opening notes for the session. I hadn't realized she was concerned that I thought she should let her work go on Dreams *and concentrate instead upon our private material, but I was quickly able to convince her that I didn't feel that way.)*

SESSION 934——August 10, 1981
8:27 P.M. MONDAY

Good evening.

("Good evening.")

Dictation to begin.

Man explored the physical world in the dreaming state long before he explored it physically. Such dreams gave him the assurance that other lands existed outside of his own, and spurred him onward into those physical expeditions in which the species has always taken a particular delight.

A man or woman might [be] while dreaming suddenly in strange territory, looking at the sky from a different viewpoint, with, say, a familiar river nowhere in sight, and with a mountain where ordinarily a plain might be. This was in a way as startling an experience as it would be to you to find yourselves on some distant planet. (You do, for that matter, explore space in the same fashion, and on at least some occasions your own "visitors from outer space" are dream travelers from other dimensions of reality. Period.)

(Long pause.) In such a fashion man learned the location of the oceans upon the earth—or at least was given the assurance that such large bodies of water existed, along with clues as to their locations, and the placement of the stars overhead.

Also in the same manner dreams were an aid in navigation, so that they served to let sailors know when land was near before it could be physically perceived—and there is no human activity to which dreams and group dreams have not contributed.

They were of great aid, of course, in human politics, so that through dreams the intents of tribal leaders, say, were known to the others. Some people within the tribe specialized in such dreams, and again, dream content was and is directed by the individual intents, purposes and interests of the dreamer. In a certain manner dreaming, then, helped sharpen such individual tendencies while still directing them toward the public value fulfillment. The person interested most in herbs and plant life would also find that nightly dreams mirrored that daytime pre-occupation, so that nightly dream excursions might find the dreamer examining strange herbs in another location than the native one. Or he might be given knowledge as to how the herbs could best be used for healing purposes. People are natural mimics, as are some animals and birds, so when tribal members related their dreams, they did not just tell them but acted them out with great mobility, carefully mimicking whatever animals or people or elements of land they may have encountered.

(8:47.) The origins of drama began in just that fashion. Tribal leaders were usually chosen only after long "dream investigations," in which the new leader's name cropped up, say, time and time again in the people's dreams. They expected to receive counsel from their dreams. Such information was then aired and shared, studied and examined along with all physical considerations that applied before important decisions were made *(all intently)*.

You do still continue such activity, again, [although] you have turned your conscious minds away from those directions. Most of it does not become conscious because you do not want it to. In some areas, however, with the acceleration of physical travel, certain kinds of dreams *(long pause)* have become more highly pertinent. Families in your society are often broken up, parents and children living quite apart in other portions of the country or in different countries entirely, so dreams that connect you with such relatives have risen to the fore, so to speak. People often keep track of changes in hometowns that they may not have visited for twenty years except in the dream state, when they familiarize themselves with the alterations that have happened, visit beloved streets and houses, or view old classmates.

Very few people make any attempt to check out such information in physical terms. There is an entire global dream network, in other words, that goes quite unrecognized—one of spectacular organization in which exchanges of information occur that give you the basis for the formation of recognized physical events.

If small families kept track of their own family dreams, for example, they could discover unsuspected correlations and sense the interplay of subjective and objective drama with which they are always psychologically involved. Notice what kind of information you seek out from the newspapers, for example. Do you read the front page and ignore sports, or vice versa? Do you read the gossip column? The obituary? Do you seek out stories of lurid crime, or look for further incidents of political chicanery? The answers will show you the kind of material you look for most often. You will to some extent specialize in the same kind of information when you dream. You will organize the contents of your mind and the information available to you according to your own intents and purposes.

(9:05.) One person's dreams, therefore, while his or her own, will still fit into an important notch in the dreams of a given family. One person might, because of his or her own interests, seek largely from dreams warnings of difficulty or trouble, and therefore be the family's dream watchguard—the one who has, say, the nightmares for everyone else. That person will also serve a somewhat similar role in the waking state, as a member of a family. The question in such instances is the reason for such a person's overconcern and alarm in the first place—why the intense interest in such possible catastrophes, or in crime or whatever?—and the answer lies in an examination of the person's feelings and beliefs about the nature of existence itself.

As far as group dreaming is concerned, however, there are still some people who have always served as watchdogs in that regard, while others even in the dream state operate as healers or teachers or explorers or whatever. There is no craft that was not first conceived of by an individual dreamer, who later transferred it to the social world of activity.

In the dreaming state, then, the needs and desires of families, communities and countries are well known. The dream state serves as a rich source for the world's knowledge, and is also therefore responsible for the outgrowth of its technology. This is a highly important point, for "the technological world out there" was at one time the world of dreams. The discoveries and inventions that made the industrial world possible were always latent in man's mind, and represented an inner glittering landscape of probability that he brought into actualization through the use of dreams—the intuitive and the conscious manipulation of material that was at one time latent.

Value fulfillment will always provide inner directions that remind man constantly of the best ways in which such technology can be used. The need to possess such knowledge is uppermost in man's mind now, and so it also becomes a vital dream topic or subject. In the dream state, then, to one extent or another man seeks solutions to the problems of his age.

End of dictation.

(9:23. See Note 1 for an excerpt from the few short paragraphs of personal material Seth gave us before saying good night at 9:35 P.M. Then see Note 2 for what is surely a pretty wild idea of mine.)

NOTES. Session 934

1. "The entire idea of the magical approach," Seth told us, "is of itself sustaining.

"It should remind you of the true effortlessness that is in a fashion responsible for your very existence. When you become overly concerned or worried in any area, remember that you are thinking those thoughts while the process of thinking is utterly effortless. That realization alone can further remind you that the conscious mind does not have to have all (underlined) the information required. It only needs to have the faith that means are available—even if those means are beyond its own scope of activity."

This material very nicely supplements information I'd quoted from the second session Seth gave in his series on the magical approach to reality. Jane delivered that session just a year ago, on August 11, 1980. In Chapter 9 of *Dreams*, see the third part of Note 7 for Session 920.

2. I couldn't help feeling sad and frustrated as I took down Seth's words on dreaming, and Jane reacted in the same way when I read them to her after the session. I'd been especially impressed by this passage (and still am): "There is an entire global dream network, in other words, that goes quite unrecognized—one of spectacular organization in which exchanges of

information occur that give you the basis for the formation of recognized physical events."

We talked about how people could be helped to consciously realize their participation in this worldwide dream organization. Why, I wondered, couldn't the nations of the world set up cooperative studies to verify its existence? At once, I told Jane, I thought that science and religion would be violently opposed to the idea, at least in the beginning, for it would challenge many rigid beliefs held by each of those disciplines. In deeper terms, of course, such a study would actually validate the sources of science and religion [just as it would confirm Seth's material on dreams, incidentally!]. The experiment has the potential for significantly broadening our conscious understanding of the world we're creating.

Setting up such a global organization to study dreams, I told Jane, with some amusement, would probably require a decade of arguing among nations. Would governments gather the information, or independent agencies? How would all of this be paid for, administered and analyzed? How long would it take to acquire statistically significant data? Would the peoples of the world cooperate? I said they most enthusiastically would, for if Seth is right the dream research would have a sound intuitive basis: It would uncover and reinforce many deeper aspects of our individual and collective beings—and I know of few things more important than that consciously we understand ourselves as well as we can in order to meet the great challenges we're creating. But, I said, imagine trying to win the cooperation of the nations of the world for such an undertaking! Actually, it would be quite an advance if we could even agree to begin talking about such a study.

As for myself, I think I've had some good results keeping informed through the dream state about people and events in my home town of Sayre, which lies just across the New York State border in Pennsylvania, and is only 18 miles from the hill house in Elmira. We have seldom visited Sayre in recent years. I dream about it often, however—sometimes with results that have been verified in unexpected ways. Jane plans to use some of those dreams in the book she's planning on Seth's concept of the magical approach to reality.

SESSION 935——August 13, 1981
8:34 P.M. THURSDAY

(We did not hold our regularly scheduled session last night. This evening both of us felt logy after our supper of veal and spaghetti—yet Jane was also restless. Eventually she decided to have the session. "Well, I feel him around," she said with some surprise at 8:33. Then:)

Good evening.

("Good evening.")

Dictation. Now: Dreams occur at so many levels of reality that it is quite impossible to describe their true scope. For one thing, that scope includes levels that are consciously unknown to you. *(Long pause.)* Dreams serve as backup systems also, for example, in the important communications between various peoples or nations—and, particularly when physical communication is cut off between such groups, dreams provide the continuation of information's flow from one part of the species to another.

There are dreams of different import, some triggered genetically, that serve as sparks for particular kinds of behavior— dreams, in other words, that literally span the centuries in that regard, coiled latently in the very chromosomes; and no level of consciousness is without some kind of participation in dream states. In that regard even electrons, for example, dream. Dreaming touches upon both microscopic and macroscopic events, or realities, and is not simply a human characteristic, appropriately appearing within your own range or within your own species. It is instead one area of subjective experience that is everywhere prevailing within the universe.

As I have mentioned many times, animals then dream, as do plants, insects, and all forms of life. All molecular constructions exhibit that certain kind of introspective activity, as if the inner working of some giant computer was intimately in touch not only with its own programming and the probabilities connected with it, but with a deep psychological awareness of the activities of the electrons and various visible and invisible particles that form its own physical construction.

(Long pause at 8:50.) You are bound to have, then, many larger dream formations that can only be called group dreams—subjective events in which your own dreams happen, and in which your own dreams take part. You expect all of the elements of the

physical world, however diverse, to fit together and form a certain kind of permanency and order. It should be no surprise, then, that this same kind of "fitting together" includes subjective life also—or that, say, your private dreams are also fragments in a vaster dream reality. They are as important to the operation of that reality as electrons are to your physical one *(long pause)*, providing inner pathways for the accumulation of wisdom and pleasure.

There are certain kinds of dreams in which the various species then communicate, and in which the energies of the environment and its inhabitants merge. These include a kind of horizontal psychological extension, the translation of one kind of dream into another kind—the transference of information from one system to another, in which the symbols themselves come alive.

I can only hope to evoke some feeling within you that is reminiscent of your own actual behavior at those hidden levels of dreaming activity, but they have remained highly pertinent in the development of all species with their environments, keeping the intents and purposes of one alive in the other. I have told you that in actuality, now, no genetic knowledge is gone from the earth. It does not vanish. It is retained in latent form within a kind of backup system, so that in terms of probabilities each species carries within its own genetic patterns the blueprints and specializations of each other's genetic sequence.

Those sequences follow the pursuits of value fulfillment so smoothly that they can be reactivated whenever the conditions are fortunate—for even the animals are not concerned with simple survival alone, nor the plants, but with what I can only call *(long pause)* emotional qualities: qualities that seek a full appreciation and creative extension of those conditions of consciousness that stamp each species as itself and yet join it with all others.

(Long pause at 9:10, then all intently:) In a fashion your own dreams operate or appear as electrons in other realities. That is, they change their form, their subjective force or direction, and become part of the working mechanics of the universe. The same applies to your own thoughts. They are not "wasted" after you have thought them *(with humor)*, or simply discarded. They do not become extinct either, but go on to serve other functions in the universe than those with which you are presently aware.

(Slowly:) This all involves a lush multitudinous creativity. The pleasure principle can probably be likened most to the latent appreciation of beauty that is everywhere apparent if you <u>look</u> for it: the ecstasy of each form of life for the wonders of its <u>own</u> existence, in which love's values go beyond themselves, and yet a condition in which each species or life form "realizes" that its own fulfillment adds immeasurably to the existence of all other forms.

End of session. We did manage at least to hint of some material that almost exists on the edge—the very edge—of any rational understanding. My heartiest regards and a fond good evening.

("Thank you."

9:32 P.M. "Wow," Jane said as soon as she was out of trance. "Now that's funny, 'cause I didn't feel that much with it when I started out. But I came to feel that I was *right with it, right close to some kind of important knowledge that I could communicate at the same time. Like you were* almost *speaking the unspeakable, you know? Quite wild. Or you stretched yourself as far as you could possibly stretch. . . . When I'm speaking for Seth, it's a different kind of knowing that you try to pull down. It's a great feeling."*

And I told her that she'd given an excellent session indeed, and that I wished such important material was common knowledge.)

CHAPTER 11

The Magical Approach, and the Relationships Between "Conservation" and Spontaneous Developments

SESSION 936——November 17, 1981
8:35 P.M. TUESDAY

(Three months ago, way back on August 13, following the outline she'd written on July 8 for The Magical Approach to Reality: A Seth Book,[1] *Jane began work on the first draft for Chapter 1 of that project. That same evening she held the final session, the 935th, for Chapter 10 of* Dreams. *Since then she's given but two short private sessions, on November 9 and 12. All through those weeks her physical states had fluctuated considerably. Seth reassured her in both sessions. In the first of the two he remarked that "Ruburt is still dealing with spin-off material following or resulting from his sinful-self data. . . ." In the second one he stressed that although Jane was still afraid of spontaneous bodily relaxation, "[Ruburt] is safe, supported and protected—that is, of course, the message that he is trying to get through his head at this time."*

Before going into our chronology of personal events for those three months, however, I want to continue my brief study of the affairs—really the consciousnesses—involving Three Mile Island, Iran, and the war between Iran and Iraq. I last dealt with those subjects in the first, 933rd session for Chapter 10.

Ever since the accident to the nuclear reactor of Unit No. 2 at TMI, 31 months ago, the reactor's great containment building and an auxiliary structure have been flooded with highly radioactive water. [It grew to be over eight and a half feet deep in the reactor building.] Utility engineers now have in operation a filtering system to decontaminate before storage the nearly one million gallons of water in the two buildings. The job is to take around nine months; the processed water will finally be disposed of in 1983; the filters holding the radioactive material will be trucked to facilities in Idaho and Washington State for testing and storage. Yet to come are the removal of the reactor's cover, its damaged core, and the decontamination of the buildings themselves.

Because of the opposition of local people and Pennsylvania officials, utility executives have not been allowed to restart Unit No. 1, which was shut down for refueling at the time of the accident. The cleanup at TMI must proceed regardless of whether Unit No. 2 is repaired or decommissioned, or whether the entire plant is closed down. The Nuclear Regulatory Commission has rejected the idea of a sealed-up radioactive power plant sitting on its island in the Susquehanna River; the danger of eventual uncontrolled contamination, including seepage into the river, is too great.[2]

The killing in Iran continues—and hardly just because of that country's war with Iraq. At the end of August, only two months after the group assassination by bomb explosions of more than 150 leading officials of the Islamic Republican Party, both the president and the prime minister of Iran were killed by another bomb; so were six other men. This time a leader of the Mujahedin-e Khalq, the largest of the resistance groups in the country, announced to some of our news media that the killings had been carried out by his organization.

Yet American specialists on Iran do not believe that even those two severe decimations of its leadership will result in the collapse of the Iranian government. In their opinions none of the guerrilla resistance organizations would be able to run the country—deal with its growing economic difficulties, say, or its other great challenges. Nor, despite Western fears, does the Russian-oriented Tudeh, Iran's Communist Party, seem anxious to take over; instead, the leaders of the Tudeh are support-

ing the government [at least so far], just as the armed forces do. Despite the appearance that the revolution in Iran—made up as it is of all of those diverse consciousnesses—is feeding upon itself in very destructive ways, in ordinary terms, civil war does not appear to be likely. Yet. And the Iraqi conflict goes on.[3]

I'd never seen Jane hesitate for so many months over beginning a new project, as she had with Magical Approach. Usually she just plunged right into her latest creative inspiration, and that she hadn't done so this time was to me a clear sign of her long-range, general physical-emotional state. I continued to reassure her [as Seth did also] after she'd finished Chapter 10, for I was deeply frustrated and concerned for her. There wasn't anything else I could offer that she would affirm. As the weeks passed she denied more than once that she was depressed. Watching my wife over the years, I'd long ago come to feel that I was observing someone who was following a chosen course with incredible ability and determination. Nor is it contradictory of me even now to note that Jane's path is quite in accord with her basically innocent, mystical nature—for her acceptance of her nature makes possible her explorations of it in her own unique ways. When she does mourn her impaired state, it's still never with that tired old question directed at a supposedly unjust and uncaring nature: "Why me?" She just keeps trying to grapple with her challenges.

And she does well at times. When she began writing Magical Approach, she even surprised me by occasionally helping me get breakfast, cooking bacon and eggs at the hot plate I'd set up for her some seven months ago on the kitchen table.[4] Although she could work at the table while sitting down, she'd given up those simple, nurturing acts of food preparation many weeks ago; her fingers weren't working well enough, she told me at the time; she didn't trust herself enough to handle hot food—and I admit that when she implied a risk, the chance of an accident, I stopped encouraging her to help me with meals.

By August, however, Jane hadn't "walked," even by leaning upon her typing table and pushing it before her, for over eight months; she was still getting around the hill house in either her wheeled office chair, or the old straight chair I'd equipped with casters last June. She'd failed in her last attempt to get on her feet a few days after I'd finished working on the straight chair.[5]

From the 19th of August through the 28th, then, Jane worked on Chapter 2 of Magical Approach.[6] Three days later, when she was writing Chapter 3, we received from an editor in the trade production

department of Prentice-Hall the frontmatter proofs for If We Live
Again. *They were easy for Jane to check, and she called in her approval
of the few little changes that had already been made.*

*Early in September—magically appearing as though from another
reality, for we'd quite forgotten about the situation—we received through
Prentice-Hall six copies of the reprinted Dutch-language edition of* Seth
Speaks. *This time the publisher in the Netherlands, Ankh-Hermes, had
not cut* Seth Spreekt.[7]

*Right after that Sue Watkins called from her home in upstate New
York to tell us that she'd just received from Prentice-Hall her first printed
copy of Volume 2 of* Conversations With Seth. *She's to send us an
autographed copy after more reach her. Both Jane and I congratulated
her on producing a fine pair of books. Even though we could hardly be
called impartial, we knew that in her long account of much that had
taken place in Jane's ESP classes, Sue had produced superior work both
for herself and for us, through her viewpoint offering new dimensions
and insights concerning what all three of us—four, counting Seth!—
had been, and still are, trying to do. Our copy of* Conversations *did
arrive from Sue early in October. Seeing it cheered Jane—yet my wife
continued to hassle [as she put it] her efforts on* Magical Approach,
*asking herself again and again whether she really wanted to do that book.
Her intuitions always affirmed that she did. It was often difficult going
for her, though:* Magical Approach *still wasn't flowing the way she
wanted it to.*

*Then on October 23 Jane's creative contentions led to her "attend"
material—in which she picked up from Seth that her only responsibility
in life is to herself: "Attend to what is directly before you." Seth told her
that she bore no onus to save the world. In relief, Jane wrote a short poem
to accompany Seth's message, then wrote further that she "realized that
like many I'd become afraid of faith itself." I've presented this cluster of
material in the frontmatter for Volume 1 of* Dreams. *Her insight helped
both of us. However, she hadn't had a session, regular or private, in over
10 weeks [since August 13], so on October 27 she recorded in her journal
the continuance of her daily creative struggles: "And once again I'm way
behind in sessions and writing. This* A.M. *I 'worked' from midnight to
3—without getting anything done. I wonder about the advisability of the
entire project* [Magical Approach]. *Where had the magic gone? Where
was my inspiration? Those were my thoughts when it occurred to me that
I should be writing them down, because they're part of the whole picture.
I felt better. . . ."*

Following her latest self-renewal of faith, Jane started to notice some physical improvements. One very unusual way these showed themselves began on the evening of October 31, when four younger people who had been members of ESP class visited us from New York City.[8] They'd been scouting the Elmira area for other ex-students, to see if any of them had old class tapes of Jane speaking for Seth and/or singing in Sumari; they had had some success in their searches, but we didn't play any of the tapes that night.[9]

Jane and I thought it most interesting that within 29 days [in October] various events—the arrival of Volume 2 of Conversations, *Jane's coming through with her "attend" material and poetry, the visit of her former students, and even her contentions with* Magical Approach— *had helped her rejuvenate her sense of physical ease and well-being on at least three separate occasions. She wrote more notes, more poetry. We kept trying to encourage her new motions, of the kind described in Note 8, but they began to taper off.*

Through all of our challenges, we were aware of at least some of the incredible variety of positive and negative world events in the news—the bombings and the peace talks, the sports contests and the religious controversies, the national strikes and the latest developments in the arts. Amid the economic difficulties in our own country, and after a number of often very expensive delays, the second flight of our shuttle spacecraft, Columbia, *came due on November 4. Of primary importance was to be the testing in space of the 50-foot-long remote-control robot arm, which had been designed to place satellites in orbit and retrieve them for service and repair. Only seconds before lift-off, however, computers shut down Columbia's flight because of a drop in pressure in oxygen tanks. Then clogged oil filters were discovered. The launch was rescheduled for November 12.*

At the beginning of these notes I wrote that three months passed after Jane finished Chapter 10 of Dreams *before she held her next session—a private one—on November 9. In that short session Seth sought to add his reassurances to Jane's own, and to mine as well.[10] On the 12th Columbia was launched as scheduled, but only after another delay caused by the failure of an electronic decoding unit. Then within a few hours after lift-off, the shuttle's crew had to deal with the malfunction of one of the ship's three fuel cells. Mission officials decided that for reasons of safety Columbia would land after a two-day flight instead of staying up for the planned five days; the 83 orbits were reduced to 36. The crew did successfully test the orbiter's multijointed robot arm, however. In the meantime, on the evening of the 12th, following his suggestion that she resume the sessions on a twice-weekly basis, Jane spoke for Seth in another private session. That one too was short.*[11]

Five nights later—at 8:35 P.M., Tuesday, November 17, 1981—she held the first, 936th session for Chapter 11 of Dreams. *Here are the notes for the session itself:*

Jane seems to be considering a switch from our Monday-Wednesday session routine to one of Tuesday-Thursday.

We have an excellent stone fireplace in the living room of the hill house, and often during the winter months I used to build a fire in it at suppertime; we ate while sitting on the couch. Jane and I really enjoyed all of the deep implications conjured up by the wood fires. We had the fireplace cleaned a couple of years ago, however, and with that break in routine I gave up using it: By then my time had become so taken up each day with what seemed like an endless list of things to do—with trying to help Jane, with working, with running the house, with answering the mail and so forth—that I just stopped making fires.

Early this morning we heard strange scratching sounds on the other side of the closed fireplace damper. These soon became intermixed with a series of musical chitterings and chatterings. A bird, or birds? We didn't think so. Next we speculated about squirrels, since there are plenty of them living in the woods out back—yet the sounds didn't seem quite right for one or more of those creatures, either. The noises stopped after an hour or so.

They hadn't resumed by session time. Jane leaned back on the couch with her feet up on the coffee table, and I sat facing her with my notebook propped up on one knee; the fireplace was only a couple of feet in back of me. Soon after 8:20 Jane began to "feel Seth around." Right away I learned that the session was to be one of her slower ones. I've indicated just a few of the many long pauses she used in trance.)

Now—

("Good evening.")

—good evening, and dictation. Beginning of the next chapter *(11),* which will be entitled: "The Magical Approach *(very long pause, eyes closed),* and the Relationships Between 'Conservation' *(very long pause)* and Spontaneous Developments"—and give us a moment.

(Pause.) In a fashion dreams allow for a curious mixture of learning processes, while at the same time serving to introduce surprising developments. Period. That is, dreams promote the

conservation of knowledge. They are an aid in the development of skills. They conserve available information by weaving it through the other structures of your experience.

At the same time dreams have their startling qualities, promoting the insertion of unexpected developments, in which case they appear to deal with the breaking down of conserving principles. In this fashion they also mirror your more exterior behavior, conserving what you know already, and yet introducing new patterns, new spontaneous orders that would sometimes seem to run against conservative issues. They reinforce the past, for example, when you dream of past situations. They also seem to undermine the integrity of the past by showing it to you in an unfamiliar light, mixing it with present and future tints.

(8:49.) Many people might wish that I would add many more methods to help you study dreams and their nature. In such a manner also dreams suggest nature's spontaneous order throughout the centuries, and allow you to look at the species in a truer light. Your lives, for that matter, are dependent upon the curious relationships that are involved. Colon: You would not get by for one day if the conserving principles and the unexpected did not exist exactly as they do. There is so much you must learn and remember in life, and so much you must spontaneously forget—otherwise, action itself would be relatively meaningless.

You perform far more actions in a day than you recall. You do not know how many times you lift your arms, speak a sentence, think a thought. With the kind of consciousness you possess, an overreliance upon conserving principles could then end up in a reduction of life's processes.

(9:01.) In private living and in so-called evolutionary terms, however, life necessitates the intrusion of surprising events, unforeseen actions, leaps of insight or behavior that could not come alone from any accumulation of knowledge or simple conservation of energy, but seem to suggest entirely different new developments.

Dreams often serve as the frameworks in which sudden remarkable insights appear that later enable a man or a woman to envision the world in a way that was not earlier predictable. The world's activities always include the insertion of surprising events. This is true at all levels of nature, from microscopic to macroscopic. As I have said before, all systems are open. The theories of both evolutionists and creationists strongly suggest and reinforce beliefs in the consecutive nature of time, and in a universe that begins in such-and-such a fashion, continuing on to such-and-such an end—but there are horizontal events that appear in the true activity of nature, and there are horizontal entry points and exit points in all experience. These allow for the insertion of unofficial new energy, the introduction of surprising events. Period.

(Long pause at 9:13.) Again, it is very difficult to explain such activities. They can affect—and do affect—the rise and fall of civilizations. You are used to reading nature in a particular manner, however, and to experiencing events at surface levels. You are naturally equipped to appreciate a far richer blend, and as I have often said, you are yourselves possessed of a need to explore the subjective ramifications of your existence.

As "the times change" you tire of the old ways. Even your dreams begin to reach out into new avenues. The relationships between nature's natural conservative behavior and nature's need for innovation are stretched. More and more remarkable events begin to occur, both in private and mass experience, in physical and mental behavior, in the events, say, of both stars and man.

People want, then, to throw aside old structures of belief. They yearn, often without recognizing it, for the remembered knowledge of early childhood, when it seems that they experienced for a time a dimension of experience in which the unexpected was taken for granted, when "magical events" occurred quite naturally. They begin to look at the structure of their lives in a different fashion, that attempts to evoke from nature, and from their own natures, some graceful effortlessness, some freedom nearly forgotten. They begin to turn toward a more natural and a more magical approach to their own lives. At such times the conserving elements in nature and in society itself do not seem as strong as they did before. Surprising events that were earlier covered up or ignored seem to appear with greater frequency, and everywhere a new sense of quickness and acceleration gradually alters the expectations of people in regard to the events of their own lives, and to the behavior they expect from others. You are in such times now.

Old honored explanations suddenly appear withered. Unpredictable remarkable events seem more possible. The kind of work done in dreams to some extent is changed. They become more active, more intrusive. Predictable behavior, even of the natural elements, is harder to take for granted. Man begins to sense more and more at such times the vaster dimensions of behavior upon which that appearance of conservation resides.

(9:43.) There are considerable changes that occur under such conditions in man's subjective experience. Man's feelings about himself change too, but little by little his trust in unpredictability grows. He is more willing to assign himself to it. The species begins its own kind of psychic migration. It begins to sense within itself further frontiers and the possibilities for action. It begins to yearn for the exploration of mental lands, and it sends portions of itself out as couriers.

End of dictation.

(9:50.) Now: Ruburt is that kind of courier. There are many in all areas of life, and this involves not only an excitement on the part of your own species, but the same kind of curiosity and excitement on the part of other species as well. Again, most difficult to explain—but those connections that exist between all species and the environment are themselves affected. The horizontal communications stretch and expand to allow for later developments in terms of probabilities, for consciousness always knows itself in more than one context, and it is possible for nature to experience itself in ways that would seem to be most improbable when the properties of conservation and learning are at their (underlined) strongest spring.

End of session.

("Do you want to say something about all of those vitamins Jane is taking these days?" We had talked about this earlier today.)

Not this evening—but I will have material for you there, and on Ruburt shortly, when some new insights on his own will allow me to make further points than those I could make at present. End of session, and my fondest good wishes.

("Thank you. Good night.")

10:01 P.M. Jane vaguely remembered Seth's puzzling continuation of book work after he'd said dictation was over for the evening. I told her I thought he'd triggered his extra material himself through talking about our species' couriers. I'm pleased that he said Jane is such a one. I don't

*remember him describing her before in just that way; it's another insight
into her chosen mystical-psychic role in physical life "this time around."*)

NOTES. Session 936

1. In Chapter 10 of *Dreams*, see the opening notes for Session
933.

2. The cleanup costs at Three Mile Island are now projected at
more than $1.5 billion, and will continue to increase. Many gov-
ernment officials and private analysts now believe that if the
operating risks associated with nuclear power generating plants
do not ultimately shut down many of them, their economic dilemmas will. I don't know whether the nuclear power industry in
the United States will die, but it's in great trouble: Various studies show that around half of the 90 reactors under construction
could be replaced by more economical coal-fired plants, containing excellent pollution-control equipment. By the late 1980s
power from those new nuclear plants will be 25 percent more
expensive than it would be if generated from coal.

There are plenty of more immediate challenges. For example:
The staff of the Nuclear Regulatory Commission has asked the
operators of more than 40 nuclear plants to check for cracks in
the walls of the vessels encasing their pressurized-water reactors
(which are the kind installed at TMI). Evidence is accumulating
that the vessels are becoming embrittled by neutron radiation
from the reactors much more quickly than their designers had
anticipated. Small cracks have been found, but not all areas are
reachable for testing. A rupture of a typical pressure vessel
could result in an uncontrollable release of radiation into a containment building not designed to handle such a situation. If the
building itself was breached, the escaping radiation could cause
some 48,000 deaths, 250,000 nonfatal cancers and injuries,
5,000 first-generation birth defects, render 200 square miles un-
inhabitable, require decontamination of another 3,200 square
miles, and damage other properties worth many billions of dollars. No protection against that kind of accident has ever been
required by the NRC. The forces of consciousness at work would
seem to be incredible—beyond our grasp.

3. When the leaders of Iraq ordered the invasion of Iran 14 months ago, they expected to win the war in three weeks. They proclaimed that the war had really begun over 1,300 years ago, at the battle of Qaddisiya in A.D. 637, when Moslem Arabs drove the Persians, who are Indo-European, from Iraq. (Iraq was called Mesopotamia then, and until 1935 Persia was the name for Iran.)

In a passionate, bloody series of events later in the seventh century, a split occurred in which the Moslem religion was divided into two main branches, the Shiite and the Sunni. Now Iran is ruled by the Shiites, and is religiously oriented; Iraq is ruled by the Sunnis, and is more secular and socialistic. Iranian leaders emphasize the religious aspects of the war, Iraq the ethnic. The rulers of each country have urged the citizens of the other to revolt against *their* leaders. There is much disillusionment in Iran over the excesses of the Shiite clergy. In Iran martyrdom is encouraged—at home, in the war, and in terroristic activity abroad. Iraq has been accused of using chemical warfare (courtesy of the Russians) against its enemy. The Moslem world, then, is hardly a monolithic entity; as within Iran itself, the myriad consciousnesses making up that whole framework are much too varied for that to be true.

At least partially because of their brutal history, Iranians—Persians—are strongly self-centered; preservation of the self is given an overriding impetus. The world is seen as being full of peril. Causality, the interrelation of cause and effect, is often ignored or misunderstood in the Iranian quest for immediate advantage. Influence counts for much more than obligation; the concept of long-term mutual trust is seen as basically adversarial; goodwill means little. Yet, such egocentric characteristics often are sublimated into the seemingly contradictory practice of martyrdom—the two are united within the Iranian interpretation of Moslem theology. In a land ruled by a body of theocratic law the needs of the country must ultimately prevail, as in the case of attack from without, say. There is no area in which Moslemic precepts do not apply.

Rather ironically, not all Moslems want the Americans to leave the Middle East, as the terrorists have announced they must do. And the government of Iran, in spite of its great hatred for our country, is pragmatic enough to join it in a very efficient exchange of large sums of money; these transactions, in part to settle business claims against Iran, are a portion of the arrangements made last January to free the American hostages.

4. Following superscript number 7 in the opening notes for Session 931, in Chapter 9 of *Dreams*, see my information on how we were trying to cope with Jane's physical difficulties back in March 1981.

5. After superscript number 14 in the opening notes for Session 931, see my accounts of tailoring the straight chair for Jane, and of her vain attempts to get on her feet.

6. My ever-present concern for Jane would certainly have turned into outright fear had I seen at once the long, untitled poem she wrote on August 26, concurrently with her work on the second chapter for *Magical Approach*. She didn't put the poem into its final form, and she didn't show it to me. Not that she tried to hide it. Neither of us may tell or show the other everything—I just hadn't been present when she wrote the poem, and she let it lie in her 1981 journal, where I "accidentally" came across it some time later. Even when I did find the poem I became sad, then frightened, then more hopeful as I read it, and I knew at once that I'd have to insert it here in *Dreams*. For Jane *had* been depressed when she wrote her poem. Perhaps it was her poetic art of expression that helped me identify so strongly with her emotions, but I suddenly felt that even I had never really understood the myriad depths of her challenges and her reactions to them. In the poem I saw expressed anew her ancient fear of abandonment, along with her dilemmas over her lack of mobility—and my fright was engendered by what I thought were signs that she might choose to leave this physical reality for good. To die. (I'd had similar feelings seven months before she held this 936th session: In Note 13 for Session 931, in Chapter 9, see my comments following the excerpts from the private session for April 15, 1981.)

Jane might have shortened her poem had she written a final draft; rather, I decided that the reader should see just how she had spontaneously and poetically contended with her challenges on a particular day. In order to save space here, however, in each stanza I'm "running together" her characteristically short lines, separating them with the diagonals, or virgules, that are standard in this kind of presentation:

Something in me / ebbs and tides, / as if I let myself /
for a while / be washed away / out to sea / while leaving /
some spidery shell / upon the shore / dry and shriveled, /
scarce alive. / [yet] with fierce / mouth and eyes /
half alive. / But ah, that half / is passionate /
and filled with / life's yearning.

The other part, / dispassionate, / flows together /
with the waves / past world and rock / dispersed as mist, /
beyond impediments / uncaring / while my heart /
in the fragile shell / calls out, / "Come back /
dear counterpart. / I am exhausted, / near dying, /
a partially empty / shell, paper-thin / with all my /
life alive / and flaming / only in my head / but nearly /
unstirring. / How can you leave me / in such a state, /
vulnerable / and exposed?"

Sometimes there is / no reply at all, as if /
my voice itself / turns into mist / or is lost in /
the waves pounding / until it seems / I am indeed /
abandoned, / separated from / some forgotten self /
who has gone elsewhere / without me, / so that the gulf /
between us / is so distant / that messages sent back /
and forth / now take so long / to reach me /
that only future / generations / of myself /
would be here to / catch their meaning.

Then I hear— / as I think I did / this morning— /
some response / that says, / "Who do you think / sent me /
on such a journey / if not yourself / who said, /
'Don't worry / about me. I'll make out / but hurry— /
go while the tide / is full and take /
advantage of its motion, / to which I'll add /
all of mine / I can afford to lend. / Let yourself be carried
where the flesh / in its sweet cowardice / would be afraid to
follow.' / And so I did."

I scarcely remember / but recognize the voice / and feel /
some distant tide of motion / turning back, /
some mythical self / carrying / a million messages /
beyond the known / and exotic treasures back /
to where I'm waiting.

And a rush of motion shifts / my dry wrists /
minute yet violent, / so that I startle (shudder) /
who have been / motionless so long. / The spidery shell that /
holds my heart / is lifted at one edge /
as if by a sudden wind / and coiled / dry tendrils /
of nerves and muscles / unwind themselves. /
My color changes, / my white parchment / skin turns coral, /
minute wrinkles disappearing. / My shape begins /
to fill out again / as I sense a / strange self returning . . . /
more swiftly now / mind-stroking / the giant waves /
of the unknown / mental sea.

Little by little / my strength arouses. / My muscles unravel /
which have been / folded tight, / saved for future use, /
and I sit up now / running brittle fingers /
through my sun-dried hair. / I say, "We went too far /
my friend. / From now on we'll / have to go together /
just out as far as I can / walk or swim—or I'll go /
mind-traveling with you. / But I won't stay home /
alone again, / appliances turned down / halfway, waiting."

"Nor will you have to." / The voice is clearer now /
until it sounds / from my own mouth / (vibrant, loud) /
no longer distant. / We chatter half / the night together /
while I shake / the webs of remoteness /
from fingers and toes. / My shell / grew soft as a web /
then it fell apart / and was whisked off sighing /
in the morning / wind. / All around us /
the beach gathers the / precious images /
that leap up suddenly / in the dark, coming in with /
the tide that unites / the tides of the heart.

My counterpart says, / "Those treasures / are marked with /
your name / and will be arriving / each day for a while, /
marvelous surprises / from the most mysterious / of places. /
But I've grown wiser too— / how good to find you /
waiting for me here. / No journey is worth /
disturbing our harmony, / the self's unity, /
and to the undivided / self / all journeys / are possible."

"Right now I just want / to stand up whole / and walk across /
the beach," I said. / And arm in arm / we did, /
smiling our double-single smile.

I cherished Jane's ending for her poem, for in it she'd reaffirmed at least the possibility of her self healing itself. Yet, my hope was tempered even as my fear lessened, for she hadn't mentioned outright the integration of a more understanding sinful self into her psyche. Jane's physical challenges, her symptoms, are with her *now*, I thought, and we must deal with them on the way to rejuvenation. I was left caught as we talked after I'd read her poem: suspended between despair for my wife and the hope that she would choose to go on living, in our terms.

7. In Chapter 2 of *Dreams,* in Volume 1, see Note 1 for Session 885, which we held on October 24, 1979. Through a series of misunderstandings, the people at Ankh-Hermes had published an abridged translation of *Seth Speaks* without having permission for the cutting from Jane and me. We still feel regret that the company had to go to all of that extra expense in order to publish a second edition of the book. I also wrote that "all concerned must wait for at least another year before a full-length version of *Seth Speaks* will be published in the Dutch language." Actually, almost two years passed before we received our copies of the new edition.

I also mentioned our challenges with Ankh-Hermes in Chapter 5 for Volume 1. See the notes opening Session 902, which Jane held in February 1980, four months after coming through with the 885th session.

8. Our four visitors had become our dear friends long ago. I was sure that, by arriving just when they did, they contributed much to Jane's latest improvements. They offered enthusiasm and faith and reinforcement to both of us, and renewed in us a fine nostalgia for old, seemingly more innocent times—even though all of us knew that that was illusory: Basically, those class days, those class years, couldn't have been any more innocent than any other times; it was just that hindsight helped!

I've slightly paraphrased portions of Jane's entry in her journal for November 2, 1981. These events show once again her body's incredibly tough, creative, and ceaseless attempts to right itself and carry on—when it was allowed to respond to faith:

"Some really beneficial and odd developments are taking place in my physical condition," Jane wrote, "generally starting last Saturday night (October 31) when the kids visited from NYC—students I haven't seen in nearly two years. During their visit I noticed that my right leg, propped up on the coffee table, would suddenly fall very quickly and unexpectedly to the floor.

Then they left. When company had gone I talked to Rob and nodded and dozed—then again my leg suddenly dropped and entire body turned independently of my will or intent to the left. This happened several times. Then in a moment of dozing I suddenly found my body moving forward, half standing, with strong energy and more or less natural motion—all by itself.

"Effects continued on Sunday. Once my right arm suddenly moved out to the left, throwing my pack of cigarettes I was holding to the floor with sudden energy. Then late Sunday night I watched TV, dozing off a few minutes at a time—I came to, frightened, to find myself half off the couch and on the floor, trying to get onto my chair; yelled for Rob, who was in another room. He helped me back. Then a long dream experience in which my body was clearing itself."

Very briefly: More so than Jane is, I think, I'm intrigued by and susceptible to nostalgia. I create a feeling for it. I used to equate the emotion with sentimentality—but leaving aside the basic merits of the latter, I've come to understand that nostalgia, growing out of its inevitable counterpart, memory, represents a facet of Seth's idea of simultaneous time. For if past, present and future exist together (and continue to develop), then I see nostalgia as expressing a legitimate searching by the conscious mind as it seeks to grasp that the past exists now, and is not "dead." The quest for nostalgia is one way to bring the living past up-to-date. The yearning I feel each time I drive past the apartment house Jane and I lived in for 15 years, just west of the business section of Elmira, represents my conscious reunification of the past with the present, and even a projection of both into the future in ordinary terms.

When I look up at those three high, old-fashioned bay windows that illuminate the living room of Apartment 4, on the second floor of that house, I visualize Jane sitting behind them at her oak table, thinking and writing, intrigued and comforted by the busy patterns of people and automobiles traversing the intersection she looks down upon: Walnut and West Water Streets. And behind those windows, at night in that living room, she paces back and forth for hours at a time after she begins to speak for Seth in December 1963. She holds ESP classes there. Accordingly, then, a Jane Roberts Butts and a Robert F. Butts live in that apartment I'm creating. I think my nostalgia for those days reinforces our activities in larger realms of consciousness, as well as in our "present" joint reality, in which my wife is now chair-bound.

(Note: All of the photographs of Jane that appear in *The Seth Material* were taken in the living room of Apartment 4 early in 1970; glimpses of the room appear in those shots. The first and last photos show Jane before the bay window that faces the northwest, with the trees and the backs of the houses lining the east side of Walnut Street in view.)

9. Jane held her ESP classes for seven and a half years (from September 1967 through February 1975). Those gatherings were disrupted almost seven years ago, when we moved from our downtown apartments into the hill house, and for a number of reasons we did not resume them. Strange it may be, but Jane and I have never conducted a search for class artifacts, as our friends had just been doing, and as other former students had done before. We grew up without modern conveniences like portable tape recorders, of course, but even so our natural creative desires had always been to express ourselves graphically, in written and printed words and in drawn and painted images. They still are. In addition, Jane's impetus is to continue driving forward; that's her way, even though each project grows—as it must—out of the past. (I've shown in *Dreams* that many of her physical symptoms have resulted from conflicts between those spontaneous urges, and entrenched beliefs that revolve around her sinful self and tell her that such activity is wrong.)

We always liked the idea, however, that others were recording class events and were keeping tapes for us if and when we wanted them; we also liked the idea that it was safer to have the tapes scattered about instead of being kept in one place. In class Jane might have listened to portions of a tape as it was being made, or immediately after class was over, but seldom would I hear her playing the same tape later—if we had a copy of it, that is. She's fascinated to hear herself speak as Seth, and sing in Sumari, but she always wants to move on. I simply have never devoted myself to collecting tapes. I don't want to overstate the issue, but neither does Jane pay that much attention to a book once it has been published. She does reread various private sessions, usually those in which Seth discusses matters relating to her symptoms. Until this year (1981) she would occasionally re-

play one of the few tapes we'd made together, or use our recorder when writing poetry. She gradually gave up working that
way, however, as it became more and more difficult for her to
exert enough finger pressure on the recorder's keys.

10. Seth dealt with our personal challenges for almost all of this
session on Monday evening, November 9. After supper Jane had
announced that she wanted to try for a session—she didn't know
whether it would be private, for *Dreams*, or on other material.
She'd just finished rereading a number of book sessions. She was
both nervous and impatient at the prospect of her first session
since last August. Here are excerpts:

"Ruburt is still dealing with spinoff material following or resulting from his sinful-self data," Seth said, "and this material
generally follows the lines of development that are fairly obvious
in the poems and notes [he has written] since that time.

"He knows what I am referring to. Some small portions are
not as yet typed, and should be, for the typing alone of that
material will act as an impetus. The entire sinful-self material
should be reviewed. He did indeed become afraid of faith itself.

"He is presently encountering that kind of feeling, uncovering
the reasons for it, and trying to recapture in a way the very
young innocent self's sense of faith. That faith existed even before churchly doctrine was imposed over it. He is trying to uncover his own natural faith. That attempt, of course, brings him
into conflict with whatever doubts still stand in his way.

"The body, again, does possess such a natural faith, and it has
nothing to do with esoteric methods, and so forth—but, again,
deals with a kind of self-evident biological knowledge. There is a
more emotional charge connected with those issues, hence the
temporary feelings of panic, for example. These should be discussed. I will have further pertinent material to add to the overall category of Ruburt's situation, but I am simply making this
evening's session to give him a sense of immediate direction.

"I know how to quicken the impetus of the psyche, to give it a
gentle nudge in the proper direction, to insert a hint of reassur-
ance, and with this session that is my intent. The sinful self's
material serves as a small psychic source at the moment: That is,
he still reacts to it, and the same material may appear from
different viewpoints."

(To me at 9:14:) "I will also have comments concerning your

own reactions, and I suggest—but only suggest—that again your usual two sessions a week be held, as a framework for the therapeutic endeavors.

"I did briefly give him a message *(on October 23, 1981):* Attend to what is before you, for it is there for a reason. In each person's life, and in your own, at each and every point of your existence, the solutions to your problems, or the means of achieving those solutions, are always as apparent—or rather as present—within your days as is any given problem itself. What I mean is quite simple: The solutions already exist in your lives. You may not have put them together yet, or organized them in the necessary ways. The solutions in Ruburt's case lie in all of those areas with which you are normally concerned—the mail, the sessions, the psychic abilities. When you attend to what is there with the proper magical attitude of mind, then the altered organizations can take place.

"A belief in a 'god who provides,' by whatever name, is indeed a psychological requirement for the good health of the body and mind. Ruburt did not want to face such issues. *(Long pause.)* He felt that they opened the door to all of organized religion's psychological quicksand of emotionalism. The sinful-self material is doing its work, opening the necessary doorways of desire and intent. When Ruburt has typed those small later poems, the path will seem much clearer to him. The innocent self is being uncovered.

"Ruburt is dealing with quite profound material involving the self's relationship with its source—this material being worked out in your current situations. The solutions will automatically lead him not only to a solution in practical terms, but toward the areas of development that he has been seeking *(emphatically),* while being afraid of them at the same time."

Jane smiled after Seth had left us. She was pleased that she'd had the session: "I still get scary after a layoff." She knew what material Seth wanted her to type. I should note our disappointment that those strange, new and quick bodily motions she'd experienced just a week ago had soon tapered off. See Note 8 for this session.

11. These insights from the material Seth gave Jane and me on Thursday evening, November 12, show how he continued to try to help us help her:

"Now: It is the effortlessness, the spontaneous relaxation, that worries Ruburt, in that it is not specifically decided upon at any given point, but seems to happen by itself.

"Ruburt's body is allowing itself to relax, particularly on the couch when his back is supported. Tension is being relieved, and often this sudden lessening of tension also frightens him. It is excellent therapy on the part of the body, of a fairly temporary nature. It breaks down, however, many strong elements of control after control continually being applied. These are of excellent benefit. Rigidity is drained from the body by such methods. He is safe, supported and protected—that is, of course, the message that he is trying to get through his head at this time. You can be of help to him by reminding him of that support and protection. The body knows what it is doing *(emphatically).*

"His ideas as he tried to explain them to you earlier this evening are excellent. They revive him psychologically, particularly with your help, as he discusses them. The sinful-self material is 'timed' in its own fashion so that although there is a good deal of material already written, its effects are periodic—that is, they are clued to spring into even greater insight, which may not be apparent at any one given time. It is important that he tells you when he does feel panicky. However, the feeling itself does not last long. Relaxation, again, is a part of the creative process.

"I hope to finish our book *(Dreams)* regardless of your publishing plans and so forth, and at this general point that will be beneficial to our friend as he sees some daily accomplishment made in that area. *(Long pause.)* I want Ruburt to see, however, that healing is taking place, that he can trust his own mind and body, and that all portions of the self are being dealt with, whether or not such is obvious at any given time. Our material on such points is not fiction. Unfortunately, in your society you need every good suggestion you can get, to offset fears and negative conditioning.

"[Ruburt] does not have to publish a book every year on the button. The creative material will flow. It flows as a result of his own characteristic nature. It is safe to express that nature. It is even safe to explore that nature, and it is safe to allow himself to take some comfort in the source of being.

"The same advice, with suitable variations, could be given to anyone, of course, and be equally pertinent."

SESSION 937——November 19, 1981
8:30 P.M. THURSDAY

(Jane hadn't operated well yesterday.[1] She did tell me that she was somewhat surprised to realize Seth might be closer to completing his work on Dreams *than she'd thought he was. My own idea has been that Seth is far from finishing the book.*

Jane held Session 900 for Chapter 5 of Dreams, *in Volume 1, some 20 months ago. In Note 1 for that session I described a most vivid dream experience—one in which, Seth told me in the session itself, I had viewed the many-faceted light of my own being and of the universe. Participating in that event had been our friend, Floyd Waterman. Floyd is an extremely generous and caring individual who has helped us many times over the years; he's the contractor who converted half of our double garage for the hill house into Jane's writing room.[2] Jane and I have each shared a number of psychic experiences with him.*

The comical series of events involving Floyd, one of his sons, and another helper had started this noon: "Hell, Rob, it's a coon!" a surprised Floyd called down to me from the roof of the house, after the beam from his flashlight had illuminated the black mask across the animal's face and made its eyes shine as it crouched at the base of the fireplace chimney. The raccoon had evidently picked the site as a secure, heated refuge from the winter weather to come. The three men vainly tried several methods to coax the half-wild, half-tame creature back up the chimney. Finally Floyd opened the damper a bit and lit a sheet of newspaper in the fireplace: The smoke immediately sent our very upset tenant scrambling up the chimney, across the roof and into the hemlock tree growing at one corner of the front porch. Then while his two helpers stood guard to keep the raccoon in the tree, Floyd lugged a very heavy flat stone up the ladder and planted it across the chimney; he's going to cement a wire mesh in place as a permanent seal against animals and birds.

I pushed Jane in her chair out on the porch, as close to the hemlock as we could get behind the floor-to-ceiling glass; we looked up at the chattering animal from only three feet away. We'd seen raccoons playing in the tree a few times, and Floyd, who lives on a farm, sees them often. This one was fully grown and bore a heavy coat of mixed black, brown, and gray hair; the colors exactly matched those of the tree trunk. In the gloomy day we couldn't see eyes in the black face. We couldn't tell the animal's sex. [I read later that females and the young live in groups, the adult males usually alone—perfectly suitable accommodations of consciousness for raccoons!] "Coons can't run fast," Floyd told us, "and big dogs will attack 'em if they catch them out in the open in the daytime. But that coon could kill even a big dog, if it got cornered." He added that if we heard a loud thudding noise on the roof tonight, it meant that an animal had managed to dislodge the stone cap on the chimney. And Floyd had been right: The raccoon stayed in the tree until dusk, then descended and ambled into the woods in back of the house.[3]

Jane's delivery for Seth was hardly fast this evening, but still she paced the session quite a bit more rapidly than she had the one for last Tuesday night. And we heard no sounds at all from the fireplace in back of me, or from the roof.)

Now: Dictation.

The same curious mixture of nonpredictable and predictable activity operates in genetic patterning also, in which the genetic systems are largely set up to achieve the retention of specific characteristics, and yet can also demonstrate behavior that seems (underlined) to be genetically unfaithful, distorted, or to introduce alterations that might appear to be travesties upon genetic integrity.

Those odd genetic happenings, however, as I have tried to explain, often provide a resiliency and a widening of probabilities that are most necessary for overall genetic balance. Dream actions can indeed—and often do—affect genetic alterations, acting as triggers for altered cellular action. There is a give-and-take between the seemingly separate mental and physical aspects of your lives at every level of experience, and at every level within nature's seeming boundaries.

There are decisions in which each individual plays a part that are made in fields of activity that you usually do not even realize exist. Period. Do you have that sentence?

("Yes," I told Seth. I was getting the rather odd impression that to some extent his material this evening would grow out of our experience with the raccoon, even if he didn't mention it.)

The people of a nation can at any given moment decide to activate or experience a particular event almost entirely in the physical realm, or to separate its elements in such a way that half of it is experienced physically and the other half in dream reality. Transformations of energy occur of course constantly, so that, say, a probable physical storm can instead appear as an economic one.

(Long pause at 8:46.) It can appear as an emotional storm on the part of large numbers of people. It can instead appear as a series, say, of frightening dreams. Period. At each point of its existence such an event can weave in and out of such manifestations, largely dissipating itself. Period. An adverse physical situation, such as an illness, may turn into "a frightening dream," yet in all such cases the necessary standards of self-integrity are maintained.

The same alterations apply of course for fortunate events, which may be experienced through full physical expression, or through a series of manifestations that might also involve social or economic happenings, or the occurrence of splendid weather conditions, dash—the insertion of excellent, almost perfect summerlike days, or whatever. The predictable and nonpredictable serve, then, to form the boundaries of physical experience.

The more open you are to such ideas the greater the flow of your experience can be.

(9:00.) As Ruburt himself often mentioned in his own book, *The God of Jane,* you should never accept as fact a theory that contradicts (underlined) your own experience. Man's experience (underlined) includes, for example, all kinds of behavior for which science has no answers. That is well and good. Science cannot be blamed for saying that its methods are not conducive to the study of this or that area of experience—but science should at least be rapped on the knuckles smartly if it automatically rejects such behavior as valid, legitimate or real, or when it attempts to place such events outside of the realm of actuality. Science can justly be reprimanded when it tries to pretend that man's experience (underlined) is limited to those events that science can explain.

It is instead, of course, quite possible that your predictable world exists not in spite of but because of those surprising, unpredictable, unofficial occurrences. Period. There is a kind of larger spontaneous order of which the seemingly unpredictable elements of your world provide their own clues.

(A one-minute pause at 9:15.) Give us a moment. . . . By taking notice of seemingly unpredictable events, by changing your focus, you can indeed begin to sense the larger patterns of such a reality. And that reality leaves many traces in your own experience. It everywhere provides hints and clues as to its own actual-

ity and your own participation in varying fields of expression that have not been given any official recognition.

Within the patterns of human experience, then, lies evidence of man's greater ability: He rubs shoulders with his own deeper understanding whenever he remembers, say, a precognitive dream, an out-of-body—whenever he feels the intrusion or infusion of knowledge into his mind from other than physical sources. Such a creature could not be the puppet of a genetic engineering accidentally manufactured in a universe that was itself meaningless. Period.

If man paid more attention to his own subjective behavior, to those feelings of identification with nature that persistently arise, then half of the dictates of both the evolutionists and the creationists would automatically fall away, for they would appear nonsensical.[4] It is not a matter of outlining a whole new series of methods that will allow you to increase your psychic abilities, or to remember your dreams, or to perform out-of-body gymnastics. It is rather a question or a matter of completely altering your approach to life, so that you no longer block out such natural spontaneous activity.

(9:35.) End of dictation.

(After giving a few paragraphs of personal material for Jane, Seth then ended the session at 9:47 P.M.)

NOTES. Session 937

1. Jane typed this entry for her journal while sitting at a card table in our glassed-in front porch:

"Wednesday, November 18, 1981. Right now I'm really blue, my eyes operating poorly; tears warmly close; yet enjoying the dark sky and street as rain threatens . . . the view of the mountains afforded by the windows; the rock music on the radio; the odd remaining odor of door varnish—deeply loving all of it yet swept through with something like nostalgia. The phone rings and at first I can't tell if the ring is really here or from the radio, and when I answer the phone the voice is distant; it asks for Rob. A flash flood watch is in effect—nothing to worry us on our hill! I wait to feel better. Rob turned off the radio so he could hear on the phone. . . . He goes out front to feed the birds. I do feel relieved some, to be writing this down. It's time for lunch; maybe I'll do a few notes afterward. . . ."

2. In Chapter 10 of *Mass Events*, see the opening notes for Session 873, which Jane held on the evening of August 15, 1979.

3. Jane and I regret that we've deprived our guest of the protected and warm—if not natural—habitat it had chosen. We had certainly enjoyed watching the raccoon. I told my wife I'm particularly pleased that even though we live within the confines of a small city, we're also in close contact with the natural world and its creatures. I think of this enjoyable proximity as an excellent way of keeping in perspective our human position upon the planet. I don't want to be simplistic here, but for some years I've been concerned that those living in large metropolitan centers miss a certain daily, vital participation in the very environment within which by far most of the life forms on earth exist. I'm not sure what percentage of the human population now lives in urban areas, but it must be high, and climbing. Yet beliefs rule all: Evidently, even with all of the challenges that crowding can set up, it's just as natural for people to congregate as it is for them to live spread out—perhaps even more so, if one facet of their behavior can be said to be "more natural" than another!

(A note: I'm not referring to the ordinary scientific concept of naturalism here—that the so-called natural world is all that exists. Indeed, Jane and I insist that the ingredients of the nature we think we look out upon are entirely creative and spiritual—a state of affairs profoundly different from that advocated in orthodox naturalism!)

4. In the Preface for Volume 1 of *Dreams*, see Session 881, with its Note 1. Then I suggest a review in chapters 1 and 2 of all of the material pertinent to evolution and creationism.

SESSION 938——November 24, 1981
9:07 P.M. TUESDAY

(We sat for the session at about 8:30. Once again Jane used many very long pauses as she spoke for Seth. I think that through Seth tonight she beautifully discusses several of her key insights into the nature of reality—and I don't think it has ever been done any better.)

Now—dictation.

(Long pause.) The entire picture of physical life as you understand it must be of course experienced from your own viewpoint,
but its complexity, its order and magnificence of structure and
design should be understood as composing but one example of
the infinite number of realities, each constructed by the propen-
sities and characteristics of its own nature and the nature of its
own consciousness.

The word "unconscious" is in a fashion meaningless. There
are endless versions [of consciousness], of course, with their own
worlds, forming organizations of meaning and purpose. Some
of these mingle with your own and vice versa. The "inner structure" is one of consciousness, and the deeper questions can eventually only be approached by granting the existence of inner
references.

(9:16.) Give us a moment. . . . The nature of time, questions
concerning the beginning or ending of the universe—these cannot be approached with any certainty by studying life's exterior
conditions, for the physical references themselves are merely the
manifestations of inner psychological activity. You are aware of
the universe only insofar as it impinges upon your perception.
What lies outside of that perception remains unknown to you. It
seems to you, then, that the world began—or must have begun—at some point in the past[1] *(a one-minute pause at 9:18)*, but
that is like supposing that one piece of a cake is the whole cake,
which was baked in one oven and consumed perhaps in an afternoon.

The inner references of reality involve a different kind of
experience entirely, with organizational patterns that mix and
merge at every conceivable point. You tune your consciousness
while you sleep as one might tune a piano, so that in waking
reality, it clearly perceives the proper notes and values that build
up into physical experience. Those inner fields of reference in
which you have your existence are completely changing themselves as your experience is added to them, and your own *(long
pause)* identity was couched in those references before birth as
you understand it.

You are one conscious version of yourself, creating along with
all of your contemporaries the realities of the times. When I use
the term "contemporaries," I refer to all of the species. You read

your consciousness in certain fashions, but it is quite possible to read the consciousness of the world in other ways also.

(Pause at 9:35. Scientists do not know how many species exist on earth—only that they total in the billions.) If you read it sideways, so to speak, you would still end up with an orderly universe, but one in which the nature of identity would be read completely differently, stressing adjacent subjective communications of a conscious kind that form other kinds or patterns of subjectivity and psychological continuity. These result in the formation of "personalities" or entities who are aware of their own identities by following different pathways than your own, while also in their way contributing to the formation of your universe even as you do.

(Very slowly.) Your numbering of the species is highly capricious. Again, you recognize as alive only those varieties of life that fall within certain ranges of attention. You objectify and diversify. The lines drawn between the self and what is nonself, between an organism and its environment, are highly arbitrary on your part. There are psychological patterns, therefore, that completely escape your notice because they do not follow the conventions that you have established. These combine what you diversify, so that you have hidden psychological values or psychological beings that combine the properties of the environment and the properties of selfhood in other combinations than those you know.

They would seem to be the spirits of nature,[2] as you would be more or less bound to interpret them from your viewpoint. They would certainly be psychological relatives, but with their own time schemes, languages, and psychological affiliations. These do exist along with the kinds of consciousness that you recognize within the structure of physical life. When you dream, however, you often come in contact with these cousins of consciousness. It is not simply that they communicate with you, or you with them, so much as it is that in sleep the conventional properties that you have learned are somewhat loosened and abandoned. You see "the lights around the corner," so to speak. You see a species of consciousness, a species that must remain unexplained in any normal explanations of evolution, and these hint at the communications that exist at all levels *(intently)*, protecting not only the genetic references necessary to your own kind, but the com-

binations of other forms of organization that exist adjacent to
your own, yet connected to them. You have often misread such
references, and many of your legends of good and evil spirits,
monsters and strange varieties of artificial creatures, appear in
folklore.

(10:05.) At one time, however, you encountered such other
formations in a different light, of course, seeing many similarities between their behavior and yours—certain characteristic
ways of perceiving at least some experience that elicited your
response and recognition.

At one time, then, you were more open in a fashion to the
kinds of consciousness that you admitted into your circle of reality. At one time, in those terms, you did not draw the lines as
finely as you do now. Instead you included such cousins of consciousness into your midst, accepting a kind of comradeship—
for to some extent at least you could see the different versions of
humanity that resulted from a change of focus, an adjacent affil-
iation of humanized energy with the environment. Quite simply, you felt that in certain terms you had other brothers and
sisters in the world that were like you but unlike you, that put together the contents of the universe in their own fashions. Such
species, of course, can nowhere appear within the dictates of
evolution or be perceived as realities except under those conditions when you relax your usual conventions of perception and
behavior.

(10:18.) Nevertheless, encounters between you occur frequently—in the dream state as stated, in alterations of your
usual focus, and in your arts, where you are less arbitrary in your
definitions. As you began to bring your own physical reality into
harder, clearer focus, you stopped with your own view of human
consciousness, shutting off completely and rather arbitrarily
those other elements in order to more clearly frame and define
the boundaries of physical order. It seems to you now that such
personalities *(long pause)* are not physically perceivable, but at
one time you could bring them into the range of your perception.

*(Jane took a very long pause in trance at 10:25—so long, in fact,
that I thought she might have fallen asleep as she sat there on the couch
with her eyes closed.)*

You ended your classifications where you did, however, preferring to see man as the king of intelligence. This meant that you abruptly drew the line where it now seems it <u>must</u> have been drawn. You continued that companionship, however, at other levels of activity, levels that are still open and that must be taken into consideration whenever we approach any discussion of dreaming and the dreaming world *(intently.*

(10:27.) End of dictation. Now give us a moment. Rest your fingers. . . .

(See Note 3 for the private balance of the session.)

NOTES. Session 938

1. According to generally accepted scientific theory these days, our solar system is some 4.6 billion years old. The universe itself originated between 10 billion and 20 billion years ago.

2. In Chapter 2 of *Dreams*, in Volume 1, see Note 5 for Session 885, as well as my comments about naturalism at the end of Note 3 for the last (937th) session.

3. As I think the ideas in the session proper are among Jane's best, so do I think those in the material she delivered for herself are equally good.

(Seth at 10:28:) "You have been of excellent help to Ruburt lately. So far in our discussion of his own situation, we have not for good reason touched upon certain material because he was not ready for it.

"As his abilities grew, however, of course he sensed the outlines of other realities, the glimmerings of other worlds. He sensed these cousins of consciousness in one way or another—these environments that seemed real but not real, these further extensions of possible experience—and he decided that he must be very cautious: He must be prudent *(long pause)*, he must take his time, he must range but carefully—and certainly to some extent such feelings cut down upon his spontaneity.

"The cautions are natural enough under the restrictions man usually places upon consciousness. Ruburt carries his protection and safety wherever he goes. It is a natural grace, characteristic of consciousness of any kind. Its protection and validity are always honored. Ruburt is safe wherever he goes. His psychological stance is honored wherever he goes.

"I will have more to say on this subject in a personal context at our next session. These few statements, however, will help him, and help him enlarge on an inner circle of acquaintanceship with friendly colleagues that belong in those other categories, but indeed are friendly colleagues as well.

"End of session and a fond good evening."

(10:45 P.M.)

To me, Jane's sensing of those "cousins of consciousness," those "friendly colleagues," and her very cautious reactions to her inner knowing, are clear signs of the consistency of her beliefs and her work through the years. And as I've shown in the notes for *Dreams*, it's also obvious that in spite of Seth's reassurances, and my own, she hasn't felt safe wherever she goes.

Her consistency of attitude was strongly reinforced for me when, as I put together the notes for this session, I came across two rough, untitled poems that she'd produced on March 19, 1977—four years and eight months ago. I think it hardly coincidental that I found them just at this time. Jane had written them in colored ink in one of her 4 by 6 sketch pads. She hadn't typed the poems for her journal, or shown them to me, but had quite forgotten about them. They're presented a little later in this note.

The freshness of those poems was so vivid to me, their contents so pertinent to Jane's situation today, that they seemed devoid of all that time that had passed since she'd written them. At once I thought of trying to explore that timelessness in the only way I could as a physical creature—by, contrariwise, taking the time to list a flow of events since she had conceived the poems, putting their creativity into perspective while still feeling it as if it were new. Arbitrarily, I chose professional events from our own lives, and thought of all of them as happening at once (as, according to Seth, in a larger framework they do). Obviously, anyone can compile such a list, involving any group of subjects. This happens to be the one I made:

Jane, then, wrote those two poems 16 days before she dictated the last session for Seth's *The Nature of the Psyche* on April 4, 1977; one month before she began dictating *Mass Events* on

April 18, 1977; two years and two months before she began *God of Jane* on May 6, 1979; two years and six months before she began dictating the Preface for *Dreams* on September 25, 1979; two years and eight months before she came up with the idea for *If We Live Again* on November 15, 1979; three years and five months before she began dictating Seth's material on the magical approach to reality in *Dreams* on August 6, 1980; four years before she began dictating Seth's sinful-self material in that book on March 11, 1981; four years and three months before she began coming through with her own sinful-self information on June 17, 1981; and four years and five months before, on August 26, 1981, she wrote the poem in Note 6 for Session 936 of *Dreams*: *"Something in me / ebbs and tides, / as if I let myself / for a while / be washed away / out to sea / while leaving / some spidery shell / upon the shore /. . . ."*

I see that expanse of time (that four years and five months), as being really an emotional bridge between Jane's poem in Note 6 for the 936th session and the two she wrote in March 1977. All three are entirely consistent not only with her beliefs and emotions, but with my own. For I feel now, in connection with the two "new" poems, the same profound sensations I had concerning Jane's challenges when I wrote in Note 6: "Perhaps it was her poetic art of expression that helped me identify so strongly with her emotions, but I suddenly felt that even I had never really understood the myriad depths of her challenges and her reactions to them." All three poems, then, are of a piece, in which she explores across time and emotion different facets of a common set of beliefs about friendly psychic colleagues and feelings of safety.

Now, however, I took another small step and understood that if the three poems reflect deep fears Jane has, revolving around her abilities, they're *also united* by her determination to press on with those gifts. Her "undeviating direction," expressed in Poem One below, is directly related to the material about her that I quoted from Seth in Note 6 for Session 931, in Chapter 9 of *Dreams*: "Nothing, however, would have kept him at the sessions for this amount of time unless he wanted them." (The session I cited had been held in February 1980, when Jane had been speaking for Seth for more than 17 years.)

Once again, as I did in Note 6 for the 936th session, I'm

running together Jane's short lines in each stanza of her poetry, separating the lines with virgules.

Poem One

If there are angry winter roots | within my many seasons |
a wildness untempered | by reason's ways— |
a force, weirder and | more elemental than |
autumn's demented fervor | (raging yet glorious, orange and |
green leaves splintered, | falling everywhere) |
then, so there is.

And as autumn's fierce | moods have their |
reasons—in nature's | deeper sanity | so must . . . |
my undeviating | direction— |
Though my thoughts' leaves singly | seem separate |
they ride in one elemental | force | carried weightless— |
Then with them let me | be so supported |
though my tumultuous journeys carry me, | like them, |
above stormy treetops. | For higher still |
the sky holds all | safely contained.

Poem Two

1

If I've gone kinky— | legs at crazy angles— |
arms half bent— | no longer walking upright— |
a physical outcast— | and a mental speed-demon— |
well, no more apologies—from me | to me.

When you bunk your head | against the sky | and it gives— |
you're tempted to back off; | suspicious, confused |
as a scared animal | treated kindly: You growl, |
pretend to lick or bite | yourself— | too scared to |
even wag your tail.

2

So now it's time to say— | "It's all right," |
and pick up the | magic bone | to try | its strange new |
nourishment. | I've prowled around it | for too long |
in circles; sniffing; | and I never did | say thanks.

3

*Someone magically / took my leash off / and I was so scared /
I pretended it was / still there even / tighter than before.*

*"Ahem," said the magic voice. / "You're free— /
didn't you notice? / Why don't you run off / like any lucky /
animal?" / And I said, "Don't tell lies. / I won't listen."*

*That was years ago. / Now I'm shivering, tired, /
tied out alone in the / black wind. / I keep tugging /
at the leash that isn't there / but seems so real.*

*Real scissors / won't cut / that kind of leash. /
So I'm making / imaginary ones / which snip /
the dream leash / into a thousand silver / pieces— /
that melt before my / dream-real eyes.*

CHAPTER 12

Life Clouds

SESSION 939——January 25, 1982
9:48 P.M. Monday

(Another two months have passed during Jane's production of Dreams. *We had a very subdued holiday season. Now the new year is almost a month old; the weather is cold but the frozen ground is practically bare of snow. Our mail is as heavy as ever. Those "unused gaps of time," those long weeks passing between recent chapters for* Dreams, *have become very worrisome to me, for they fall outside of Jane's natural creative rhythms. She hasn't even had many private sessions during those breaks in book work; she gave but two private sessions between chapters 10 and 11, and four between chapters 11 and 12. That very infrequency itself is an obvious "symptom" of our psychic and physical challenges.*

I regard the first one of the four sessions Jane held before starting Chapter 12 as being a key session, an excellent one indeed for us. We feel that it marks a turning point—yet, paradoxically, we're not at all sure that we can turn in the right direction! Jane came through with the session just a week after giving the last session for Chapter 11 [on November 24, 1981], and I'm presenting it here in Note 1.

We discussed that session thoroughly the next day, December 2, and Jane ended up defending herself from what I had written in some of my notes. She showed more animation than I'd seen her display for some time, and I was glad to agree that she made some good points; others I disagreed with. I asked her to type a summary of her remarks for inclu-

sion with our next session. At the same time, I tried to make it easier for her to do the typing itself. I've made things for her before.[2] *Recently she had been having trouble comfortably lifting her hands high enough to reach her typewriter as it sat upon either the oak table in her writing room, or upon her standard metal typing table. I took the time to build a lower, very solid table whose top rides just above her knees as she sits in her office chair; she can operate her typewriter much more easily at that lower level. She makes mistakes typing because her fingers aren't working well, but is anxious to improve her accuracy through working. [Nor is her handwriting as steady as it used to be.] As she typed on December 3: "Rob just made a new wooden typing table, right height, etc, and I am trying it out now. It worked great, want to start up journal, want to start project . . . want to get sessions started up again too or tell myself so anyhow."*

However, she did not type the summary I'd asked her for. That evening she held the second of the four private sessions she was to give before starting Chapter 12 of Dreams.[3]

Our program of discussing Seth's material, as well as our own ideas—which included our taping suggestions for Jane to listen to daily—had come out of those sessions for December 1 and 3. Obviously, we were trying to encourage Framework 2 activity. I spent the next day rearranging all of Jane's working paraphernalia in her writing room, following her directions, and that re-creation of her world helped also. "Rob and Seth started us on a new program and though we've hardly begun, I do feel some relieved more peaceful," she typed in part on the morning of the 5th as she sat at her new low table. "yesterday i felt the place clicking about me. P.M. I did a little mail but didn't really get into the notes which are to be a part of the program. My typing is still pretty poor but do know this will improve. I don't feel any flow in these notes but I do feel a submerged flow rising and i do feel . . . centered, more content . . . as I get this far I feel a definite block of expression and some mild enough panic but recognize the fact that a feeling of repression came as I decided to do my notes . . . writing down at once and will tell rob."

And a very positive event took place that afternoon. Jane received from Prentice-Hall the first copies of her book of poetry: If We Live Again: Or, Public Magic and Private Love. *We had looked forward to seeing that handsome little volume ever since she first conceived of it well over two years ago, before she had a title.*[4] *If possible, Jane was even more pleased at the publication of* If We Live Again *than she had been when her book of poetic narrative,* Dialogues of the Soul and Mortal Self in Time, *came out in 1975.* If We Live Again *once more carried her back to her earliest days of creative work, which in turn had led to her teenage dreams of becoming a published poet [she was born in 1929]. As I've shown in various notes in the Seth books, through the art of her first love, poetry, Jane presents her beliefs with an amazingly simple clarity, combining her mystical innocence and knowledge with her literal-minded acceptance of physical life.*

"I begin as best I can . . . read sessions," Jane typed on December 7, as she recorded her efforts, and mine, at carrying out our program for her. We played the tape of suggestions we'd made. "I do feel a blockage of expression; my ass hurts typing—a sweet soreness of joints I sit on that brings tears briefly; yet it is a stretching sensation. same right arm. so much I'd like to write down," she noted later in the day. For although we didn't know how they'd done so, our suggestions had helped her tune into a number of dear images of her girlhood in her hometown of Saratoga Springs, New York: She'd seen herself at an amusement park— Kaydeross—located on the shore of Saratoga Lake, just outside of town; she'd seen herself "jumproping very young" in the recreation field across the street from the Catholic grade school she had attended; she'd seen and interacted with family members, all dead now. That night she had very vivid dreams.

Jane's "early spontaneous Saratoga images," as she called them, her re-creation of her own past, had continued the next day. I found her visions particularly poignant, because in them she had seen herself as having the full and unconscious freedom of physical motion that the very young so take for granted. I wondered whether a part of her might be viewing her childhood in order to remind her of that mobile heritage, to help her regenerate it in the present.[5] "see myself jumproping [again] . . . but the places themselves seem more significant to me [today] rather than people," she wrote. "they are fairly extensive, in color and i look out from them at the view thus going inside them to a degree; must cover the . . . time period when I was about three. . . . vague ideas that when I was around five an older man died in the neighboring house where I'd played on the porch and that someone took me to see the body—my first such experience. . . . Well, now I'll read a magical approach session. rob and I together read recent session this a.m. . . . ." And she had more strong dreams that evening.

Five months ago, in the opening notes for Session 936 in Chapter 11 of Dreams, *I wrote that by the end of August 1981 Jane had roughed in the first three chapters of* The Magical Approach to Reality: A Seth Book. *In all of the weeks following she did only some very loose work on three more chapters. On Wednesday, December 9, my idea that she would probably never finish the book was reinforced by her own note.*[6]

That evening Jane came through with the third of the four private sessions she held before beginning Chapter 12. Her hearing and visual difficulties were continuing. Once again Seth offered us material relative to our daily program—but that's not the only reason I decided to present the full session in Note 7.

Jane worked less and less as the holiday season approached, although on December 15 she gave her fourth private session; its most evocative subject matter—art and child psychology—is separate from our themes for Dreams. *We saw only a few friends. I was busier than ever, however: running the house, preparing for Christmas, helping my wife in various ways, working on the earlier notes for* Dreams *and trying to accumulate some painting time. Jane didn't do any more on her manuscript for* Magical Approach, *nor anything about obtaining the medical help she'd mentioned on the first of December. Our program of self-help gradually began to diminish, as had many of them before.*[8] *Finally, in an effort to cheer up Jane one day as she sat idly at the typing table in her writing room, I tried a variation of a tactic that had worked so well for her inception of Seth's* The Nature of the Psyche *almost six and a half years ago: This time, standing in back of her, I put my arms around her and rolled a clean sheet of paper into her typewriter—but here's the note she wrote the next day:*

"*A dark morning. I feel a definite reluctance about myself and a merging of other feelings. The smell of the heat coming out of the air ducts is faintly comfortable as it blends with the still lingering odor of Rob's varnish. Suddenly the sunlight splashes out of the sky. My body is sore, arms hurt as I type. Rob it seems to me is utterly silent in his studio. I think of the one experience in particular that I'd wanted to note down: Yesterday's vision. Yesterday morning I felt a good deal like i do this morning; middling poor mood, sore body, yet aware of the need to break the spell, move about.*

"*After lunch yesterday with a mild sense of horseplay, Rob had put a piece of fresh paper in my typewriter. 'Just title it Chapter 1 and start in on a new project,' he'd said. He went back to his studio and I closed my eyes trying to visualize my [psychic] library;*[9] *nothing, I tried again and just as suddenly I saw a woman seated opposite me [at] the living room table.*"

That note is Jane's last entry in her journal for the year, and she did not date it. Although she told me she had enjoyed having the vision, she said little about it and made no notes. I made a mistake: I should have insisted upon a detailed oral or written account from her, and made my own notes if necessary. I did remember her describing an older woman in shabby clothes, whose lips were moving as though she was talking to Jane; there was no sound. The vision had been very brief but quite real. Note that Jane had felt herself transported from her writing room into the living room. Regardless of any of that, however, my attempt to use direct positive suggestion to help her cut across her doubts and concerns failed. She didn't start any new long-range writing project.[10]

After the holidays Jane worked on several small acrylic paintings of flowers that friends had given us for Christmas. She wrote a few notes and tried some poetry; her handwriting continued to be unsteady; she still made many errors typing. However, she also began to occasionally manifest an upsetting new development—a slight tremor in her voice. I then realized that each time I heard that certain agitation her speech slowed down slightly. We thought the voice effects were connected to her hearing and vision difficulties, which also fluctuated to some degree. Jane was concerned and not concerned, and once again I saw in her that innocent acceptance of the reality she was creating—the one I often had such trouble understanding [as well as my own participation in creating it!]. Not that she uncomplainingly welcomed this physical challenge, but that she overlaid its arrival with a frame of mind in which she kept going as best she could. I tried not to alarm her as we talked, while mentally I speculated about whether the vocal changes could be a further sign of her withdrawal from the world. Before we held the private session for last December 1, I had admitted to her my fear that she was gradually cutting down on her communication with the world.[11]

Neither of us knew how such a tremor and slowdown might influence the sessions, for example: Jane hadn't spoken for Seth in several weeks, so we had yet to find out! I took comfort in remembering her excellent vocal power when delivering the private session for December 3.[12] *Her voice is a powerful and dramatic connective among realities for her, charged with energy and emotion whether she's speaking for herself, for Seth, or speaking or singing in her trance language, Sumari.*[13] *That vocal steadiness and power, coming out of someone whose weight hovers around 100 pounds, has always been most reassuring to us. We tried what Seth had suggested many times: After discussing her voice effects we gave Jane gentle suggestions that they could be greatly minimized, then turned our attention away from them. Actually, I hoped that our almost childlike trust—which I felt was closely related to at least some of the psychological elements involved in her acceptance of the voice challenges to begin with—would make possible their complete disappearance.*

Over two weeks passed after the holiday season before Jane finally hand-lettered the first formal entry for her 1982 journal:

THE NEW JOURNAL
Jan. 15, 1982
FRIDAY

(On the next page she wrote:

"Things I love"	"My Good Qualities"
Rob—	honest
house—	good-looking
views—	talented many ways
sunlight—	writing
nature—	psychic
cats—	poetry
some people—	good mind
writing—	good-hearted
many more—	

Things I'd
Like to do
soon:
Finish Seth book

Such lists can always be extended. At once, however, I thought of adding these qualities to Jane's attributes:

powerful singer in Sumari
a fine dramatist
literal-minded
unbelievably stubborn
basically innocent

I think most people would agree that Jane's singing in Sumari is extraordinarily original, and that she's an excellent natural dramatist.

It's easy to miss, or skip over, the drama in her lifework because it's so pervasive in all of her creative endeavors. She was fully aware that that quality became much more obvious in her class singing and sessions, but she didn't have to consciously evoke it—the drama was just there. In its own form each time, it still underlies our sessions, and her poetry, writing, and painting.

Some would argue, however, over whether the next three characteristics on my list are assets of Jane's, or hindrances. I believe that any of those can be either or both, depending upon circumstances. My position is that all of the qualities listed, by both Jane and me, represent creative portions of her as she is—*and I accept them all.*

Jane had noted on the 15th that she wanted to finish Seth's book soon. She made no more entries in her journal over the next ten days. She did more painting. Rather than intensify, her voice tremors lessened on some occasions and disappeared on others. The slowdown in her speech was more persistent, although it didn't become more pronounced in any manner. Following our own suggestions, we did fairly well at not dwelling upon those vocal challenges; we sent out no signals to Seth, asking him to discuss them. And Jane did have the energy to firmly begin dictating Session 939 for Chapter 12 of Dreams *at 9:48 P.M. on Monday evening, January 25:)*

Now—good evening.

("Good evening.")

Dictation. We will begin a new chapter *(12),* entitled: "Life Clouds."

(Pause.) Joseph *(as Seth calls me)* used the term today in a discussion, and it is an excellent description of the way in which your universe was "initially" seeded.[14]

Understand, however, that the term "dream cloud" would serve as well. [Yet] it is an evocative reference to the way that All That Is packaged itself in the formation of its numberless realities. Such life clouds "still" exist—and you had better put the word "still" in quotations. Each seed of life, of living, contains within itself its own protective coating, its own placenta of necessary nourishment and environmental circumstances, its own system and branches of probabilities.

Those branches of probabilities act like remote sensors, seeking out those conditions that will be suited to the seed's best value fulfillment and development. In the simplest of terms, the life clouds will send forth their contents *(pause)* where circumstances best meet their own requirements. On the other hand, the life clouds can seed their own worlds completely. Space itself already speaks of a creation "begun," for no matter how empty space may seem to be it simply appears like a vast cathedral, or tent or pyramid of form, for the moment perhaps vacant inside, with walls so distant that they go unperceived.

Probabilities may be swirling everywhere, yet remain of course unperceived in any given instant, so that you might in this odd strange analogy *(pause)* hear a dim brief whirr, as in the whirling of winds, and think it unimportant—while what you heard instead was an entire world of probabilities speed past where you stood *(intently).*

Your own entire structure of life, therefore, with its acute and precise definitions in the package of reality, is a living life cloud that may or may not be perceived in other realities. That cloud contains within it ever-freshening sources of new creativity. When you dream or sleep or think, you automatically add to other dimensions of a life cloud or dream cloud that emerge from the very actions of your own subjective motions.

(A one-minute pause at 10:10.) Even infinity is being everywhere expressed in each moment, for infinity itself is not something apart from what the universe is. As the universe is a portion of infinity's creativity, in that light there are new species appearing all of the time, whether or not your own situation allows you to perceive that emergence. You yourselves may be portions of that emergence. From your threshold or focus you would be relatively unaware of your own motion on a new time threshold— for to the beings on that threshold you would have already arrived, while to you in your present their existence would at best be theoretical, as if they were future selves. From your standpoint they would be, of course.

At other levels your dreams mix and intertwine not only with those of your contemporaries, but with those of all times and places, living or dead in your terms. Each universe—such as the one you know—serves as a small colony of existence, and is infinite within the characteristics of its own nature.

Some of this evening's material will only have meaning to you in the dream state, for that matter, and the words of the book may stir some of those meanings into your attention. Each portion of all such life clouds seeks value fulfillment, again, but that term itself is woefully inadequate to express the nature of life's diversity, purpose, or meaning.[15]

(*10:28.*) This purpose or meaning does not exist apart from your own existence, however. You are a part of life's meaning and purpose—but those purposes, "coming from" (*long pause*), coming from the source of your own being, are too great to be expressed or described within the structure of your personhood as you understand it. Such understanding is often experienced or sensed, however, sometimes as you are listening to music or when you are deeply stirred by emotion, and when you do not place a great distance between it and yourself.

Attending to the life that you have with love, beginning "where you are," will best allow you such a feeling for your own meaning.

What do I mean by such attention? Attention to the moment as it is presented. Attention to the table of rich reality as it appears before you. Attention to the kind of person you are, and to the loving appreciation of your own uniqueness. To attend to your life in such a fashion brings you into a clearer communication with the inner action of your own existence.

End of dictation.

(*10:39. After giving a few paragraphs of material for Jane, Seth ended the session at 10:58* P.M.)

NOTES. Session 939

1. Eight weeks later, I'm presenting only a summary of my very long notes for this private session, which Jane held on Tuesday evening, December 1, 1981. The notes stemmed from the unexpected discussion we began at about 8 o'clock, a few minutes after Jane had told me she wanted to have a session on herself. I returned to the living room and found her leaning back on the couch, asleep—and with a lighted cigarette in her hand. A long cone of ash fell into her lap as she woke up with a start: "I never *never* do that when I'm here alone!" she exclaimed, chagrined. Yet she dozed again when I went out to her writing room after her office chair, which I use while taking notes for the sessions. I thought her sleeping after saying she wanted a personal session was a poor sign. Yet I think that in this session Seth reached core

beliefs of ours that we have yet to fully grasp, let alone surmount. He can do better for us only if Jane allows him to, but after we've struggled for so many years I'm no longer sure that she can.

I'm afraid that I did most of the talking in our "discussion," but once again we tried to view our lives in some sort of joint mental and physical perspective. We didn't fight, or even argue. We never do, yet I said things that later I wished I hadn't. Such regrets are inevitable, I suppose, but if I can tell my wife about the storms of consciousness that I think are so active in the Middle East, for example, then certainly I feel like discussing my feelings about our own challenges. Both of us are as concerned as ever about her situation. Jane's feelings of panic, which she had today, and which I tried to help her through, generate their counterparts within me—no doubt about it. At times I couldn't believe myself as I talked tonight, even while I was driven once again to think that on the deepest levels Jane's mystical way *is* bringing her just what she wants. (In Chapter 9, see Note 13 for Session 931.)

I told her I think that on those levels she really doesn't want to hold the sessions anymore, that we're surrounded by clues to that effect, that such a strong part of her is now so against her psychic work, so afraid of its implications—of being swept away, of going counter to her early religious imprinting—that her fear has put her in an impossible position physically. Since she's becoming more and more helpless, I said, we can hardly say we're solving our challenges in ordinary terms. "And don't tell me your present state means that you're getting better, like Seth says, because you're not," I said. "You haven't walked for how long?—two weeks over a year now, I think it is. Not even with your typing table. I'm aware that you may be coping with certain lifetime challenges through the psychic method, so the question becomes one of how far you want to carry the thing. In this probability I put physical survival first, obviously, but do you? Sweetheart, I'll have to admit that sometimes I wonder. . . ."

Jane listened to me go on and on: "I'm on the point again— very close—of refusing to help you with the sessions any longer. I know I've said that before, but this time I don't know what else to do. If we don't see some pretty drastic improvements within the next few sessions, you may end up talking to the wall if you want to have one, or into a recorder if you can operate it. I can't stop you from speaking for Seth by yourself, or doing it with someone else, but I *can* refuse to encourage you myself.

"What I think about illness," I said, "is that as a people we know so little about it consciously that we're still literally in the dark ages in that respect. I've felt that way for a long time now—that our understanding of what human beings really are is minute at best. Seth offers the greatest insights I've ever heard, and I'm more grateful for those than I can say. I think it's very dangerous to take too hard a position on anything we think we've learned as a species, for I can't imagine that in future millennia we'll ever cling to very much of it. In the meantime we're groping around in the dark. To ask any one person to figure it all out now, and to prove it to the world and cure oneself at the same time, may just be asking too much. Learning about our abilities is a social and cultural affair, and you—anyone—need help. Lots of it. Only where do you get the help while trying to learn a few things?

"I'm *not* trying to blackmail you into going into the hospital," I told Jane several times. "I gave up on that last summer, when Floyd *(Waterman)* and I and the others couldn't talk you into it—"

"I don't want to do that," Jane said. "I wouldn't mind trying some things on my own here at the house, like getting an eye, ear, nose and throat doctor here, or an orthopedist—but no hospital. But I'm shocked at what you're saying about giving up on the sessions."

"I didn't plan to say all of this tonight."

And so for the first time that I could remember, Jane actually said that she was considering medical help, even if only under certain conditions. Just recently she began having difficulties with occasional double vision and with hearing. The latter impairment has already cut down on our communication, for almost automatically these days I think twice about speaking to her unless we're face to face. (The last time in *Dreams* that I mentioned trying to get her to accept medical care was five months ago, in June 1981: In Chapter 9, see the opening notes just preceding superscript number 18 for Session 931.)

Jane's main puzzlement, however, is that even with Seth's and her own sinful-self material her physical symptoms persist to such a degree, in spite of an occasional lessening. Evidently, she said, *both* of us are still consciously unsure of what our challenges and fears are on certain levels. Obviously, I'm as deeply involved in her symptoms as she is. We talked about the many delays involved in our producing *Mass Events* and *Dreams*. She's "felt good" about finishing Chapter 11 of *Dreams* a week ago, but has done little on *Magical Approach* recently, except to reread her rough work for the beginning of that book. (She began to slack off from *Magical Approach* early last October—two months ago— after working well on the first three chapters.) Tonight, I even speculated, admitted my fear, that in a way she's embarked upon a long-range campaign to at least drastically reduce, if not elimi- nate, her *communication* with the world, for one sacrifice follows another in an order that can hardly be accidental, Jane revealed that she'd had similar thoughts.

I explained that lately I've been thinking about what can hap- pen when a person chooses to be born with very strong gifts, but then discovers that for whatever reason or reasons he or she cannot use them, or has to pay a high price to do so. At first I thought it contradictory that such conflicts can arise within na- ture's framework—then I realized that they must happen all of the time, and so, actually, *are* natural after all. I used to think that nothing could keep an individual from showing a great ability. Now, I told Jane, I realize that things are far from being that simple. The use or nonuse of an attribute can have as many ramifications as there are human beings who possess whatever version of it: ranging all the way from being completely buried in a life, to being simply left alone, used just "as is," or thor- oughly transformed in expression.

(*Seth, beginning at 9:45 P.M.:*) "I have some comments to make on your discussion—rather brief for now.

"Ruburt does not owe me anything. If he decided not to have sessions, or not to operate in the so-called psychic arena, this does not mean that he would be a failure in any way. He does not owe me a sense of commitment. The material I have given on his health I will, however, stand behind, whether or not it is difficult for you to understand, or whether or not you can bring your- selves to accept it.

"I do admit that from your standpoint—or viewpoint—that it

may be very difficult to accept some of the statements that I make [which] appear perhaps even to be directly contradictory to your observation of Ruburt on a daily basis, and to his own experience of himself.

"It certainly does not seem to either of you that he is getting better. It often seems instead that the opposite is true. You may presently just find it too difficult to take the leap of faith required without more evidence to back it up—this despite the quite frequent feelings of release that Ruburt does experience, along with the much more apparent difficulty. If those feelings go no further, then what good are they? So you both are bound to wonder.

"I know that they are indicators of the body's healing energies, and I also quite understand that in the overall you find such a statement unacceptable.

(Very long pause beginning at 9:59.) "I would never stand in the way, however, of Ruburt's recovery as you understand it. Nor would I feel that Ruburt has let me down, or that you had in any way. Ruburt does need a return to an earlier orientation. That sense of beauty, that reorientation, can relieve the feeling of responsibility that he has at times taken upon himself. He needs an orientation toward the simpler issues—those that carry within themselves a simpler childlike magic. He needs to turn away from an overconcern with life's more 'weighty problems,' to lose the feeling that it is up to him to solve those problems for himself and you and for the world.

(More and more slowly:) "Most of that should be obvious to you. The stresses and strains are in a fashion not simply those of one person and that person's relationship with his own nature. Those (underlined) issues are compounded by Ruburt's understanding, as of now, of other people's lives as they write to you. At the same time, he does not deal directly with such people, so he cannot follow through, for example, as a therapist might. His class gave him some direct encounters through the years as he personally helped to direct others, and could watch the results through their achievements or behavior.

"He certainly expects more of himself than is required, and I have given a good deal of such material, several months back, I believe. I will, however, sort through his experience with your questions in mind, and see what other information I can give you. The other comments are simply handy bandaids, so to speak, but are extremely healthy along the way. When he feels panicky your loving touch—a light quick massage or embrace— acts as quickly on the nervous system as anything else, and far faster than any medicine. Animals even have long been aware of such immediate therapeutic action.

(Very long pause beginning at 10:21.) "The statements I have made regarding the innate nature of the spontaneous self can be of the greatest service if they are accepted. You are trying to redefine the very definitions of personal identity—no easy task. Not just Ruburt alone, but the people of the world are, one way or another, now in the process of just such a redefinition. It is impossible to assign some time element to that (underlined) kind of assignment.

"In the meantime, Ruburt experiences the stress in a certain fashion.

"There is little else this evening for me to say, but I will indeed make whatever further connections I might make, and I will add my own help and energy to him at whatever levels they can be most useful."

(10:28. Sitting very quietly on the couch, Jane took another long pause. Her eyes were closed. Then she began to gently snore: She was asleep, of course. After my first surprise I debated over whether to call her. Finally, as I began to put away my notebook, she came back to her Seth consciousness with a start:)

"I will bring the session to a close, then. I have ranged within it on several occasions this evening, to see what other glimmerings might have immediately come to my attention, and I wish you as always a fond good evening."

(I told Seth good night at 10:32 P.M.)

As I did for the opening notes for the session, I'm summarizing the closing notes. Jane remembered sleeping, but nothing that might have taken place during that time. We understood how she could drift into sleep from her trance state—if she was tired, say, or deeply dissociated—but in spite of my questions she had no idea of why she "woke up" in trance instead of in her usual awake state of consciousness. She'd even resumed speaking for Seth. She dozed again while I put away my notebook and fed the cats. I helped her get into her chair from the couch.

"But that would be awful to give up the sessions," she exclaimed as I wheeled her into the bathroom.

"Don't worry, hon." I laughed. "I know none of it's going to happen. Maybe I'm wrong about all of it anyhow. I fully expect you to go right on with *Dreams*. And other psychic stuff too—though I don't know about *Magical Approach*."

But I was afraid as I thought of what could happen to her while she kept on working. We talked about starting up another daily program of reading and discussing Seth's ideas. It's not that we disagree with him, really, or find his material unacceptable. It *is* that we cannot make it work for us the way we want it to—that is, to evidently supersede deep and powerful inner goals. Probably, also, there are things left unsaid because Jane may unwittingly block them. I told her that Seth had said nothing at all about what I regard as the central conflict: the one between her sinful self, so-called, and her spontaneous self. I even agree that our challenges may well be successfully handled in one or more other probable realities, that in those terms that's an entirely acceptable way for us to learn. Such a course, however, may leave us with something much less than the solution we want in *this* reality. And there must be resolutions possible here too, I do believe. Where is our faith? We have much to learn.

2. Six months ago, I described how Floyd Waterman had helped me rebuild a narrow old straight chair for Jane, and equip it with casters, so that I could more easily steer her into certain parts of the hill house. In Session 931 for Chapter 9, see the opening notes following superscript number 14.

3. After the personal session of December 1 (see Note 1), I'd suggested to Jane that we initiate a daily program of reading and discussing Seth's material. In keeping with that idea, two nights later Seth recommended that we begin studying the sessions on the magical approach to life and on the sinful self. Then he commented in general on the cyclic and beneficial nature of such undertakings:

". . . certainly it must seem to you both that you begin many therapeutically designed programs only to have them disappear. There is a rhythm to such programs, however, and it is natural for the self to rouse at certain times, begin such activities, then apparently (underlined) discard them.

"They begin with a certain impetus, give you a certain kind of progress, and regardless of how great or small that progress may be, there is a necessary time of assimilation—that is, the stimulation over a period of time is more effective when it is in a fashion intermittent, when certain methods are tried out, applied, and so forth—but by the very nature of the healing process there is also the necessity of letup, diversion, and looking away.

"Left alone, the self knows how to utilize such rhythms. If you trusted the characteristics of the basic natural person, you would not need such sessions as ours, generally, in the world at all—for such knowledge would be part of it and implied in its cultural organizations, and the daily habits of the people."

How ironic, I thought, that Seth could say he'd be unnecessary if generally we human beings did a better job of creating our reality!

I'd also written in the notes for the last session (of December 1) about our difficulties producing *Mass Events*, and that Jane has "done little on *Magical Approach* recently. . . ." Seth this evening:

"The sessions on the magical approach . . . can serve as valuable springboards to release from your own creative areas new triggers for inspiration and understanding, and hence for therapeutic development. That should be part of the program, in other words, regardless of what Ruburt intends to do bookwise with those sessions.

"Another point: Regardless of any seeming contradictions, the beneficial aspects of any particular creative activity far outweigh any disadvantages. The nature of creativity, regardless of any given specific manifestation, is reflected in an overall generalized fashion that automatically increases the quality of life, and such benefits are definite regardless of what other conditions also become apparent. I mean to make clear here that regardless of any complications that may seem only too apparent to you, in the production and distribution of my last book, and Ruburt's *(Mass Events)*, the benefits far outweigh any disadvantages.

"You cannot know what would have happened, for example, had it not been produced *(as I'd speculated to Jane late this after-*

noon), or distributed, so the question might seem moot. In the same fashion, the publication of my next book, or rather the one we are working on *(Dreams)*, is bound to bring you greater advantages than disadvantages. Expression is far preferred, of course, to repression—but more than this, the matter of repression cannot be solved by adding further repression as a therapeutic measure. That is, the problem [of Ruburt's symptoms] would have popped up in a different fashion regardless of the apparent trigger.

"If the apparent trigger of a difficulty is a creative accomplishment, then the difficulty itself is 'loaded' also with its own natural therapeutic solutions."

Very clear in Seth's material, I told Jane after the session, is his message that it would be a great mistake for us to give up the highly creative endeavor of the sessions, regardless of whether they were ever published. I said that I was delighted to retract the observation I'd made before the last session—that on deeper levels she didn't want to hold the sessions any longer. I added that once again we could try searching the creative matrix of the symptoms themselves for the solutions to her challenges, and mine as well, for that is where those solutions will be found.

4. I first mentioned what was to become *If We Live Again* early in the Preliminary Notes for the Preface to *Dreams*—those leading off the private session of September 13, 1979. By the time I wrote the opening notes for Session 886 in Chapter 2, three months later, Jane had decided the book would contain "some of the poetry she has dedicated to me over the years since we met in February 1954." Seth agreed. Rather immodestly, I present below the first verse of a love poem Jane wrote for me on November 5, 1965. It's in Section Two, which section bears the title of *If We Live Again* itself. Jane often reworks her poetry, but for the book she changed only two words and added one in this verse which she wrote over 16 years ago. She was 36, and we'd been married for 11 years:

Past Lives (to Rob)

In what past lives
did we live before?
My cells remember
what my brain does not recall.

Your touch
sends images flying up
like leaves rising in a wind
from silent layers
underground.

I like that entire poem, of course—but in a different way I like just as much the untitled poem Jane wrote on a different subject almost 15 years later (on August 25, 1980). She was 51. I borrowed this poem for the opening notes for Session 920, in Chapter 9 of *Dreams*, and urged her to give it a title and present it in *If We Live Again*. Jane did so on both counts, in Section Six: "Strange Liberty." She also changed the format of the poem, but not the words of what I consider to be one of her best creative insights.

Reason's Source

It's not that my mind knows less
than it did before,
but that its reason
finally deduced
the magic of its source,
and sensed beneath
the logic of its ways
the deeper spontaneous
order
that powers its own thought.

5. It was inevitable that Jane's images would remind me of the note I'd written well over two months ago, on re-creating the past, or updating it, through nostalgia. In Chapter 11 of *Dreams*, see Note 8 for Session 936. Her images led me to search out the collection of battered black-and-white snapshots of her that somehow, some way, she'd managed to save from her early childhood. Along with scraps of her youthful poetry, the pictures are the only physical remnants she possesses of her first years, and studying them anew I realized just how valuable they really are. I talked of having them copied and enlarged by a professional photographer; I speculated about eventually having some of them reproduced in a book. That idea may have to wait, however: For some years Jane hasn't cared to be photo-

graphed—or have pictures of herself shown, no matter when they had been taken.

6. I'd always encouraged Jane to write *Magical Approach*, but my hopes that she would ever finish the book had been declining for some weeks. I didn't give her any negative suggestions when I read the note she typed for her loose-leaf journal, but I did think the book was dead in spite of the qualified optimism she expressed at the conclusion of her entry. Except for a couple of minor corrections, I'm presenting the note just as she wrote it, spelling errors and all:

"December 9, 1981. Each time I think of beginning MAGICAL APPROACH I feel this reluctance; I'm not sure what bugs me, the copying of records, putting together the days events or what—but i want more of the fun and magic of it for myself, and less hard work. I'd planned a consecutive story line book including some of robs dreams with interpretations yet feel strain there now, showing how this detail or that one fits the picture, this noon it came to me that the approach seemed to rational at this time; i wanted one that was lighter in tone, quicker yet more expansiveso if anything the books technique would be magical itself. . . . forcing the reader to make some connections from other-than-time frameworks. a possibility came to me of a part 1 consisting of the original abridged sessions one after the other with robs notes included but nothing of mine at all. This followed by a part 2 with chapters following an intuitive shape favoring more association, the sinful self stuff too, showing the portions of psychic motion. could start with a chapter 1 very like the one I have organized and then just have a session or so a chapter until part 2. i don't know, its a thought . . .

"i read over that chapter 1 this a.m. and thats about all i did and think about these ideas . . . and so far this is all i've done this afternoon. want to look chapter over again . . .

"Now after reading over rough chapter 1 again, this time it seems fine! so I'll look over rest I have and see what I think. . . .

"Now instead i am impatient with sinful self syndrome, want to ally myself with magical self;"

Finally: After considering my interpretation of Jane's note—that she wouldn't complete her book on Seth's magical approach to reality—I began to speculate about eventually putting together such a work myself. . . .

7. Seth not only designed his material in this excellent session to help Jane and me, but others as well. In my opinion, he also answered my wife regarding the note she'd written earlier in the day (see Note 6, above). Aside from all of those points, however, I think it quite remarkable that despite her physical hassles Jane approached the rolling cadences, the inspired certainty of delivery, that she'd achieved over two years ago in some of her sessions for chapters 1 and 2 of *Dreams*.

(Seth, starting at 8:49 P.M.:) "Ruburt is truly beginning to understand that the magical approach is indeed the natural approach to life's experience.

"It is the adult's version of childhood knowledge, the human version of the animals' knowledge, the conscious version of 'unconscious' comprehension. I told you that Frameworks 1 and 2 were actually united. They seemed to be so disunited that it is almost impossible to discuss them using any other terms. To understand that much alone, to comprehend the simple idea of Framework 2's indisputable existence is strongly important, however."

(Long pause at 9:03.) "You do not have to worry in an overly strained way about putting the new principles of life into practical experience at once. You do not need to worry or deride yourselves for stupidity if it appears *(very long pause, eyes closed)*, looking over the long annals of work that we have done together, that it should have been obvious that our ideas were leading in certain directions—for not only have I been trying to divest you of official ideas, but to prepare you for the acceptance of a new version of reality: a version that could be described in many fashions. It has been during the annals of history, but many of those fashions also indisputably, and with the best of intentions, managed to give a faulty picture: You ended up with your gods and demons, unwieldy methods and cults, and often with the intellect downgraded. I hope, of course, that our 'model' avoids many of those pitfalls.

"In those annals there is legend after legend, tale after tale, history after history describing civilizations that have come and gone, kings risen and fallen, and those stories have always represented c-u-l-t-u-r-e-s *(spelled)* of the psyche, and described various approaches used by man's psyche as it explored its intersection with earthly experiences.

"Some mountain climbers, when asked why they climb a certain peak, respond: 'Because the mountain is there to be climbed'—so the natural approach, the magical approach, is to be used because it exists, and because it represents an open doorway into a world of reality that is always present, always at the base of your cultures and experience. Theoretically at least, the magical approach should be used because it represents the most harmonious method of life (underlined). It is a way of living that automatically enhances all of your abilities and accelerates your comprehensions.

"To some extent tonight's relatively brief session should remove senses of urgency on your parts, or of self-criticism, that make you question when or how [you] can 'learn to make' the magical approach work in any specific way—that is, why you cannot learn to make the approach work in, say, helping Ruburt's condition in a faster, more effective fashion."

(9:24.) "You should understand that the approach is the best one to use in life, generally speaking, but it will improve all conditions, even if you still have difficulties in certain areas, and its use cannot help but promote the overall quality of your lives. That recognition takes the pressure off, so that you can to some extent relax your old attitudes enough so that you allow the magical approach *(long pause)* to work in those areas that have been bones of contention.

"The magical approach puts you in harmony with your own individual knowledge of the universe. It puts you in touch with the magical feeling of yourself that you had as a child, and that is familiar to you at levels usually beyond your physical knowledge of yourself. It is better, then, to use the approach because you recognize it for what it is than to use it specifically in order to get something that you want, however beneficial. *(All very intently:)* There is no doubt at my level that use of the approach can clear up Ruburt's difficulties naturally and easily. If it is used because you recognize its inherent rightness in yourself, its inherent 'superior stance,' then it automatically puts you in a position of greater trust and faith. It opens your options, enlarges your vista of comprehension, so that the difficulties themselves are simply no longer as important—and vanish from your experience in, again, a more natural manner."

(9:37.) "In a fashion, all of the material that I have given you

in the annals of our relationship was meant to lead you in one way or another to a place where the true nature of reality could at least be glimpsed. You are at that point now.

"In a manner of speaking, Ruburt's physical condition represents the bruises, the wounds inflicted upon any individual in his or her long journey *(long pause)* toward a greater comprehension of life's experience. In religious terms, you begin to glimpse a promised land—a 'land' of psyche and reality that represents unimpeded nature *(again, all very intently)*.

"The 'proper' question to ask is not: 'Can I enter that land?' The land is here, where you are, and it always has been. The methods, the ways, the beliefs, the modes of travel to a destination create the destination itself. *(A one-minute pause.)* It is impossible for you to operate without beliefs in your present mode of existence *(another minute)*, 'for beyond' those glittering packages of beliefs, however, there exists the vast reservoir of sensation itself, the land that does indeed exist 'beyond beliefs.'

"The universe is not dependent upon your belief in it in order that it can exist. It contains within itself its own comprehension of its own knowledge, its own magical recognition of itself, its own harmonious laws and orders, its own cabinetry. It possesses and holds intact even the smallest probability, so that no briefest possible life or creature or being is ever lost in the shuffle of a cosmic mechanics.

"To even sense the existence of that kind of reality, however, you must have already 'opened the doorway' to Framework 2, and begun to use the magical approach as your natural instinctive way of dealing with experience."

(With a smile:) "End of session, and a fond good evening."

(10:05 P.M. "Good night, Seth.")

8. Seth had commented earlier this month on some of the reasons for such cyclic behavior. See Note 3 for this session.

9. In *Psychic Politics*, which Prentice-Hall published in 1976, Jane describes in detail how she learned about the many aspects of her psychic library.

10. Jane had responded beautifully to my suggestion when she began dictating Seth's *The Nature of the Psyche*: I'd playfully told her at suppertime that she was going to start a new Seth book in the session which was due that evening—and three hours later

she did just that. Although she was writing her own *Psychic Poli-tics* while I worked on the notes for *"Unknown" Reality*, she was between Seth books, and I wanted her to have one in progress so that it "could underlie her daily life like a foundation." See the opening notes for the first session in *Psyche*—the 752nd for Monday evening, July 28, 1975. We held that session four months after moving into the hill house.

11. In Note 1 for this Session 939, in Chapter 12, see the open-ing notes for that December 1 session.

12. See Note 7 for this Session 939.

13. In Jane's *Adventures in Consciousness,* see Chapter 7 for her thorough discussion of how she began to speak and sing in her trance language, Sumari, in November 1971.

Jane initiated Sumari in ESP class, and largely let it go when we ended class and moved to the hill house four years later. As with her speaking for Seth, her greatest power and drama in singing was engendered in class. For the most part in our regu-lar, private, and book sessions, Seth speaks to me with a quieter, businesslike energy; I always feel his vigor and humor, but he isn't nearly as loud or quick or boisterous as he was in class. Jane was obviously sensitive to the infusion of energy from 30 or more people during those gatherings, and through her Seth responded masterfully. The same was true of her singing, when she ranged from the most delicate soprano trills and nuances to powerful, much deeper emanations.

I have come to feel that I should have encouraged Jane to speak and sing much more often in Sumari, either when we were alone here at the house, or on a Friday night, say, when we had company. I gave up doing so partly because I hesitated to add to her pressure to perform, whether or not the material might be recorded, and partly because, except on rare occasions, she didn't *offer* to sing—or to have a session—as she used to sponta-neously do in our downtown apartments.

Once in a while, Jane will sing to herself as she sits at her table in her writing room and looks east through the sliding glass doors at the side street rising into the woods to the north. Across the street is the white clapboard house of our neighbors, whom we love and who love us. Our friends have a large yard beside their house. It's filled with trees and flowering shrubs—a view Jane cherishes, and one she has painted and written about a number of times. Indeed, she was looking out at that view at four o'clock on a foggy morning in June 1979 (over two and a half years ago) when she was inspired to name that certain part of her "that is as clear-eyed as a child" the "God of Jane." Out of that insight she titled the book she had started a few weeks earlier *The God of Jane: A Psychic Manifesto*. In Chapter 9 of *Mass Events*, see the opening notes and Note 1 for Session 860.

Occasionally Jane will record a Sumari song when I'm out of the house; I may hear her play it later, but I don't "bug" her about sharing it with me. With the increase in her symptoms her songs have become more subdued, more poignant. Although she seldom translates them into English, I know their subject matter. As Seth does, they represent one portion of her psyche offering reassurances to another more conscious portion, in our terms; they deal with her questioning of the reality she's creating in the finest personal detail—her wanting to know why she's made her choices, her determination to press ahead, her embracing of our beloved earth and our universe. Sometimes her singing carries from her writing room at the back of the house, through the kitchen, around the corner and down the hall into my studio. And sometimes I hear her voice break in mid-song. She is overwhelmed with her yearning. She stops singing.

14. When Seth quoted me as referring to a "life cloud," he went back to the discussion Jane and I had at lunch today, concerning recent news reports and articles: Some prominent astrophysicists, mathematicians, and astronomers have announced their belief in a theory of "panspermia"—that in ordinary terms of time life on earth was "seeded" from space, instead of arising by pure chance in some primordial ooze or sea on our planet. Those men believe in evolution—that once it originated, life, as Charles Darwin proposed, has ever since been growing in complexity and "evolving" through natural selection and random mutations, or DNA copying errors, into the life and beings we see and are today. Among other signs, the rebel scientists cite the evidence for vast clouds of microorganisms in space, and the identification in certain meteorites of bacterial and fungal microfossils, along with a number of amino acids. They claim that

even at 4.6 billion years, the earth mathematically is not old enough for life to have had the time to evolve (beginning about 3.8 billion years ago) into its enormously complex current forms. That lack of ordinary time in evolutionary theory is a question Jane and I have often wondered about.

The panspermian theory is that life reached the Earth from a living organization permeating our entire Milky Way galaxy, and that there *is* a creator, or intelligence, or God out there. In talking with Jane this noon I went the step further by saying that the galaxy *itself* is alive—not merely full of life. Jane and I discussed various ways that All That Is could have seeded life on earth through the roles of probabilities, and how certain successive forms could take root upon the earth when environmental and psychic conditions were right, and so give the appearance of an evolutionary progression. All That Is, I said, might have offered those same incipient forms to the living earth many times, only to have the earth reject them or fail to develop them for many reasons. But even these latest scientific theories are based upon ideas of a past, present, and future; their proponents do not consider that basically time is simultaneous—that the universe is being created *now*. We had an interesting discussion. In Chapter 1 of *Dreams*, see sessions 882 and 883.

15. Seth may think that his own term, "value fulfillment," "is woefully inadequate to express the nature of life's diversity, purpose, or meaning," but over two years ago, in Chapter 2 of *Dreams*, he gave what I think is an excellent interpretation of that quality. In Session 884 for October 3, 1979, he came through very emphatically in one of Jane's best sessions:

"Value fulfillment is most difficult to describe, for it combines the nature of a loving presence—a presence with the innate knowledge of its own divine complexity—with a creative ability of infinite proportions that seeks to bring to fulfillment even the slightest, most distant portion of its own inverted complexity. Translated into simpler terms, each portion of energy is endowed with an inbuilt reach of creativity that seeks to fulfill its own potentials in all possible variations—and in such a way that such a development also furthers the creative potentials of each other portion of reality."

SESSION 940——February 3, 1982

8:52 P.M. WEDNESDAY

(We missed holding the last two regularly scheduled sessions. Jane's vocal difficulties have been minimal, but her handwriting hasn't been too steady as she answered mail and worked on some poetry. After supper tonight she suggested that I get the session notebook ready, although when I joined her in the living room at 8:30 she said she didn't feel Seth around at all.

Two and a half years ago I wrote in the closing notes for Session 869, in Chapter 10 of Mass Events, *that she had finally received from Seth the full title for this book:* Dreams, "Evolution," and Value Fulfillment. Mass Events *was published eight months ago, and we have been receiving a steady flow of inquiries as to when* Dreams *will be issued. We're glad to try to answer questions like that, but our correspondents cover many topics and express many viewpoints—and some are hard for us to handle. As we waited for the session Jane gave me two very long letters she had received yesterday. I felt sad after reading them. We think that both writers express extreme points of view, and that both are much too adulatory of us. To answer one letter would draw its author to our doorstep at once: "I am your Seth," and: "I will visit you as soon as I hear from you." The writer of the other letter, while praising our work, is caught up in questions of conventional religion: "I keep wondering over and over again whether Seth is a demon or a deception. What do you have to say about this?" We don't feel like justifying ourselves.*

Reluctantly, I agreed with Jane that she'd better not answer the letters. I could sympathize with their writers, though, for each one had communicated with us out of a deep need, and is searching for insight into the creation of a personal and mass reality. Often I remind myself that each note I write in connection with the Seth books, or send to a correspondent, represents my attempt as I compose it *to grasp a little bit better the interior and exterior realities I am creating for myself. My trust is that this self-examination helps others.*

On the envelope of the letter containing the queries about Seth's validity, Jane had penned a few lines as she sat at her desk yesterday afternoon:

> If you stand
> at your porchstep
> you can sense the

universe
at your fingertips.

Neither of us expected that Seth would develop his session out of that idea—or even that he would give material for Dreams. *Note that when he uses the pronoun "you" this evening he refers not only to Jane and me in particular, but to readers in general.)*

Good evening.

I have not given you a multitude of methods or suggestions, telling you how to decipher or understand your own dreams, though I have mentioned such topics often in this book and others.

I have not given you complicated methods concerning out-of-body travel, and yet all of our books, by changing your attitudes, will help you bring about changes in yourselves that will automatically enhance such activities. They will begin to take their natural places within your world. No methods will help you otherwise.

I do not want you to think that the answers to your questions lie prepackaged in the dream state, either, relatively inaccessible except to those *(long pause)* who possess unique talents or some secretive knowledge of the world of the occult. Many people, long before the time of printing or reading, learned to read nature very well, to observe the seasons, to feel out "the seasons of the soul." The answers, therefore, lie as close as your own back-door steps, for at the thresholds of your beings you automatically stand in the center of knowledge. You are never at the periphery of events.

Regardless of your circumstances, your condition in life, your training or your aptitudes, at your own threshold you stand at the center of all realities—for at your center all existences intersect. You are everywhere part of them, and they are of you. Each portion of the universe carries the knowledge of all other parts, and each point of a reality is (underlined) that reality's center. You are, then, centered in the universe.

Again, even your dreams and thoughts go out to help form new worlds.

(Much slower after a long pause at 9:10:) Such considerations should naturally spark within you far vaster and yet far more intimate insights—insights in whose light the hazy rhetoric of

prepackaged knowledge begins to disappear. As it does, so the speakers within each of you can rise to the surface of ordinary consciousness without being considered blabbermouths or mad men and women, or fools, without having to distort their information simply to bring it to your attention. The speakers are those inner voices that first taught you physical languages. You could be equally correct in calling them the voices of electrons or the voices of the gods, for each is a representation of All That Is, overflowing like a fountain both with knowledge and with love.

(Long pause at 9:22, then intently yet humorously:) When you stand at your physical doorstep you look inward at an incredible glowing psychological venture. I am not using symbols in such statements, and hidden within them are important homey clues. Period. Each spoon that you touch, each flower that you rearrange, each syllable that you speak, each room you attend to, automatically brings you in touch with your natural feeling for the universe—for each object, however homey or mundane, is alive with changes and comprehension.

(9:30.) I do not, therefore, want you to concentrate your efforts in memorizing methods of perceiving other realities, but to realize that such insights are everywhere within your grasp. If you understand that, then you will rearrange the organization of your own thoughts quite by yourself. You will begin to read your own thoughts as easily as you now read a book. It is far more important to read your own thoughts than it is to learn to read the thoughts of others, for when your own feelings are known to you, you easily see that all other feelings are also reflected in your own. When you look away from the world you are looking at it more closely. When you read sentences like the last one you are somewhat freeing your own minds, opening greater organizations. Your life is one dream that you are remembering.

You are remembering it and creating it at once, watching it grow from the attention of your own love and knowledge, and as you seem to stand at its center, so you stand at the center of all of your dreams, which then spin themselves seemingly outward.

Your physical universe began, again, then, from a dreaming center.

(Long pause.) End of dictation. A fond good evening—though you can expect some homey sessions also, of course, which are on the way *(heartily and with humor.)*

("Good night."

9:45 P.M. I found Seth's abrupt end of the session to be unexpected, in spite of Jane's many long pauses. "He is ending," she said, meaning this book. "I can always tell. Or I think I can. To me, it starts to get some kind of resounding ring to it.")

SESSION 941—February 8, 1982
9:01 P.M. MONDAY

(This afternoon Jane and I outlined a "credo" for her that we hoped she could follow back to the productive endeavors she loves so much: writing, poetry, painting, the sessions, the mail, cooking, feeding our cats, Billy and Mitzi, and so forth. (We still receive from 30 to 50 letters and packages a week.) After supper I wrote a version of the credo, stressing Jane's ability to write prose and to handle the mail. I don't know what I think about whether the statements will have any beneficial effects for her.

In this last session for Dreams, *Seth continued to speak to that all-embracing "you":)*

Dictation.

You have lived in a world in which you believed you must struggle to survive—and so you have struggled.

You have believed that the natural contours of nature were somehow antagonistic to your own existence, so that left in the hands of nature alone you would lose your way. You have believed that in the very framework of your psychology. In your experiences, therefore, all of these things have largely proven true.

Nothing taught that you were creatures. I have been trying to lead you into a new threshold of perception, where the old myths of evolution can be seen as outmoded, ancient or forsaken castles amid a forest of beliefs—a forest that is indeed itself a magically formed one. *(Very long pause.)* The forest is the world of your imagination, surely, the imagination of your minds, and yet given force and power by the innate creativity that rises up from an inner world that represents much more truly the origins of man and beast. That world has been largely hidden by the camouflages shed by science and religion alike, but in your times the landscape began to appear so dark and threatening, so forbidden and alien to your own desires, that its end seemed all the more inevitable and swift.

I hope I have given you in this book a far more gallant and true picture, that represents the origin of your life, structure and being and thought. The inner world of reality, the world of dreams, presents a model of existence in which new energy, vitality, and being is everywhere apparent, ready to come forward to form new transformations, new combinations of energy and desire.

That inner psychological universe is a psychic gestalt, propelled, formed, sustained or driven by value fulfillment, love and desire, by the loving values that have no limit *(intently)*. The universe does not give up on itself, or on any of its creatures. It is ruled by a different set of principles, a different set of values, and by inner cooperative exuberance.

(A one-minute pause at 9:23.) You may need some time before the old beliefs become less prominent, and finally fall into their proper decay—a decay, incidentally, that does indeed have its own kind of majesty, energy, and beauty. But the inner natural leanings of all of consciousness within the realms of your being now yearn for constructive change, clearer vision, to experience again their inherent sense of corporal spirituality, physical and psychic grace. They want to sense again the effortless motion that is their natural birthright.

(All more intently:) I hope that this book to some extent or another puts each of you in touch with your own inner psychological motion, your creative breath, so that you are invigorated and sense within your own minds and spirit a new promise, a new intent, and the exhilaration of earthly and spiritual strength. You dwell in a state of natural grace that is quite alive and vital whether or not science decrees that consciousness possesses its own intent. Nature is supernatural all the while, of course.

End of chapter. End of session. End of book.

(9:33.) Return to your own discussions. They serve you well, because they help clear communication at your end.

(Long pause.) The sessions on magical approach do indeed represent the most "natural truths" about the nature and structure of your world, to the extent that you understand them and put them into practice.

I will continue with whatever schedule of sessions that meets your desires, needs, and purposes. End of session.

("Thank you."

9:37 P.M. After she came out of trance, Jane and I simply stared at each other. Dreams *was done at last! We felt sad, for several reasons. Even though Jane had remarked at the end of last Wednesday evening's session that Seth was close to the end of the book, his actual completion of it still hit us. I congratulated her; I told her that she had created another fine work which would help many people.*

However, all of our reactions were much more subdued than they had ever been before when she had finished a book, either by herself or with Seth. No matter what other challenges we had created for ourselves over the last two years and four months, the knowledge that Dreams *was in process had served as a comforting foundation in our lives. That had been true even during those long delays in its production. We regret that that support is gone. And we know that as the creation of* Dreams *begins to recede from our immediate perception other challenges will inevitably move forward. Basically, things have come down to our hopes that Jane can keep going from day to day, and that our new credo will offer her support now that Seth and she are through with their book.*

My own role in the physical production of Dreams *is far from over, however. In notes at the end of this session I'll briefly consider the latest expressions of large-scale consciousnesses concerning Three Mile Island[1] and the countries of the Middle East,[2] and then will unify those discussions by explaining how I think those great events of consciousness have counterpart relationships, just as "living" entities do.[3] I'll also refer to our country's space-shuttle program.[4] Next, I have to put into final form the complicated notes I began for a number of sessions for* Dreams *as Jane delivered them. After that will come the job of typing the finished manuscript for this massive two-volume work; I do not know when I'll have it ready for our publisher. And therein lies another reason for our somber moods: Our dear friend and editor, Tam Mossman, almost certainly will not see* Dreams *through the publishing process. Tam has grown restless; he needs a change; he plans to leave Prentice-Hall.[5]*

In Note 1 for Session 939, in this Chapter 12, I quoted myself as telling Jane last December 1 that she hadn't walked for "two weeks over a year now, I think it is. Not even with your typing table." In the opening notes for that session, I quoted her as writing on December 7: "I do feel a blockage of expression; my ass hurts typing—a sweet soreness of joints I sit on that brings tears briefly; yet it is a stretching sensation." At the finish of Dreams, *her span without walking has increased to 14 months and 22 days. She is still uncomfortable sitting—more so, even, and I fear that her flesh will break down from the constant pressure; I've seen what I interpret as signs of that happening.*

Jane hasn't contacted a doctor. Her hearing and handwriting remain impaired. Her voice tremor and slowdown remain mild and intermittent; she's done well during sessions. And as I write these closing notes I remind myself once again, as I often do, of those promises we made each other when we married in 1954—"that neither one of us would interfere with the other's creative approach to life, no matter what resulted from the actions we individually chose. . . . Yet as the years passed I still had to learn the obvious—that Jane's creative powers are inextricably a part of her whole approach to life, including her symptoms. How could it be otherwise?"[6]

  In Volume 1 of Dreams, *see the first session in the Preface. Well over two and a half years ago, I wrote in the opening notes for that session that Jane had "some 17 chapters in fairly good shape for her third Seven novel,* Oversoul Seven and the Museum of Time." *She had laid it aside to begin work on* God of Jane. *Although she considered resuming work on* Seven Three *at various times while she was producing* Dreams *with Seth, she never did; the status of that novel remains the same. Recently, however, she's talked about finishing it, and I expect that she will.*[7]

  I can't note the same for The Magical Approach to Reality: A Seth Book—*the very promising work that Jane and I first discussed a year and a half ago [in August 1980], after Seth had started his group of excellent private sessions on that subject.*[8] *I watched Jane try to write the book a number of times; last month, in Note 6 for Session 939 [in this chapter], I finally expressed the opinion that she wouldn't finish the job. Or, to put it another way,* Magical Approach *has yet to undergo a resurrection by her! But obviously Jane has the freedom to engage in any project, and she chooses not to follow through with some of them. I think* Magical Approach *would have been a fine book as she planned it—but that it ended up squelched by at least two major factors: She was too inhibited by the subject matter [her physical symptoms] out of which the magical approach material had grown, and she was bothered because she had chosen to emulate the plodding way in which I put together the Seth books. That way didn't allow her the creative freedom to spontaneously plunge ahead. As I wrote in Note 6 [for the 939th session], eventually I might try assembling such a work myself.*

Even so, Jane had the magical approach in mind two days later, when she typed a rough last note for her journal on February 10: "Still annoying problems with fingers . . . hoping to clear this up, using in part robs new suggestion page [credo] for me. typing weth right hand. as I see it even that can be utilized in magical approach. again, Seth finished his book monday."

A note added a month later: Jane's journal entry is indeed a last one, for on the 26th of February, 18 days after finishing her work for Dreams, *she was admitted to a local hospital for treatment of hearing difficulties, rheumatoid arthritis, and several other afflictions. Jane's and my hospital experiences have already become so involved that I've begun to think of describing them—and whatever they may develop into—in a series of chronologically ordered introductory essays for* Dreams, *instead of the more conventional introduction I'd been expecting to write. The shocks have been great for us, and are continuing. Without knowing anything, I know that we'll need much time in which to understand all of the deeply moving and conflicting emotional, psychic, and intellectual events connected with this development. Each day as I look at my lovely wife lying in her hospital bed after years of struggle, I feel the surge of those events—and I* see *them in Jane, and* feel *them in her!*

In a way our joint world came crashing down upon us on February 26, yet we continue to live amid the welter of our beliefs. Again and again in the notes for Dreams *I've indicated how Jane and I tried to understand the probable reality we've created. With the hospital experience, I'm telling myself that if I can write about the storms of consciousness involving whole nations, I can certainly describe and reflect upon our own storms of consciousness. Jane and I must still have an unbelievable amount to learn, even though I think that in more basic terms certain portions of each individual's reality are consciously unknowable. As Seth said three years ago: "Consciousness attempts to grow toward its own ideal development, which also promotes the ideal development of all organizations in which it takes part.*[9]

What, then, are those "ideal developments" Jane and I are growing toward? Questions like that must intrigue Seth even more than they do us; his dealings with us—but especially with Jane, of course—are as much learning experiences for him as they are for us. After all, here he is, engaged in a "lifelong" process with my wife, and just as dependent upon what he can get through her psyche, as she is upon what she can get from him and then let through to me and to others! What storms of consciousness, as well as peaceful reaches, must Seth travel through in order to help her even as much as he does? As far as he's concerned those storms and reaches aren't physical, but instead consist of intensities of feeling—as they do for us us too, basically.

From her mystical orientation Jane chooses what she wants to learn and use from what Seth has to offer. I think that if one isn't a mystic, such a state of being can only be approximated: There are obviously many variations possible, but the mystic chooses challenges that the rest of us can really understand only in the vaguest of terms. Jane's mystical creation of her universe is just her own. It always has been and it always will be; she has expressed her way over and over again in her deceptively simple poetry, as well as in the sessions. That way is a fount of creativity I can only partially grasp. No matter that right now our joint reality seems quite opaque to me as Jane lies bedridden. I know that it appears much more translucent to Seth, and that he sees our great active potentials as we cannot at this time.

Although Jane has had intimations from Seth in the hospital, she hasn't spoken for him, and I do not know whether she will or not.

Now—and I borrow the greeting of a certain energy personality essence: I can note some three and a half years later, shortly before Dreams *goes to press, that copies of many items from our estate have been transferred to Yale University Library. These include the thousands of pages of the Seth material, regular and deleted [or private]; Jane's and my own journals and other miscellaneous manuscripts, written records, and notes; ESP class tapes; some of Jane's poetry and art, and some photographs of each of us. I have also sent to the library the originals of many thousands of letters from readers. And the transfer continues.)*

NOTES. Session 941

1. In Chapter 10 see Note 1 for Session 933, which Jane held six months ago. I described asking her if Seth could give us some information on the consciousness connected with nuclear energy. She promised me that he would discuss it soon—but we have yet to receive any such commentary. This is as much my fault as hers; I let the question get away from me amid our day-to-day activities. Now that *Dreams* is finished, we'll probably not get the information for use in this book. (However, I do have a few related remarks of my own to offer in Note 3 to come.)

I last discussed the cleanup at Three Mile Island, and nuclear power challenges in general, including safety and costs, in the opening notes for the 936th session, with its Note 2. That was almost three months ago, in November 1981; see Chapter 11. Lesser accidents, or "events," as they are called within the nuclear-power industry, have continued to happen within the context of that primary accident at TMI—the loss of coolant for the nuclear reactor of Unit No. 2. I call the whole series of accidents "events of consciousness," and think of them as unfolding in an orderly way from that initial large-scale event of consciousness, which took place on March 28, 1979. Early in January of this year (1982), for example, decontamination workers in a pair of buildings located between the plant's two reactors triggered alarms when they inadvertently blew radioactive dust into the buildings from a drain filled with contaminated particles. The "unusual event" was not serious, although a small amount of radiation was released into the atmosphere through a ventilating system.

The process of decontaminating and storing the great amount of radioactive water which had collected in the containment building housing Unit No. 2 is well under way, as it is in an auxiliary building next door. Yet in mid-February the president of the company operating TMI announced that leakage from a tank used to store some of that water had contaminated groundwater at the site. The radiation is low-level, however, and well below federal safety limits.

In Note 2 for the 936th session, I also described how the NRC had asked the operators of certain nuclear power plants to check for cracks in the vessel walls of their pressurized-water reactors, which are the kind installed at TMI. Now problems with corrosion are being announced. The reactor for Unit No. 1 at TMI is undamaged; it had been shut down for maintenance and refueling at the time of the accident to its twin, nearly three years ago, and a series of delays has kept it idle ever since. In February, again, company officials revealed the discovery of extensive corrosion in the bundles of small-diameter tubes in the two steam generators powered by Unit No. 1, which will delay any restarting of the unit for another six months to a year. The tubes circulate hot radioactive water from the reactor throughout the steam generators. Replacement of at least several thousand such tubes will cost millions of dollars; if engineers simply plug the damaged tubes, the reactor will operate well below capacity. (Steam generators at some other plants have a new problem: the accumulation of a corrosive sludge at their bases.)

The NRC is under a court order that prevents it from relicensing the start-up of Unit No. 1 at TMI until the psychological health of the communities surrounding the power station has been studied.

Company projections are that the entire cleanup at TMI won't be completed until the end of 1988—more than nine years after the accident took place. Current plans are that once the radioactive water is drained from the containment building of Unit No. 2, engineers will conduct remote investigations of the core of the reactor itself. A specially designed video camera will be inserted into the core so that the actual damage to the pencil-thin fuel rods can be assessed; and hundreds of thousands of sonar readings, taken through openings already present in the reactor, will be assembled by computer into images of the core. Several major steps must follow, all of them on an enormous scale: the lifting of the 160-ton metal "head," or cap, of the reactor; the removal of the upper plenum assembly, the 55-ton mechanism which makes possible the raising and lowering of fuel control rods into the 100-ton reactor core, thus regulating the intensity of its nuclear reactions; and eventually, the difficult piece-by-piece removal of the damaged core itself. Even then, the core will still be so radioactive that most of the work will have to be done by remote-controlled devices. Finally, the cavernous containment building itself will be cleaned, again by remote control.

Yet from the very day of the accident, this question has existed along with each step of the cleanup process, and will continue to do so: What to do with Three Mile Island, that enormously complicated human creation that now has its own consciousness, and that has in its own way exerted the force of that consciousness throughout our civilized world? To dismantle TMI seemingly would solve the "problem"—but only partially, for once born its consciousness will (like all others) continue to live. I repeat, however, that in this country no public citizen has been either seriously injured or killed in an accident at a commercial nuclear facility (as have a few workers).

2. "The killing in Iran continues—and hardly just because of that country's war with Iraq," I wrote in the opening notes for

Session 936, in Chapter 11 of *Dreams*. Some three months later the killing goes on, and with even more ramifications of violence, intrigue, and power politics—involving not only Iran but that unhappy country's neighbors in the Middle East.

It's quite clear, of course, that the nations of the West, including that "Great Satan," the United States, are, with Japan, keeping the fanatical Iranian mullahs (Moslem religious teachers) in power, so that their country will not be taken over by the Tudeh, Iran's Communist Party; that most unwelcome development could place Iran under Russian domination. Iran's economy is actually at a very low point because its leaders have squandered much of its already reduced oil income on the war with Iraq, and on revolutionary institutions and food imports, while devoting little to the nation's long-term interests. There's plenty of oil available from around the world; were the West to stop buying Iranian oil, the regime would quickly collapse. The United States doesn't want either Iran or Iraq to win their war. In the grimmest of political realities, our side is using Iran to block Russian expansion into the Middle East, and is using Iraq to block Iranian domination of its other, weaker oil-producing neighbors. The Iranian-Iraqi war promises to be the bloodiest one in centuries between the two countries; the West is working for a stalemate that over the years will degenerate into "harmless" border clashes. And Russia continues its remorseless occupation and subjugation of Afghanistan.

Just as the native mujahedin—resistance fighters—of Afghanistan consider it their religious duty to battle the Russian invaders (even while thousands of their countrymen take refuge in Pakistan to the east and in Iran to the west), so do the Iranian fundamentalists think it *their* religious duty to export their revolution until an Islamic empire extends from the Mediterranean to the Persian Gulf.

The mixing of consciousnesses in the Middle East, then, ultimately revolves around the great overall clash of ideologies between the United States and Russia. At the same time, Iran's mullahs want a continuing war with Iraq to help consolidate their total power; they do not want victorious, high-ranking military leaders back home from the front to challenge their undisputed power (as internal resistance groups like the Mujahedin-e Khalq are doing). Iran has become a totalitarian religious theocracy. I wrote in Note 3 for Session 936, in Chapter 11, that despite their egoistic orientations, ultimately Iranians bow to the ancient power of their religion, including the demands of martyrdom. They continue their revolution even with their short-sighted military and economic policies, the war, the assassinations of scores of their leaders, and their country's isolation by the free world. They export terrorism with a vengeance. They hate both the East and the West. With equal fervor they demand the downfall of the United States, France, Russia, Israel, and Iraq, among other nations. And for their grimly creative focus of revolutionary consciousness they unabashedly take full credit.

Some ideas came to me as I was taking a walk late one evening during the days I worked on this note. "We don't want it thought," I wrote when I got back to the hill house, "that the overall consciousness of Iran is playing with the individual consciousnesses of its people, say, as with toy soldiers, setting its citizens up against the world only to have them knocked down. Nor would this be true of any other country. Rather, we want to relay to the reader that the great consciousness of Iran is made up of the individual consciousnesses of its people—that within that chosen national context the individual does have whatever freedom of creativity is possible. The mental and physical freedoms available will vary widely, according to time, nation, and history, but they will always be chosen. This is hardly new thinking. Indeed, it's quite obvious, but it's the best way I can put it into words at the moment. . . ." Once again, I refer the reader to Seth's excellent material on violence as quoted in Note 2 for Session 933.

As I finish this note—and *Dreams*—I believe it quite safe to predict that whenever this book is published the reader will find that the general situation in the Middle East is essentially the same: The consciousnesses of the countries involved, then, will continue to resist all outside overtures to "sanity" that do not help perpetuate the exploration of their long-term goals. In the Middle East (as anywhere else on our planet) there's plenty of "time" for peace later! There are endless variations of peace to be ultimately explored, to be held in delicious abeyance, to be savored by each consciousness there, no matter how great or small, like the knowledge of a fine wine or a rich dessert still to come. . . .

3. "I am not assigning human traits to energy. Instead, your human traits are the result of energy's characteristics—a rather

important difference," Seth told Jane and me almost two and a half years ago. In Chapter 1 of *Dreams*, in Volume 1, see Session 884 for October 3, 1979.

For this note I'll touch upon what I believe are some other characteristics of energy—the consciousnesses associated with warfare and nuclear energy, and the counterpart connections among those great states of being. Then I'll refer to the concepts of perception theory and privation theory.

I think the main idea we're trying to bring to consciousness as a species is that we've chosen to move beyond the limits of the ordinary, safe world we've always created. Until the development and use (by the United States, no less!) of the atom bomb four decades ago, we could routinely kill each other while knowing that most of us, and our homelands, would survive. We're still fighting our conventional wars, but now we have to face the threat of national or species disaster through the escalation of an "ordinary" war into one in which nuclear weapons are either accidentally or deliberately used.

Even the damage that potentially can stem from a peacetime nuclear accident, as at TMI, can be great indeed. In Note 1 for Session 933, in Chapter 10 of *Dreams*, I speculated about nuclear energy being an earthly analog of the illimitable loving being of All That Is. Now I believe that it is. My conviction was triggered late the other night after I had been struggling with this note. I relaxed by watching a television travelog; I saw a great waterfall in an isolated jungle setting; the cameraman zoomed in on the foaming, surging water leaping at the base of the waterfall— and staring at that eruption of energy I suddenly realized the obvious: It's not the *force* of any nuclear reaction that we fear, but the *consciousness* of the event. We must mature quickly enough to learn to "control" the contradictory potentials of the nuclear energy that we've helped guide into being. We have barely started to use that great power for peaceful purposes. I believe, then, that unwittingly we're translating compartmentalized glimpses of All That Is through the extraordinary consciousness of nuclear energy. Isotopes of some of the elements involved with that energy have "half-lives" of millions of years— far longer, quite possibly, than our species will exist in those terms of time. Those reaches of time are so great, so *timeless*, that I see them as another earthly analog of All That Is.

Our relationship with nuclear energy, then, as it has been with warfare, is mainly adversarial: We still crave protection from our own creations. Now no one on earth is "safe"—in this probable reality our species has given at least unconscious permission (through the dream state, for example) for the great nuclear experiment to continue.

According to Seth, and Jane's and my own experiences, each individual is a member of a group of "counterparts"—each is psychically connected to other men and women alive on earth now, in various countries, who are exploring related lifetime themes in ways that no individual could ever do. Counterparts may or may not meet, yet all share intuitive connections. Although Seth hasn't gone into the idea yet, I believe that *events* have counterparts also, just as does any "living" organism, whether human or not. The counterpart notion is Seth's timeless version of his concept of consecutive incarnations. (And yes, I think that events have reincarnational histories also, but in this note I'm confining myself to the counterpart thesis.)

Moreover, I believe that counterpart relationships do exist between wars and nuclear energy. (Such associations also apply to large geological and geographical events, for example, and I wish I had the time and space to go into *those*!) But if Jane and I, say, as counterparts are exploring certain long-range connections through our own adventures in consciousness, then the consciousnesses of related major events must have much greater abilities and desires for fulfillment. Consider the following group of events as seen through a narrow window of ordinary time; consider the moral, economic, and diplomatic impact they have had—and are still having—upon our own national interests (let alone the interests of other nations). These events must interact with each other on many levels: The revolution in Iran came to a head with a change of leadership in February 1979, after a ruler long favorable to the United States had been deposed; the accident at TMI took place in March 1979; the American hostages were taken in Iran in November 1979; Russia invaded Afghanistan at Christmastime 1979; and less than 10 months later Iraq invaded Iran. This list can either be expanded almost indefinitely, or compressed—but, I think, these events and states of being all are psychically related. Many fascinating connections could be traced out.

The ordinary violence involved with these events leads me to comment upon the theological concept of privation theory, and the military one of perception theory—for again, I think the two are closely related, not only to each other but to the points I've made in this note. In mundane terms, both represent long-standing distortions in perception of the great basic creativity of All That Is. I suggest that the reader review Seth's material on the basically creative use of violence as I quoted it in Chapter 10; see Note 2 for Session 933.

Privation theory has for many centuries been a main tenet of theology: Evil is not a power in itself, but only the absence of good; it is not-good. Room is made for the existence of the devil, who rebelled against the God who created him and constantly inveighs others to follow him in choosing the not-good. I believe that the only devils we know are those we originate ourselves. Through privation theory religion has created unanswerable questions for itself as it seeks to explain man's inhumanity to man. To me, privation theory is a beautiful example of how man projects his fears of the world he's created out upon that very world. His focus is much too limited.

Man's focus is equally limited in perception theory, which is a deadly psychological game played by the United States and Russia. It's deadly because nuclear weapons are involved. Perception theory rests upon the assumptions of large groups of people in the two countries, including many of their leaders, and by the political rulers of many other nations, that it is vital for the United States and Russia to possess numerically balanced arsenals of nuclear weapons. Both countries passed the point of potential overkill years ago, but that doesn't matter. What does matter in perception theory is that whenever one side is seen as pulling ahead in the arms race, the other must match that progress, then do better, even though militarily it's quite unnecessary. Indeed, military leaders in the United States, and evidently in Russia, concur in playing out the illusion of perception theory for their own psychological and political purposes.

To me, privation theory and perception theory are interchangeable; they represent consciousnesses deeply exploring the misperceptions I've listed concerning violence, and the relationships involving the counterparts of nuclear energy and warfare.

I don't mean at all to put down everything we've created in our world, and to proclaim that Seth's concept of All That Is is the magical solution that mankind has been searching for throughout his existence. I *do* mean to relate the self-created elements of our interior and exterior, individual and mass worlds to a larger whole of consciousness. It's inevitable that we'll grow. *How* we'll grow is the question!

Ironically, as individuals and nations we talk about casting off old beliefs while cherishing them as long as possible. Why have large segments of consciousness chosen to operate in such a fashion? I think we're creating a probable reality in which consciousness has the absolute freedom to explore all facets of itself—every one we can think of, and therefore create. Within our national orientations, within our religious and secular, scientific and artistic structures, we are choosing to go to the extremes of "good" and "bad," and to deal with the consequences, all stewing together in what seems like an impossible mix of reason and emotion, learning and joy, pain and violence, and life and death. Naturally, many of us don't like certain facets of our creations, yet we must deal with all of them if we are to make any sense out of our reality. Otherwise, our growing will be too limited; we'll remain slaves to our animosities.

I do think that through her mystical understanding and interpretation of our probable reality, Jane has indeed offered much to us, and that she will continue to do so. We'll have to resolve our great challenges through voluntary group and international efforts, though. No one nation or entity can impose its way of consciousness upon the rest, without violating the very concepts it's trying to espouse for one and all.

It should be obvious in this mere sketch that I'm groping for answers through which to understand Jane's and my own joint world. I cannot make the words express my thoughts and feelings the way I want them to.

4. The troubled, brief second flight of our country's shuttle spacecraft, *Columbia*, took place three months ago, and I described it in the opening notes for Session 936, in Chapter 11 of *Dreams*. However, Seth-Jane finished this book before the third flight, which probably will be launched early in April, could begin. A fourth flight could go in June.

In Note 3 for this session I referred to what I think are a couple of earthly analogs of All That Is. To Jane and me, our species' venturing into space is another such analog: Our physical motion off the planet is certainly an objectified version or translation of our tentative explorations of inner space. In conscious terms, we have barely touched upon the fantastic inner complexities of All That Is, from which all else emerges, and which for a number of reasons we still fear.

5. Jane has worked with Tam ever since he encouraged her to write *The Seth Material* 13 years ago; that book was published a year later, in 1970. One of Tam's many generous acts was his initiating our contact with officials at Yale University Library just over three years ago. As a result, Jane and I have arranged that upon our deaths our estate—including the Seth material—goes to the Manuscripts and Archives division of the Library. My plan in the meantime has been to transfer copies of as much of our work as possible to Manuscripts and Archives, so that the material can be indexed and made available to researchers and to the public. I have yet to begin the work of copying, however, although I hope to start it soon now that I can see an end to my involvement with *Dreams*. In Chapter 2 of *Dreams*, in Volume 1, see Note 1 for Session 887, which Jane delivered in December 1979.

6. In Chapter 9 of *Dreams*, see Note 2 for Session 920, which Jane held on October 6, 1980.

7. I last quoted Jane about *Seven Three* in the opening notes for Session 920. I also referred to the very slow-moving production of a motion picture based upon Jane's first Seven novel: *The Education of Oversoul Seven.*

8. In Chapter 9 of *Dreams*, see the opening notes at superscript number 5 for Session 920, which Jane held on October 6, 1980. Then see Note 5 itself, as well as sections C, D, and E of Note 7 for that session.

9. In Chapter 8 of *Mass Events*, see Session 860 for June 13, 1979.

Index